“十三五”高等职业教育规划教材·国际经贸系列

# 外贸函电实务

（第二版）

# Correspondence in Foreign Trade Practice

王　宁　编著

对外经济贸易大学出版社
中国·北京

图书在版编目（CIP）数据

外贸函电实务：英文 / 王宁编著. —2 版. —北京：对外经济贸易大学出版社，2019.8 （2023.7 重印）
“十三五”高等职业教育规划教材. 国际经贸系列
ISBN 978-7-5663-2075-9

Ⅰ. ①外… Ⅱ. ①王… Ⅲ. ①对外贸易–英语–电报信函–高等职业教育–教材 Ⅳ. ①H315

中国版本图书馆 CIP 数据核字（2019）第 158399 号



**外贸函电实务**（第二版）

**Correspondence in Foreign Trade Practice**

王 宁 编著

责任编辑：高 卓

对外经济贸易大学出版社
北京市朝阳区惠新东街 10 号 邮政编码：100029
邮购电话：010－64492338 发行部电话：010－64492342
网址：http://www.uibep.com E-mail：uibep@126.com

北京市泰锐印刷有限责任公司印装 新华书店经销
成品尺寸：185mm×260mm 14.5 印张 335 千字
2019 年 8 月北京第 2 版 2023 年 7 月第 3 次印刷

ISBN 978-7-5663-2075-9
印数：5 001－6 000 册 定价：36.00 元

# 前　　言

本书第一版自 2016 年 5 月出版以来，被多所高职院校选为教学用书。在本书使用过程中，结合教师与学生的反馈，本次再版做出如下修订。

（1）删除了部分示范信函，使得示范信函更具有代表性。

（2）更新了练习的内容，增加了有代表性的句子，为相应情境下信函的写作提供更多的素材。

（3）新增了商务拜访、客户满意度调查和新产品介绍与促销三个有代表性的业务情境作为学习任务。

本书具有以下几方面的特色。

1. 整体设计

本书以进出口企业与它的某一客户的交易为背景，以一笔商品交易的过程为线索组织教学内容，包括交易磋商、订立合同、履行合同、商务关系维护中的往来商务函电。该设计增强了教材的可读性，避免了因缺乏业务背景而使学习过程变得困难和乏味。

2. 结构

本书采用模块教学，分为外贸函电基础知识、交易磋商及合同的签订、合同的履行、商务关系的维护四大模块，共十三个学习任务，对应外贸业务过程的典型环节。

十三个学习任务包括：建立业务联系、询盘与发盘、还盘与接受、合同的签订、信用证与付款、样品与货物的检验、货物的包装及运输标志、货物的装运、交单与付款、投诉与索赔、商务拜访、客户满意度调查、新产品介绍与促销。每个学习任务都包括七个部分：学习目标、背景知识、写作提示、示范信函、练习、技能训练、补充阅读。

学习任务之间保持着连贯性和一致性，同时，在每个学习任务内部各个部分之间也存在着内在的联系。每个学习任务中七个部分的功能和联系陈述如下。

（1）学习目标使学习者明确每个任务需要掌握的知识和技能。

（2）背景知识介绍了相应业务环节的国际贸易业务知识，使学习者更容易进行商务信函的阅读与写作。

（3）写作提示给出了每个任务的典型业务情境和信函的写作要点，有助于学习者进行商务信函的阅读与写作。

（4）示范信函是本书的主体，包括信函的业务背景、信函、注释和译文。通过示范信函的学习可以获得相应业务情境中商务信函的阅读和写作技能。

（5）练习是针对词句层次的练习，以示范信函的学习为基础，并通过变式练习使学习者提高对示范信函的理解，同时，也为后面的技能训练打下基础。

（6）技能训练是给定业务背景和信息的信函写作练习，主要作用是提高相应业务背景下商务信函的写作能力。

（7）补充阅读选取了不同行业和不同风格的商务信函，其作用是增加阅读量，既可供课堂练习使用，也可以供学习者自学使用。

3. 内容

本书的示范信函、补充阅读材料均以真实的外贸业务为背景。

本书注意取材的广泛性。示范信函以纺织品、木材加工两个行业中商品的交易为背景；补充阅读的信函以草编工艺品、钢管、智能玩具三种商品的交易为背景。学习者可以了解不同行业业务信函的特点。

示范信函的长度和数量根据相应业务环节的特点有所区别，做到重点突出、轻重分明。示范信函的语言通俗、简单、易学，避免使用过于正式、难度大的词汇和句式，目的在于使读者避免因语言障碍而失去学习的信心和兴趣。

4. 形式

本书适当插入了表格、图片和附件，改变了传统的外贸函电教材只有文字、没有或少有插图、表格、附件的风格，讲究图文并茂，增强可读性。

为便于学习者学习，本书部分采用了中英文混编方式。本书的示范信函译文、练习答案、教学 PPT 等作为教学资源提供给使用本书的教师及学习者，如有需要，可以登录出版社网站（www.uibep.com）下载。

本书在编写过程中得到了山东崇德服饰有限公司业务部经理董春英女士、利源集团实业有限公司总经理陈少文先生的协助和支持。在此表示衷心的感谢。

本书可以作为高等职业院校或应用型本科院校的经济贸易类专业、商务英语专业的教材使用，也可以作为从事对外经济贸易工作人员的培训教材或参考书。

**王　宁**
**2019 年 5 月 6 日**
**潍　坊**

# 目　录

# Contents

# 目　　录

# Contents

# 外贸函电基础知识

# Basics for Correspondence in Foreign Trade

## 商务函电与国际贸易

### 一、商务函电在国际贸易业务中的作用

在国际贸易业务中，买卖双方及相关当事人如银行、货运代理、保险公司之间的沟通是必不可少的，沟通方式主要是通过口头和书面两种方式进行的。

口头沟通包括面对面的交流、电话沟通。其优点是能够体察到对方的表情、语气等；缺点是由于口头沟通是即时沟通方式，往往不允许当事人对沟通的内容进行太充分的准备，而且，限于条件，有时无法采用面对面沟通或电话沟通。

书面沟通是买卖双方沟通的另一种主要沟通方式。优点是沟通的内容有据可查，当事人有较充分的时间准备和修改书面沟通的内容；缺点是往往不能得到即时反馈。书面沟通在国际贸易业务中起着重要的作用，其在国际贸易中的主要形式是商务函电。狭义的商务函电包括商务信函和电传。广义的商务函电除了商务信函、电传，还包括寄送的纸质书面材料，如合同、信用证、有关货物的单据等。

当代商务往来的商务函电，主要形式是通过互联网传递电子信函，有时也会采用电传和寄送纸质书面材料的方式。

### 二、商务信函的特点

（一）从内容看，同一业务情境的信函内容有大致相同的写作要点

虽然外贸业务情境随行业、产品、客户的不同而千差万别，但外贸业务流程有大致相同的业务环节，每一业务环节又有许多常见的业务情境。如在交易磋商阶段，有建立业务联系、询盘、发盘、还盘、接受等环节；在合同成立后，有信用证的开立与修改、样品寄送与反馈、货物的检验、包装、装运、交单与付款、投诉或索赔等环节。在同

一业务环节中，在进行书面的沟通时，有常见的业务情境，同一业务情境有着大致相同的写作要点[①]。

（二）从语言规范程度看，多数商务信函用词、句式较为正式

相对于日常交流，商务信函的语言往往较为正式，这表现在用词和句式上。但从贸易实务中使用的商务信函看，口语化的用词、句式也很多[②]。

（三）从语言风格看，商务信函具有简洁的特点

商务活动中，时间对于交易双方都十分珍贵，所以，商务信函应尽可能简洁、明了，以节省双方的沟通时间。信函的写作以说明沟通的要点为目标，切忌拖沓冗长。

## 三、国际贸易业务环节、情境与商务信函

商务信函是伴随着具体的业务环节及相应的业务情境而产生的。

按照外贸业务流程（出口业务流程见图 1），大致有如下一些业务环节。

（1）建立业务联系；

（2）询盘与发盘；

（3）还盘与接受；

（4）签订合同；

（5）信用证与付款；

（6）样品与货物的检验；

（7）包装及运输标志；

（8）装运；

（9）交单与付款；

（10）投诉或索赔。

其中，（1）至（4）项属于交易磋商及合同的签订阶段，（5）至（10）项属于合同的履行阶段。

每一业务环节中，有一些常见的业务情境和相对固定的写作要点。比如在交易磋商阶段建立业务联系环节，常见的业务情境包括：出口商发出的建立业务联系的信函；进口商发出的建立业务联系的信函。其中，出口商发出的建立业务联系的信函的写作要点包括：说明获得对方信息的来源和写信的意图；介绍公司及产品；主动给对方寄去产品目录、价格单或告知公司网址；希望与对方建立业务联系；期待回信。又如，在合同履行阶段信用证的开立与修改环节，常见的业务情境包括：出口商催开信用证的信函；进口商告知卖方信用证已经开立的信函；出口商要求买方修改信用证的信函；进口商回复卖方提出的要求修改信用证的信函。其中，出口商催开信用证的信函的写作要点包括：提及合同号或订单号；说明合同中规定的关于开立信用证的时间；说明仍然没有收到信用

① 本书每个任务的写作提示部分对相应业务环节中信函写作情境和写作要点都进行了归纳。

② 本书示范信函使用的语言既相对规范，同时又尽量通俗易懂，以贴近实际业务。

证；提醒对方及时开立信用证，以免耽误交货期；其他事项（比如，信用证的内容要与合同保持一致；寄送信用证开立申请书供卖方核查，以免日后修改信用证等）。此外，交易双方需要维护好商务关系，从而进行商务拜访、客户满意度调查及新产品介绍与促销等活动，在这些情境中，也需要进行书面沟通或口头沟通。

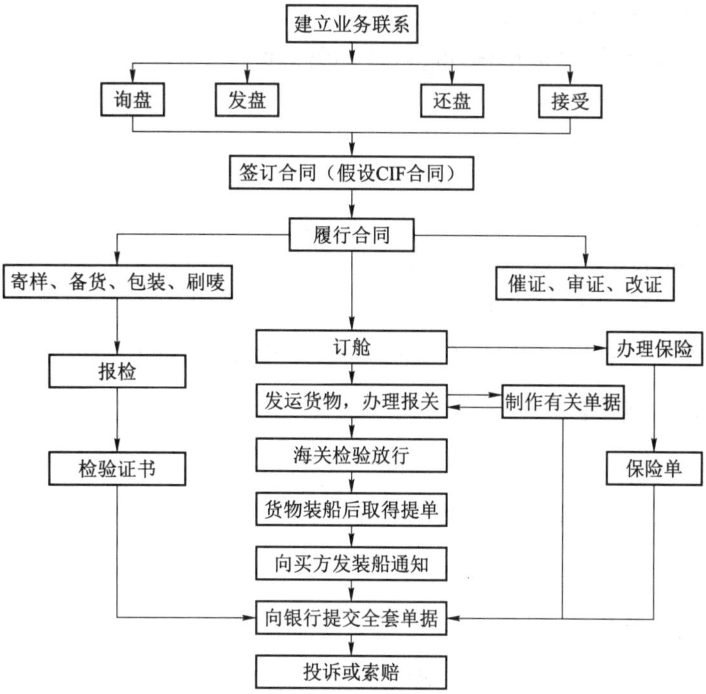


**图 1　出口业务流程**

## 商务信函的结构

### 一、示范信函

以下是一封示范信函[①]，主题是建立业务联系。

From: albert@163.com

To: salesdepartment@hotmail.com

Date: 2019.02.12

Subject: establishing business relations

Dear Sir,

Having obtained your name and address from the Commercial Counselor's Office of Embassy of China in Australia, we are writing to you in the hope of establishing business

① 本书采用当代国际贸易业务中最常使用的书面交流方式——电子邮件，作为示范信函的形式。

relations between us.

We have been an importer of fibreboard for many years. At present, we are interested in various kinds of Australian fibreboard, and we would appreciate it if you send us your latest catalogues and quotations. We trust that business can be done if your prices are competitive and the goods are of good quality.

We are looking forward to receiving your early reply.

Best regards
Albert
Purchasing Manager
Beijing Lucky Fibreboard Trading Co., Ltd.
Tel: 86-010-65771234; Fax: 86-010-65771233
Address: Room 801, International Trade Center, No. 92 Jianguo Road, Chaoyang, Beijing, China

## 二、信函的结构

以上面的示范信函作为例子，说明国际贸易业务中信函的基本结构。

信函内容可以分为必要部分和可选部分。

### （一）必要部分

1. 信头（heading）

信头包括发信人电子邮箱地址、收信人电子邮箱地址、信件的日期、主题。如：

From: albert@163.com
To: salesdepartment@hotmail.com
Date: 2019.02.12
Subject: establishing business relations

2. 称呼（salutation）

如果是第一次写信且不知道对方的姓名，那么可以用“Dear Sir”或“Dear Madame”；如果已经知道对方的姓名，那么可以用“Dear ××”。

3. 正文（body）

正文是信件的主体，根据表达的意思来分段，层次要清晰。

Having obtained your name and address from the Commercial Counselor’s Office of Embassy of China in Australia, we are writing to you **in the hope of** establishing business relations between us.

We have been an importer of fibreboard for many years. At present, we are interested in various kinds of Australian fibreboard, and we would **appreciate** it if you send us your latest catalogues and quotations. We trust that business can be done if your prices are competitive and the goods are of good quality.

We are looking forward to receiving your early reply.

4. 结束敬语（complimentary close）

常用的结束敬语有 Best regards、Regards、Best wishes、Yours sincerely、Yours truly、Yours faithfully。

5. 签名（signature）

写信人的姓名，如：

Albert

6. 职位和公司信息（position and company's information）

职位和公司信息包括写信人在所在公司的岗位，如采购经理、销售经理、总经理、销售代表等和所在的公司名称、地址、电话、传真、电子邮箱等，如：

Purchasing Manager

Beijing Lucky Fibreboard Trading Co., Ltd.

Tel: 86-010-65771234; Fax: 86-010-65771233

Address: Room 801, International Trade Center, No. 92 Jianguo Road, Chaoyang, Beijing, China

### （二）可选部分

附件（attachment）。附件是邮件的可选内容。在国际贸易中，许多信件里包含有与信件内容有关的图片、文档、表格等，是邮件的附加内容。

## 练习

以下面的各项内容为基础，整理并形成一封商务信函。

1. Sender's information:

   Li Wei

   Sales Manager

   China Light Industrial Products Imp. & Exp. Corp.

   Address: 128 Taiping Road , Beijing, China

   E-mail: liwei008@163.com

   Tel: 86-10-75334267

   Fax: 86-10-75335268

2. Receiver's information:

   John Smith

   General Manager

   H.G. Wilkinson Company Limited

   Address: 587 Lombart Street, Lagos, Nigeria

   E-mail: Wilkinson@hotmail.com

   Tel: 234-1-6587925

   Fax: 234-1-6587928

3. Date:

   March 23, 2019

4. Subject:

   sewing machines

5. The message:

   We thank you for your letter of March 20 enquiring for sewing machines.

   The enclosed catalogue contains details of all our sewing machines and will enable you to make a suitable selection.

   We look forward to receiving your specific enquiry with keen interest.

# 情境一　交易磋商及合同的签订
# Business Negotiation and Contract Signing

# 任务一

# 建立业务联系

# Establishing Business Relations

## 学习目标

1. 了解与客户建立业务联系的主要途径;
2. 掌握建立业务联系信函的写作要点;
3. 熟悉建立业务联系信函中常用的词语和句子;
4. 能够阅读与撰写建立业务联系的信函。

## 背景知识

在国际贸易中，我们可以通过以下几个渠道获得潜在客户或供货商的有关信息：互联网、展览会、国内外商会、中外使馆商务参赞处等。

电子商务网站是现代国际贸易中生产企业寻找客户、产品需求企业寻找供应商的主要途径之一，可以分为B to B（企业对企业）、B to C（企业对用户）、C to C（用户对用户）三类，企业可以根据经营性质选择相应种类的电子商务网站。

表1.1是常用国际贸易网站，图1.1是阿里巴巴网站截图。

**表1.1　常用国际贸易网站**

| 网站中文名称 | 网　址 |
|---|---|
| 阿里巴巴网 | www.alibaba.com |
| 环球资源网 | www.globalsources.com |
| 中国制造网 | www.made-in-china.com |
| 中华人民共和国商务部 | www.mofcom.gov.cn |
| 印度市场 | www.indiamart.com |

续表

| 网站中文名称 | 网　　址 |
|---|---|
| 到迪拜去 | www.godubai.com |
| 易贝网 | www.ebay.com |
| 敦煌网 | www.dhgate.com |

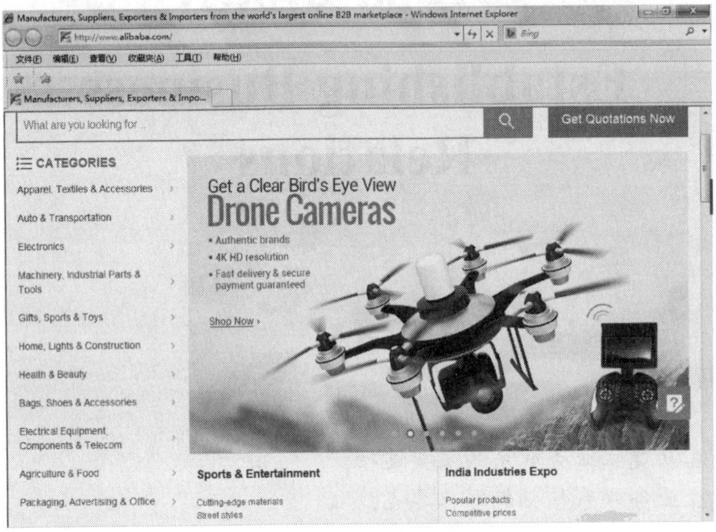


**图 1.1　阿里巴巴网站**

商品展览会也是企业寻找客户、产品需求企业寻找供应商的主要途径之一。商品展览会种类繁多，由各种展览公司主办，遍布世界各地。商品展览会可以分为综合性展会和专业性展会两类。综合性展会包括许多行业的展品，专业性展会针对某一行业的产品。

表 1.2 是部分国际商品展览会的信息，图 1.2a 和图 1.2b 分别是广交会的场馆和展厅的照片。

**表 1.2　部分国际商品展览会**

| 名　称 | 主办单位 | 地点 | 官方网站 |
|---|---|---|---|
| 中国进出口商品交易会<br>China Import and Export Fair | 中国对外贸易中心 | 中国广州 | www.cantonfair.org.cn |
| 中国华东进出口商品交易会<br>East China Import and Export Fair | 上海外经贸商务展览公司 | 中国上海 | www.eastchinafair.net |
| 德国法兰克福春季消费品展览会<br>AMBIENTE | 法兰克福展览有限公司 | 德国法兰克福 | www.messefrankfurt.com/frankfurt |
| 法兰克福国际家用及室内纺织品展览会<br>HEIMTEXTIL | 法兰克福展览有限公司 | 德国法兰克福 | www.messefrankfurt.com/frankfurt |
| 法国巴黎 JEC 国际复合材料展<br>JEC World Composite Show | 法国 JEC 集团 | 法国巴黎 | www.jeccomposites.com |

续表

| 名　称 | 主办单位 | 地点 | 官方网站 |
|---|---|---|---|
| 美国纽约全美文具国际博览会<br>NSS（National Stationery Show） | Emerald Expositions | 美国纽约 | www.nationalstationeryshow.com |
| 英国伦敦文具展览会<br>London Stationery Show | First Events Company | 英国伦敦 | www.stationeryshow.co.uk/contact |
| 贝宁（西非）中国商品展览会<br>Benin（Western Africa Chinese Commodity Exhibition） | 中国商务部 | 贝宁科托努 | |

图 1.2a　广交会场馆

图 1.2b　广交会展厅

有的网站专门发布各种国内、国外展会信息，如中国展会网（www.chn-expo.com）。获得客户或供货商的联系信息后，可以通过电话、电子邮件或面对面进行沟通。

## 写作提示

建立业务联系的信函要点：

### 一、出口商发出的建立业务联系的信函

（1）说明获得对方信息的来源和写信的意图；
（2）介绍公司及产品；
（3）主动给对方寄去产品目录、价格单或告知公司的网址；
（4）希望与对方建立业务联系；
（5）期待回信。

### 二、进口商发出的建立业务联系的信函

（1）说明获得对方信息的来源和写信的意图；
（2）介绍公司的经营范围；
（3）向出口商索要产品目录、价格单或样品等。
（4）希望与对方建立业务联系；
（5）期待回信。

## 示范信函

本书分别以生产、出口纺织品的公司（潍坊宝达纺织品有限公司）和从事纤维板进口的贸易公司（北京幸运纤维板贸易公司）与其客户在一笔商品交易中的往来信函作为案例，供学习参考[①]。

# CASE 1 Weifang Baoda Textiles Co., Ltd.

### 一、信函的业务背景

#### 潍坊宝达纺织品有限公司简介

潍坊宝达纺织品有限公司（图 1.3 展示的是该公司的生产车间）是一家高档色织衬衫面料生产企业，产品具有很强的市场竞争优势。公司拥有世界一流的生产设备和一流的生产技术及先进的管理手段，公司的产品已达到世界领先水平，产品远销美国、加拿大、德国、法国、意大利、西班牙、日本、马来西亚、南非等三十多个国家和地区。与美国的 OXFORD、POLO、PVH 和英国的 M&S、BURBERRY 以及日本的伊藤忠、丸红

① 本书的示范信函之间具有连贯性，展现了一笔商品交易过程中的全部信函。

等世界著名公司建立了长期的业务关系。

图 1.3　潍坊宝达纺织品有限公司生产车间

阿尔伯特先生是宝达纺织品有限公司的外贸业务人员，为了开发新的客户，在得知潜在客户——总部位于孟加拉国达卡的缝得好服装有限公司的信息后，向该公司发出建立业务联系的电子信函。

## 二、潍坊宝达纺织品有限公司的业务信函

建立业务联系（baoda-out 1）

From: Albert albert@163.com
To: Lisa lisa@stitchwell.com
Date: 2019.02.12
Subject: establishing business relations
Attachment: catalogue

Dear Miss Lisa,

We obtained your name and address[1] from www.alibaba.com and learn that you are a buyer of fabrics. We are seeking the chance to establish business relations with you[2].

We are a manufacturer of fabrics in Shandong, China. We mainly produce yarn-dyed fabrics for shirts, tablecloths and sheets, etc. And our products are for middle-end and high-end market[3].

In order to give you a general idea of our products, we are enclosing[4] a copy of our latest catalogue[5].

If you are interested in any of the items[6], please let us know as soon as possible. We will send you quotations[7] upon receipt of[8] your inquiry.

Best regards
Albert
Sales Manager
Weifang Baoda Textiles Co., Ltd.

附 1.1 潍坊宝达纺织品有限公司产品目录截图

## Notes

1. obtain your name and address 获得你方的名称和地址

   类似的表达方式还有：

   learn your name and address from...

   come to know your name and address through...

2. establish business relations with you 与你方建立业务联系

   类似的表达方式还有：

   establish trade relations with you

   enter into business relations with you

3. middle-end and high-end market 中高端市场

4. enclose *v.* 附上

   e.g. I would enclose the latest price list of our products for reference.

   我方将附上最新的产品价格单供你方参考。

5. catalogue *n.* 目录

6. item *n.*（清单上的）一项；一条；商品，产品（注：在本函中指商品/产品目录中所列出的商品/产品中的某项商品/产品）

7. quotation *n.* 报价

   e.g. Thank you for your quotation for 100 MTs rice.

   谢谢你方对 100 吨大米的报价。

8. upon receipt of your inquiry　一旦收到你方的询盘

类似的表达方式还有：

after receipt of your inquiry

after receiving your inquiry

e.g. We will offer you our best price after receipt of your inquiry.

我方将在收到你方的询盘后向你方报出最优惠的价格。

# CASE 2　Beijing Lucky Fibreboard Trading Co., Ltd.

## 一、信函的业务背景

### 北京幸运纤维板贸易公司简介

北京幸运纤维板贸易有限公司（图 1.4 展示的是该公司销售的产品）是一家经营纤维板的公司，进口并销售澳大利亚、智利等国家生产的纤维板。

图 1.4　北京幸运纤维板贸易有限公司销售的产品

玲玲是北京幸运纤维板贸易公司海外采购部经理，为了购买到优质而适合销售的纤维板，玲玲搜集了许多纤维板供应商的信息。本信函中澳大利亚松树纤维板工业有限公司（Pinetree Fibreboard Industries Co., Ltd.）就是其中一个供应商。为了与松树纤维板工业有限公司建立业务联系，玲玲向松树纤维板工业有限公司发出了建立业务联系的信函。

## 二、北京幸运纤维板贸易公司的信函

建立业务联系（lucky-out 1）

From: Lingling lingling@163.com

To: Sales Department salesdepartment@pinetree.com.au

Date: 2019.05.16

Subject: entering trade relations

Dear Sirs,

Having obtained your name and address from Anderson Company, Australia, we are writing to you in the hope of[1] entering trade relations with you[2].

We have been an importer of fibreboard for many years. At present, we are interested in various kinds of Australian fibreboard and would appreciate[3] your catalogues and quotations.

We trust that business can be realized[4] if your prices are in line with[5] the prevailing market level.

We look forward to[6] receiving your early reply.

Best regards
Lingling
Purchasing Manager
Beijing Lucky Fibreboard Trading Co., Ltd.

## Notes

1. in the hope of 希望
2. entering trade relations 建立贸易关系
3. appreciate *v.* 感激
   e.g. I appreciate your kind help.
   感激你的友善帮助。
4. realize *v.* 实现
5. in line with 符合
   e.g. The price is not in line with the current market level.
   价格与当前的市场水平不相符。
6. look forward to 期待
   e.g. I look forward to receiving your quick response.
   期待你尽快回复。

## 练习

**一、将下列句子译成中文。**

1. We obtained your name and address from the website of Global Sources.
2. We learn your company from China Import and Export Fair.
3. We are a state-owned corporation specializing in the export business of canned goods.
4. We are a private company dealing in fibreboard.
5. We would like to establish business relations with you.
6. As the goods supplied by your firm falls in the scope of our business, we shall be pleased to enter into business relations with you at an early date.
7. We are airmailing to you a copy of our brochure so as to make you have a better

understanding of our products.
8. Would you send 2 meters of sample No. exw-2001 to us?

**二、将下列句子译成英文。**

1. 我方在广交会上得知了贵公司的名称和地址。
2. 我方从阿里巴巴网站上得知了贵公司的名称和地址。
3. 我公司有 10 年的服装生产经验，尤其是儿童针织服装的生产。
4. 我公司从事密度板贸易已经 15 年了。
5. 我公司对贵公司生产的木材感兴趣，请寄产品目录和报价单。
6. 我们对样品号 OS-201 和 OS-202 的商品感兴趣，请报价格及交货期。
7. 我们过去从德国进口汽车，现在转从日本进口。
8. 请寄轮胎产品目录，并注明你方要求的付款条件及能给的最大折扣。

## 技能训练

### 根据业务情境和信息写信①

（一）业务情境

江苏通达轮胎有限公司（Jiangsu Tongda Tires Company Limited）（图 1.5 展示的是该公司生产的产品）是一家生产汽车轮胎的企业。企业意图开拓美国市场。公司的业务员李辉通过参加广交会认识了美国进口汽车轮胎的贸易公司——大力神轮胎贸易公司（Hercules Tires Trading Corporation）的总经理大卫 • 桑德伯格。

**图 1.5　江苏通达轮胎有限公司产品**

李辉回到公司后，主动写信给大卫 • 桑德伯格，希望与该公司建立业务联系。

① 本书技能训练部分的“根据业务背景和信息写信”，设计了一笔完整的商品交易作为业务情景。

（二）信息

出口方：江苏通达轮胎有限公司

1. 公司简介：江苏通达轮胎有限公司是一家专业化、规模化的轮胎生产企业，连续多年入围“世界轮胎企业 100 强”。

2. 联系方式

李辉

江苏通达轮胎有限公司

地址：江苏省无锡市金龙路 888 号

电话：13375365688

（0086-0510）8268868

邮箱：tongda@tongda.com.cn

网址：www.tongdatyers.com

3. 产品：通达牌汽车轮胎

进口方：大力神轮胎贸易公司

1. 公司简介：大力神轮胎贸易公司是一家专业经营轮胎进口的公司，主要进口货车轮胎和轿车轮胎。

2. 联系方式：

David Sandberg

Hercules Tires Trading Corporation

Freistadt Road Germantown, WI 53022, USA

Phone: +1 262 255 7896

Fax: +1 262 255 7898

E-mail: david@hercules.com

（三）任务

假定你是江苏通达轮胎有限公司的业务员李辉，根据给定的业务情境和信息，撰写试图与大力神轮胎贸易公司建立业务联系的信函。

信函应该包括如下要点：

1. 如何获得了大力神轮胎贸易公司的信息；
2. 介绍自己所在的公司（江苏通达轮胎有限公司）与产品；
3. 希望与大力神轮胎贸易公司建立业务联系；
4. 附上公司的产品目录并告知公司的网址；
5. 期待大卫・桑德伯格回信。

## 补充阅读

信函 1：建立业务联系

业务背景：中国一家钢管生产企业（淄博海来特锥形钢管有限公司）销售经理大卫向印度的潜在客户（印度 API 钢管有限公司）发出建立业务联系的信函。

图 1.6 展示的是淄博海来特锥形钢管有限公司的产品之一。

**图 1.6　淄博海来特锥形钢管电杆**

From: davidli@steelpipechina.com
To: mundra@indiapipe.com
Date: 2019.03.12
Subject: establishing business relations

Dear Sir,

Your company has been recommended to us by Miss Liu Jing as a prospective buyer of tapered steel pipes.

As we are in this line, we are pleased to enter into business relations with you.

In order to give you a general idea of various kinds of tapered steel pipes we produce for export, we enclose a brochure. Quotations will be offered upon receipt of your specific enquiry.

We look forward to hearing from you soon.

Regards
David Li
Sales Manager
Zibo Highlight Tapered Steel Pipe Co., Ltd.
Address: No. 1251 Nanshan Road, Zibo, Shandong, China
Tel: 86-0533-8265184; Fax: 86-0533-8265173

信函 2：建立业务联系

业务背景：中国的一家贸易公司（青岛鱼山贸易有限公司）打算从日本的一家智能玩具生产企业（三友智能玩具公司）进口智能玩具。青岛鱼山贸易有限公司的总经理爱丽斯向三友智能玩具公司销售经理呐呐先生发出了建立业务联系的信函。

图 1.7 展示的是日本该智能玩具生产公司的产品之一。

图 1.7 三友智能玩具公司智能玩具

From: alice0512@yushantrading.com
To: tunkis@smarttoy.com
Date: 2019.10.12

Subject: establishing business relations
Dear Mr. Okada Nana,

I met you at the 25th East China Fair and got your contact information from your booth.

We are an importer of Japanese toys in Qingdao. Now there is a strong demand here for different kinds of smart toys. And therefore we write to you in the hope of establishing mutually beneficial business relations with you.

It will be greatly appreciated if you could send us samples of smart toys available together with your price list, so let us have a better understanding of your products.

We are anticipating your early reply and believe that we are able to do business together in the near future.

Yours sincerely
Alice Chen
General Manager
Qingdao Yushan Trading Co., Ltd.
Address: No. 6381 Yushan Road, Qingdao, Shandong, China
Tel: 86-0532-8185678; Fax: 86-0532-8185677

# 任务二

# 询盘与发盘

# Enquiry and Offer

## 学习目标

1. 了解询盘与发盘的基本知识；
2. 掌握询盘与发盘信函的写作要点；
3. 熟悉询盘与发盘信函中常用的词语与句子；
4. 能够阅读与撰写询盘与发盘的信函。

## 背景知识

### 询　盘

### Enquiry

询盘是进口商为了了解供货情况而进行的，是交易磋商的开端。

按内容和目的划分，询盘分为一般询盘和具体询盘。

如果进口商想对出口商所提供的产品或商品进行大概的了解，他可以要求出口商向其寄送商品目录（catalogue）、价格单（price list）和样品（samples），这就是一般询盘（general enquiry）①。

如果进口商有意购买某具体产品或商品，他可要求出口商对此产品或商品报价或发盘，这就是具体询盘（specific enquiry）。

对于进口商的一般询盘，出口商可根据进口商询问的事项做出回复，如寄送商品目录、价格单和样品，并说明本公司及产品的优势，希望进口商进一步做出具体询盘；对于进口商的具体询盘，出口商的回复便是发盘。

① 一般询盘类似于进口商向出口商发出的建立业务联系的信函。

# 发　盘

## Offer

发盘是买方或卖方向对方提出各项交易条件，并愿意按这些条件与对方达成交易。

发盘可以由进口商向出口商发出，也可以由出口商向进口商发出；发盘可以是出口商在收到进口商询盘后做出，也可以不经进口商询盘由出口商直接向进口商发出。

发盘有两种：一种是实盘，另一种是虚盘。

实盘是发盘人在规定的期限内，愿意按提出的贸易条件与受盘人达成交易的表示。在有效期限内，发盘不能撤销，也不能更改。一旦受盘人在有效期内接受发盘，交易即达成。

虚盘是发盘人做出的非承诺性表示，发盘人不受发盘中贸易条件的约束，无有效期限，贸易条件不如实盘那样完整。虚盘常常注明“经发盘人最后确认后生效”。

发盘的主要内容包括商品的名称、规格、品质、最低起订数量、价格、支付条件、交货期等。

## 写作提示

### 一、一般询盘信函所包含的要点

（1）自我介绍并说明写信的意图；

（2）询问商品的一般信息；

（3）索取所需商品目录、价格单或样品；

（4）期待对方的回复。

### 二、具体询盘信函所包含的要点

（1）自我介绍并说明写信的意图；

（2）说明感兴趣的具体商品的名称、规格等；

（3）希望对方报出商品的最低起订数量、价格、交货期、付款方式等；

（4）期待对方的回复。

### 三、发盘信函所包含的要点

（1）提及或感谢对方的询盘；

（2）列出主要贸易条件：商品的名称、规格、品质、最低起订数量、价格、支付条件、交货期等；

（3）实盘：注明发盘的有效期；

　　虚盘：注明“经发盘人最后确认后生效”；

（4）希望对方进一步询问或下订单。

示范信函

# CASE 1　Weifang Baoda Textiles Co., Ltd.

## 一、信函的业务背景

### 缝得好服装有限公司简介

缝得好服装有限公司（Stitchwell Garments Co., Ltd.）（图 2.1 展示的是该公司的生产车间）是一家生产服装的工厂，总部在孟加拉国达卡，主要为澳大利亚的凯玛特（Kmart）、美国的沃尔玛（Wal-Mart）等零售商供货。

**图 2.1　缝得好服装有限公司生产车间**

丽莎是缝得好服装有限公司面料采购部的经理。在收到宝达纺织品有限公司建立业务联系的信函后，丽莎向宝达纺织品有限公司的阿尔伯特发出了询盘。阿尔伯特对丽莎的询盘进行回复，即做出发盘。

## 二、潍坊宝达纺织品有限公司的业务信函

（一）询盘与发盘（baoda-in 1）

From: Lisa lisa@stitchwell.com
To: Albert albert@163.com
Date: 2019.02.18
Subject: enquiry[1]

Dear Sir,

Thank you for your e-mail and catalogue on February 12 about your products.

I am Lisa, the purchasing manager[2] from Stitchwell Garments Co., Ltd.

We are a garment manufacturer[3] in Dhaka[4] of Bangladesh and are looking for yarn-dyed fabrics[5] in China market.

We are especially interested in flannels[6] according to the orders we are engaged in. In order to let us know the material and workmanship[7] of your products please send us samples of the following items and quote FOB[8] prices.

Cotton flannelette （single-side）

(1) XS-FLANNEL-01: 21*21, 64*54, 57/58

(2) XS-FLANNEL-03: 21*21, 80*60, 57/58

(3) XS-FLANNEL-09: 32*32, 80*68, 57/58

If the price and quality are competitive[9] and delivery time[10] is acceptable, we will place a trial order with you[11].

Best regards
Lisa
Purchasing Manager
Stitchwell Garments Co., Ltd.

## Notes

1. enquiry *n.* 询盘

   enquiry 是 inquiry 的英式拼写。

2. the purchasing manager 采购经理

3. garment manufacturer 服装生产厂家

4. Dhaka 达卡

   达卡是孟加拉国（Bangladesh）的首都。

5. yarn-dyed fabric 色织布

   色织布是面料的一种，先把纱线染色，再织成布，区别于印染布。

6. flannel *n.* 法兰绒

   法兰绒是面料的一种，常用棉或羊毛制成，面料表面有绒毛。

7. workmanship *n.* 做工

8. FOB 贸易术语，全称 Free On Board

   贸易术语是一种国际贸易惯例，由国际商会制定。贸易术语一方面对买卖双方承担的责任、费用、风险进行规定，另一方面也表明了交易商品的价格构成。

9. competitive *adj.* 有竞争力的

   e.g. Our products have strong competitive advantage.

   我方的产品有很强的竞争优势。

10. delivery time 交货期

    e.g. What is your request for delivery time?

    你方对交货时间的要求是什么？

11. place an order with you 向你方下订单

    e.g. We would place an order with you for 12 MTs rice.

    我方将向你方订购 12 吨大米。

（二）询盘与发盘（baoda-out 1）

From: Albert albert@163.com

To: Lisa lisa@stitchwell.com

Date: 2019.02.23

Subject: RE: enquiry

Attachment: price list[1]

Dear Lisa,

Thank you for your enquiry on February 18 about our products.

We have sent the samples you requested by DHL[2] with its tracking No.[3] 20190611 to your address today, and they will reach you in due course[4].

Please find the price list in the attachment[5]. And we are sending you the latest catalogue by airmail.

The following is other main trading terms[6] subject to[7] your reply reaching us in 10 days.

Payment terms: 30% invoice value[8] by T/T[9] before production, 70% invoice value by T/T after we send you the copy of B/L[10].

Shipment: in August.

Minimum quantity[11]: 3,000 yards each item.

If you have any further inquiry about the products please let us know.

Yours sincerely

Albert

Sales Manager

Weifang Baoda Textiles Co., Ltd.

Address: No. 688 West Ring Road, Weifang, Shandong, China

Tel: 86-0536-8885678; Fax: 86-0536-8885677

**附 2.1　潍坊宝达纺织品有限公司的价格单**

**price list**

cotton flannelette single-side

(1) XS-FLANNEL-01: 21*21, 64*54, 57/58 FOB QINGDAO USD1.3/Y

(2) XS-FLANNEL-03: 21*21, 80*60, 57/58 FOB QINGDAO USD1.8/Y

(3) XS-FLANNEL-09: 32*32, 80*68, 57/58 FOB QINGDAO USD1.6/Y

## Notes

1. price list　价格单

   生产厂家将主要产品的价格列在一张清单上，供买方参考、订货。

2. DHL 敦豪航空货运公司

   DHL 是国际上一家著名的快递公司。其他有名的国际快递公司有联邦快递（Federal Express）、马士基（Maersk）、日通（Nippon Express）、联合包裹服务（UPS）、美国邮政服务公司（USPS）等。

3. tracking No. 运单号

   运单号是快递公司对每一笔业务的编号，快递公司的运单号一般在网上可以查询。

4. in due course 在（将来）适当的时候

   e.g. The goods will arrive in due course.

   货物将在适当的时间到达。

5. attachment　*n.* 附件

   电子邮件中，除了正文，还可以将文本、图片、视频等放在附件里。

6. trading terms 交易条件

   交易条件包括价格、数量、包装、检验、支付方式、交货期等。

7. subject to 取决于

   e.g. The plan is subject to the decision of the general manager.

   计划取决于总经理的决定。

8. invoice value 发票金额

9. T/T（Telex Transfer）电汇

   电汇是国际贸易常用的支付方式，由汇款人委托银行（汇出行）用电报、电传等方式向收款人所在地的银行（汇入行）发出付款委托书，委托汇入行将款项付给指定的收款人。电汇是国际贸易主要的支付方式之一，其他支付方式包括开立信用证、托收等。

10. B/L（Bill of Lading）（海运）提单

    （海运）提单指用以证明海上货物运输合同和货物已经由承运人接收或装船，以及承运人保证据以交付货物的单证。提单是国际贸易中非常重要的一种单据，是卖方必须提交的单据之一。

11. minimum quantity 最低订货量

    工业品贸易中，卖方往往规定最低订货量，因为产量少会导致生产平均成本过高。

# CASE 2　Beijing Lucky Fibreboard Trading Co., Ltd.

## 一、信函的业务背景

### 松树纤维板工业有限公司简介

松树纤维板工业有限公司（Pinetree Fibreboard Industries Co., Ltd.）（图 2.2 展示的是该公司的生产车间）是一家生产纤维板（密度板）的公司，总部位于澳大利亚墨尔本。该公司的产品品牌是“松树”，以品质优良而著名，产品出口中国、日本等国家。

**图 2.2　松树纤维板工业有限公司生产车间**

比尔是松树纤维板工业有限公司的销售部业务员，在收到了北京幸运纤维板贸易有限公司采购部经理玲玲关于建立业务联系的信函后，进行了回复。

接着，玲玲发出了具体询盘，要求对方报出价格及其他交易条件，并寄样品供检验。

随后，比尔针对玲玲的具体询盘进行了发盘。

## 二、北京幸运纤维板贸易有限公司的信函

（一）询盘与发盘（lucky-in 1）

From: Bill salesdepartment@pinetree.com.au

To: Lingling lingling@163.com

Date: 2019.05.19

Subject: Re: establishing business relations

Attachment: catalogues

Dear Lingling,

Thank you for your kind enquiry on May 16.

We are a manufacturer[1] and supplier[2] of high quality MDF[3] and the plant is located in Victoria. The "pinetree" brand is recognized for consistency[4] and quality. We can also offer competitive prices.

Regarding[5] our products, I will be glad to offer[6] you our latest catalogues, which you can find in the attachment.

If you are interested in some items please don't hesitate[7] to let me know.

Look forward to receiving your further enquiry.

Best regards
Bill
Sales Department
Pinetree Fibreboard Industries Co., Ltd.

**附 2.2　澳大利亚松树纤维板工业有限公司产品目录截图**

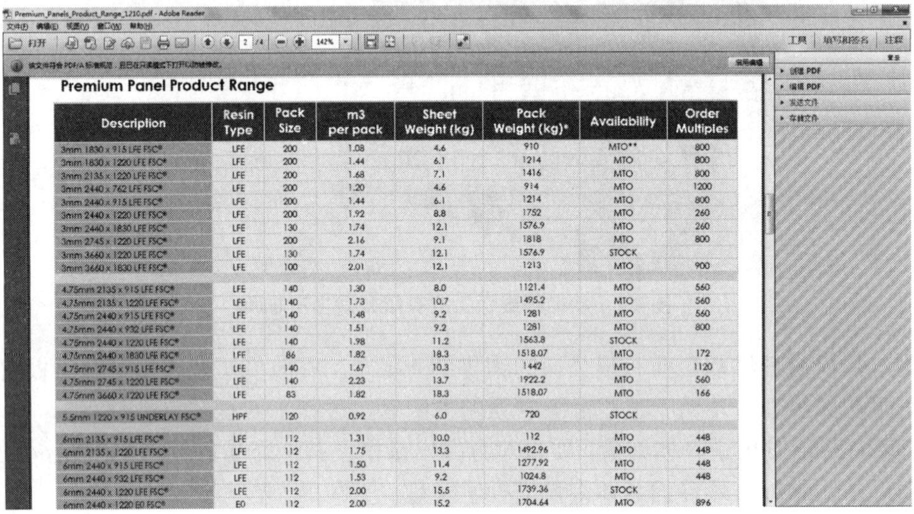

Premium Panel Product Range

| Description | Resin Type | Pack Size | m3 per pack | Sheet Weight (kg) | Pack Weight (kg)* | Availability | Order Multiples |
|---|---|---|---|---|---|---|---|
| 3mm 1830 x 915 LFE FSC* | LFE | 200 | 1.08 | 4.6 | 910 | MTO** | 800 |
| 3mm 1830 x 1220 LFE FSC* | LFE | 200 | 1.44 | 6.1 | 1214 | MTO | 800 |
| 3mm 2135 x 1220 LFE FSC* | LFE | 200 | 1.68 | 7.1 | 1416 | MTO | 800 |
| 3mm 2440 x 762 LFE FSC* | LFE | 200 | 1.20 | 4.6 | 914 | MTO | 1200 |
| 3mm 2440 x 915 LFE FSC* | LFE | 200 | 1.44 | 6.1 | 1214 | MTO | 800 |
| 3mm 2440 x 1220 LFE FSC* | LFE | 200 | 1.92 | 8.8 | 1752 | MTO | 260 |
| 3mm 2440 x 1830 LFE FSC* | LFE | 130 | 1.74 | 12.1 | 1576.9 | MTO | 260 |
| 3mm 2745 x 1220 LFE FSC* | LFE | 200 | 2.16 | 9.1 | 1818 | MTO | 800 |
| 3mm 3660 x 1220 LFE FSC* | LFE | 130 | 1.74 | 12.1 | 1576.9 | STOCK | |
| 3mm 3660 x 1830 LFE FSC* | LFE | 100 | 2.01 | 12.1 | 1213 | MTO | 900 |
| 4.75mm 2135 x 915 LFE FSC* | LFE | 140 | 1.30 | 8.0 | 1121.4 | MTO | 560 |
| 4.75mm 2135 x 1220 LFE FSC* | LFE | 140 | 1.73 | 10.7 | 1495.2 | MTO | 560 |
| 4.75mm 2440 x 915 LFE FSC* | LFE | 140 | 1.48 | 9.2 | 1281 | MTO | 560 |
| 4.75mm 2440 x 932 LFE FSC* | LFE | 140 | 1.51 | 9.2 | 1281 | MTO | 800 |
| 4.75mm 2440 x 1220 LFE FSC* | LFE | 140 | 1.98 | 11.2 | 1563.8 | STOCK | |
| 4.75mm 2440 x 1830 LFE FSC* | LFE | 86 | 1.82 | 18.3 | 1518.07 | MTO | 172 |
| 4.75mm 2745 x 915 LFE FSC* | LFE | 140 | 1.67 | 10.3 | 1442 | MTO | 1120 |
| 4.75mm 2745 x 1220 LFE FSC* | LFE | 140 | 2.23 | 13.7 | 1922.2 | MTO | 560 |
| 4.75mm 3660 x 1220 LFE FSC* | LFE | 83 | 1.82 | 18.3 | 1518.07 | MTO | 166 |
| 5.5mm 1220 x 915 UNDERLAY FSC* | HPF | 120 | 0.92 | 6.0 | 720 | STOCK | |
| 6mm 2135 x 915 LFE FSC* | LFE | 112 | 1.31 | 10.0 | 112 | MTO | 448 |
| 6mm 2135 x 1220 LFE FSC* | LFE | 112 | 1.75 | 13.3 | 1492.96 | MTO | 448 |
| 6mm 2440 x 915 LFE FSC* | LFE | 112 | 1.50 | 11.4 | 1277.92 | MTO | 448 |
| 6mm 2440 x 932 LFE FSC* | LFE | 112 | 1.53 | 9.2 | 1024.8 | MTO | 448 |
| 6mm 2440 x 1220 LFE FSC* | LFE | 112 | 2.00 | 15.5 | 1739.36 | STOCK | |
| 6mm 2440 x 1220 E0 FSC* | E0 | 112 | 2.00 | 15.2 | 1704.64 | MTO | 896 |

## Notes

1. manufacturer　*n.* 制造者，厂商
   制造者、厂商的其他表达方法：producer。
2. supplier　*n.* 供应者，供应商
3. MDF　中密度板
   MDF 是 medium density fibreboard 的缩写。
4. consistency　*n.* 一致性
   此处指产品的品质稳定。
5. regarding　*prep.* 关于

“关于”的其他表达方法：with regard to，in respect of，with reference to，as to，concerning。

6. offer *v.* 提供

   e.g. They manage a company offering advice on mergers and acquisitions.
   他们经营一家公司，提供有关公司合并和收购的建议。

7. hesitate *v.* 犹豫

   e.g. Please do not hesitate to contact us when you have any problems with our products.
   如你方对我方的产品有疑问，敬请联系我方。

（二）询盘与发盘（lucky-out 1）

From: Lingling lingling@163.com
To: Bill salesdepartment@pinetree.com.au
Date: 2019.05.23
Subject: enquiry on fibreboard

Dear Bill,

Thank you for your catalogue and price list.

We are interested in your premium[1] panel[2] and the specifications[3] required are as follows.

| Commodity | Grade | Length (mm) | Width (mm) | Thickness (mm) |
|---|---|---|---|---|
| fibreboard | premium | 2,400 | 1,200 | 3/6/9/12 |
| fibreboard | premium | 2,400 | 1,400 | 3/6/9/12 |
| fibreboard | premium | 2,700 | 1,200 | 3/6/9/12 |
| fibreboard | premium | 3,000 | 1,200 | 3/6/9/12 |
| fibreboard | premium | 3,600 | 1,200 | 3/6/9/12 |

Please quote[4] us your best price CIF[5] Xingang and shipment date etc.

Meanwhile, please send samples[6] of the required fibreboard to us for test[7].

Best regards
Lingling
Purchasing Manager
Beijing Lucky Fibreboard Trading Co., Ltd.

## Notes

1. premium *n.* 优质

   它是指产品的质量好，相当于 high quality。

   e.g. They offer premium British potatoes.

   他们提供优质的英国土豆。

2. panel *n.* 木板
3. specification *n.* 规格

   它是指对产品的具体特征的描述。

4. quote *v.* 报价

   quote 与 offer 类似，但仅限于价格方面。

   e.g.（1）A travel agent quoted us RMB10,000 for a tour from Beijing to Hong Kong.

   一家旅行社向我们报出从北京到香港的旅游价格为 10 000 元人民币。

   （2）Please quote us CIF Qingdao price for truck tire D918.

   请向我方报出型号 D918 卡车轮胎的 CIF 青岛价格。

5. CIF 贸易术语的一种，商品的价格不但包括成本，并且包括运输费用和保险费用。
6. sample *n.* 样品

   样品是在一批货物中抽取的有代表性的产品，其品质可以代表整批货物。

7. test *v.* & *n.* 测试，检验

（三）询盘与发盘（lucky-in 2）

From: Bill salesdepartment@pinetree.com.au

To: Lingling lingling@163.com

Date: 2019.05.25

Subject: Re: enquiry on fibreboard

Attachment: specification and prices of premium panels

Dear Lingling,

With reference to your enquiry on May 23, we are making you offer[1] subject to your reply reaching us before May 30. Please see the attachment for specifications and prices of premium panels. The prices we offer are on CIF Xingang basis[2].

The following are other trading terms we propose.

Payment: by irrevocable Letter of Credit[3] at sight, remaining valid[4] for negotiation[5] in Australia for further 21 days after shipment

Shipment: within one month after receiving the relevant[6] Letter of Credit

Meanwhile, the samples you required have been sent to you today by FEDEX with tracking No. 65478012. I hope that the samples will reach you in due time[7] and be satisfactory[8] to you.

We look forward to receiving your order.

Best regards
Bill
Sales Department
Pinetree Fibreboard Industries Co., Ltd.

**附 2.3 优质木板的规格与价格**

| Specifications and Prices of Premium Panels | | | | | | |
|---|---|---|---|---|---|---|
| Specification | | | Price（USD/$M^3$） | | | |
| Grade | Length | Width | Thickness (MM) | Thickness (MM) | Thickness (MM) | Thickness (MM) |
| | | | 3 | 6 | 9 | 12 |
| premium | 2,400 | 1,200 | 500 | 450 | 440 | 420 |
| premium | 2,400 | 1,400 | 550 | 500 | 480 | 460 |
| premium | 2,700 | 1,200 | 560 | 500 | 480 | 450 |
| premium | 3,000 | 1,200 | 600 | 580 | 560 | 550 |
| premium | 3,600 | 1,200 | 620 | 600 | 580 | 560 |

Notes:
1. the prices are based on CIF Xingang;
2. minimum quantity: 30 $M^3$

## Notes

1. make you offer 向你发盘
   e.g. We are making you offer for 10MT apples.
   我方向你方就 10 吨苹果做出发盘。
2. on CIF Melbourne basis 以 CIF 墨尔本为条件
3. letter of credit 信用证
   信用证，英文缩写为 L/C，国际贸易业务中主要的付款方式之一，开立信用证的银行承担第一付款责任。信用证、电汇、托收是国际贸易业务中的三大支付方式，可以结合在一起使用。
4. valid *adj.* 有效的
5. negotiation *n.* 议付；磋商
6. relevant *adj.* 相关的
   e.g. Please send relevant documents by forwarder to us as soon as possible.
   请尽快通过货运公司向我们寄送相关的单据。
7. in due time 在适当的时候
   e.g. He will arrive here in due time.
   他将在适当的时间到达这里。

8. be satisfactory 令人满意的
   e.g. His performance this year is quite satisfactory.
   今年他的表现令人非常满意。

## 练习

一、将下列句子译成中文。

1. We shall be very pleased to place our order with you if your quotation is competitive and the goods are of good quality.
2. Please quote us CIF Xingang China for the following articles.
3. We are glad to receive your inquiry for 5,000 Changhong television sets.
4. Enclosed please find the latest catalogue and price list for your reference.
5. We now make you the following offer, subject to your reply reaching us before September 30.
6. Referring to your inquiry of May 24, we are making you the following offer, which is subject to our final confirmation.
7. We can give you discount if the quantity you order is in large size.
8. As we have been receiving a lot of orders now, we advise you to place your order as soon as possible.

二、将下列句子译成英文。

1. 请向我方寄送你公司的轮胎样品，以便于我方熟悉你公司的产品质量。
2. 请报产地为马来西亚的菠萝 CIF 首尔价格。
3. 我方接到你公司 3 月 20 日对核桃仁的询盘，现回复如下。
4. 我公司的产品目录及报价单请见附件，供你方参考。
5. 现向你方就 100 台长虹牌电视机报盘，以我方的确认为准。
6. 现报盘长虹牌液晶电视机 5 000 台如下，以你方 10 日内回复我方有效。
7. 随函附上根据你方 3 月 15 日的询价所开立的报价单，期待你方的确认。
8. 对于以上发盘，商品的价格很有可能在近期上涨，因此，尽快订货符合你方的利益。

## 技能训练

### 根据业务情境和信息写信

（一）业务情境

大力神轮胎贸易公司（Hercules Tires Trading Corporation）总经理大卫·桑德伯格在收到江苏通达轮胎有限公司的业务员李辉发出的建立业务联系的信函后，立即进行了回复。

在收到大卫·桑德伯格的询盘后，李辉进行发盘。

（二）信息

大卫·桑德伯格在查看了江苏通达轮胎有限公司的产品目录和网站上发布的产品后，对型号 D928 的卡车轮胎特别感兴趣。

询盘要点如下：

1. 商品的名称：卡车轮胎 D928
2. 商品的规格：10.00R20
3. 最低起订量、FOB 上海价格、交货期等

李辉在收到了询盘后，进行发盘，要点如下：

1. 商品的名称：卡车轮胎 D928
2. 规格：10.00R20
3. 最低起订量：100 条
4. 价格：USD65/PIECE FOB 上海
5. 交货期：收到信用证后的 2 个月内发货
6. 付款方式：不可撤销即期跟单信用证

（三）任务

根据以上的业务情境和信息写信。

1. 大卫·桑德伯格给李辉发出询盘。

信函应包括以下要点：

（1）感谢李辉的来信；

（2）表示对型号 D928、规格 10.00R20 的卡车轮胎感兴趣；

（3）希望对方报出最低起订量、FOB 上海价格、交货期等；

（4）期待对方的回信。

2. 江苏通达轮胎有限公司的业务员李辉回复大卫·桑德伯格的询盘。

信函应包括以下要点：

（1）感谢大卫·桑德伯格的询盘；

（2）报出型号 D928、规格 10.00R20 的轮胎的最低起订量、FOB 上海价格、交货期、付款方式等；

（3）期待对方回信。

## 补充阅读

信函 1：询盘

业务背景：法国的一家手工艺品贸易公司（优雅贸易有限公司）的总经理海伦向中国的一家草编工艺品生产企业（青岛兴旺手工艺品有限公司）的销售经理李华发出询盘。

From: helen1219@hotmail.com

To: lihua@handicraftschina.com

Date: 2019.03.16

Subject: enquiry

Dear Sir,

We have learned from the website of Global Sources that you manufacture and export straw knitting handicrafts.

We are a company importing various handicrafts from China in France. As there is demand for China straw knitting handicrafts, we would like you to send us your catalogues along with samples and other information about your products.

Please quote your lowest price on CIF basis and delivery time as well.

Should the quality be good and the price be reasonable, we will place an order with you.

Your quick response will be appreciated.

Yours sincerely
Helen Keller
General Manager
Elegance Trading Limited, France
Address: No. 1203 Garden Road, Paris, France
Tel: 33-1-8185678; Fax: 33-1-8185677

信函 2：发盘

业务背景：中国的一家草编工艺品生产企业（青岛兴旺手工艺品有限公司）的销售经理李华回复法国的一家手工艺品贸易公司（优雅贸易有限公司）总经理海伦的询盘，并做出发盘。

图 2.3 展示的是该草编工艺品生产企业的部分产品。

图 2.3 草编工艺品

From: lihua@handicraftschina.com
To: helen1219@hotmail.com
Date: 2019.03.18

Subject: RE: enquiry

Dear Helen,

Thank you for your enquiry on March 16. At your request, we are making you the following offer subject to your reply reaching here before March 28, 2019.

Article: straw knitting handicrafts

Price: USD4.5/piece, CIF Marseille, France

Minimum Quantity: 1,000 pieces

Shipment: one month after receiving L/C

Packing: 25 pieces per carton

Payment: by irrevocable documentary Letter of Credit in favor of us

We are sending you our latest catalogue and some samples to you by airmail.

We hope that the above will be acceptable to you and are waiting for your order.

Regards

Li Hua

Sales Manager

Qingdao Xingwang Handicrafts Co., Ltd.

Address: No. 1251 Xingwang Road, Qingdao, Shandong, China

Tel: 86-0532-8745618; Fax: 86-0532-8745617

# 任务三

# 还盘与接受

# Counter-offer and Acceptance

## 学习目标

1. 了解还盘与接受的基本知识;
2. 掌握还盘与接受信函的写作要点;
3. 熟悉还盘与接受信函常用的词语及句子;
4. 能够阅读与撰写还盘与接受的信函。

## 背景知识

### 还　盘

### Counter-offer

出口商或进口商收到对方的发盘后,如果不同意发盘的各项交易条件中的某些内容,可以对发盘的内容提出修改意见，即是还盘。

还盘是受盘人对发盘的拒绝，意味着原发盘失效，原发盘人不再受原发盘的约束;同时，还盘也是原受盘人做出的一项新的发盘。

对于一方的还盘，另一方可以再进行新的还盘，即“反还盘”。如此过程，在商品交易中，往往不是一个回合就结束，而是多个回合。

### 接　受

### Acceptance

如果经过交易磋商，其中一方表示接受对方提出的各项贸易条件，即是接受。这时，标志着交易成立，双方可以签订书面合同。

在受盘人表示接受时，往往要将前期交易磋商中双方商定的各项交易条件全部列出，以供对方最终确认。

## 写作提示

### 一、还盘的写作要点

（1）表示收到卖方（买方）发盘；

（2）针对卖方（买方）发盘的内容，对自己不同意的贸易条件提出自己的条件并说明原因①；

（3）希望还盘被接受。

### 二、接受的写作要点

（1）表示接受对方的发盘或还盘；

（2）列出主要的交易条款以供对方最后确认；

（3）买方（卖方）告知对方准备签订书面的合同。

## 示范信函

# CASE 1　Weifang Baoda Textiles Co., Ltd.

### 一、信函的业务背景

潍坊宝达纺织品有限公司的阿尔伯特向缝得好服装有限公司做出了发盘后，缝得好服装有限公司的丽莎针对阿尔伯特的发盘做出了还盘。

阿尔伯特接受丽莎的还盘吗？双方又进行了哪些交易磋商呢？

### 二、潍坊宝达纺织品有限公司的业务信函

（一）还盘与接受（baoda-in 1）

From: Lisa lisa@stitchwell.com

To: Albert albert@163.com

Date: 2019.03.01

Subject: counter-offer

---

① 还盘信函写作要点中，第二点是中心内容。

Dear Albert,

Thank you for your letter and samples sent on February 23.

We are glad that our customers are satisfied with[1] the quality and design[2] of your samples, but we have to discuss the prices and other trading terms[3] in detail[4].

First, the price for XS-FLANNEL-03 (21*21, 80*60, 57/58 FOB QINGDAO USD1.8/Y) is higher than expected. There are suppliers who can offer us better price on this article, so please quote the best price[5] you can offer.

Second, we can not agree with[6] the payment terms by T/T. As you know, our government has strict control on foreign exchange[7], and only L/C can be the payment terms when conducting foreign trading.

So you have to accept L/C 120 days after sight if you do business with Bangladeshi firms[8].

Third, we do not accept shipment in August because the delivery time[9] requested by our customer is very pressing. We propose[10] that the goods are to be delivered in June.

Fourth, the fabric must be tested by authorized[11] textile inspection institute[12] approved by[13] us before shipment.

I look forward to hearing from you soon.

Best regards
Lisa
Purchasing Manager
Stitchwell Garments Co., Ltd.

## Notes

1. be satisfied with 对……满意

   e.g. We are satisfied with the design and quality of the sample fabrics you sent to us.

   我方对你方寄送给我方的面料样品的设计和质量感到满意。

2. design *n.* 设计
3. trading terms 交易条款

   交易条款指交易的主要条件，如商品的品名、价格、数量、包装、装运时间、付款条件、检验等。

4. in detail 详细地
5. quote the best price 报最优的价格
6. agree with 同意

   e.g. I agree with you on paying by T/T.

   我同意你用电汇的方式付款。

7. foreign exchange 外汇

外汇指外国货币、外币存款、外币债券、外币股票等，尤其指可以自由兑换的外国货币，如美元、欧元、英镑、日元等。

8. firm *n.* 公司；商行

firm 与 company、corporation 意义相似。

9. delivery time 交货时间

在 F 组和 C 组贸易术语中，交货时间与装运时间的含义相同。

10. propose *v.* 提议

e.g. I propose to pay by T/T.

我提议用电汇的方式支付。

11. authorized *adj.* 授权的

e.g. General Administration of Quality Supervision, Inspection and Quarantine of China is the authorized institute for commodity inspection of import and export.

中国质量监督检验检疫总局是对进出口商品进行检验的权威机构。

12. institute *n.* 机构

13. approve by 由……认可

e.g. The inspection institute must be approved by us.

检验机构必须是我们认可的。

（二）还盘与接受（baoda-out 1）

From: Albert albert@163.com

To: Lisa lisa@stitchwell.com

Date: 2019.03.02

Subject: RE: counter-offer

Dear Lisa,

With reference to your counter-offer[1] on March 1, we reply you as follows[2].

In your letter, you requested price reduction[3] on article XS-FLANNEL-03 and proposed payment terms, shipment period.

First, we can not reduce the price of this article[4] due to[5] the rising cost of labour and cotton. If you can lower the quality standard[6], that is, if you allow us to use carded cotton[7] material for production we will consider reducing the price[8].

Second, we accept the payment by L/C, but we can not accept L/C 120 days after sight because of high interest rate[9] and the risk of foreign exchange rate. We prefer to accept L/C at sight[10].

Third, we agree to change the shipment period to June, but the goods shall be shipped in 45 days after we receive the L/C in favor of[11] us.

Fourth, we usually choose Guangzhou Fibre Product Testing Institute[12] as fabric testing institute.

Look forward to hearing from you.

Yours sincerely
Albert
Sales Manager
Weifang Baoda Textiles Co., Ltd.

## Notes

1. counter-offer　*n.* 还盘
   还盘是对发盘的某些条件提出反对，并给出自己的条件。
2. as follows　如下
3. price reduction　价格减让
4. article　*n.* 物品
5. due to　由于
   其他表达方法有 because，since，as。
6. quality standard　质量标准
7. carded cotton　普梳棉
   普梳棉与精梳棉（combed cotton）相对，较粗糙些，用于质量要求一般的织物。
8. consider reducing the price　考虑降低价格
   consider doing sth.　考虑做某事
   e.g. I am considering applying for that job.
   　　我正在考虑申请那个工作。
9. interest rate　利率
   利率指银行的存款或贷款利率。
10. L/C at sight　即期信用证
    从付款时间上分，信用证分为即期信用证和远期信用证。即期信用证是开证银行在收到符合信用证要求的汇票和单据后立即给予付款的信用证。
11. in favor of us　以我方为受益人
    在进出口贸易中，受益人一般是出口商。
12. Guangzhou Fibre Product Testing Institute　广州纤维产品检测院

（三）还盘与接受（baoda-in 2）

From: Lisa lisa@stitchwell.com
To: Albert albert@163.com
Date: 2019.03.03
Subject: RE: RE: counter-offer
Attachment: Purchase Order[1]

Dear Albert,

Referring to your letter on March 2, we reply you as follows.

First, as to[2] the price, we accept your offer about XS-FLANNEL-03 (21*21, 80*60, 57/58 FOB QINGDAO USD1.8/Y) though it is higher than our expectation. We compromise[3] on the price term to develop long-term[4] business relations with you.

As to the payment term, the best we can do is 60 days L/C[5].

We accept the fabric test institute mentioned in your letter.

Meanwhile, we require the following documents[6].

Documents required:

(1) Signed Commercial Invoices[7] in 3 copies

(2) Signed Packing List[8] in 3 copies

(3) Full set of Bill of Lading

(4) Certificate of Origin[9] issued by authorized institute of China

(5) Test Report[10] issued by Guangzhou Fibre Product Testing Institute

(6) Shipping Advice[11] showing the name of the vessel, voyage No., date of shipment, marks, quantity, net and gross weight etc. to applicant within three days after the date of shipment

If you agree on the above terms, we shall place an order with you[12].

We are enclosing the Purchase Order in the attachment.

Best regards

Lisa

Purchasing Manager

Stitchwell Garments Co., Ltd.

**附 3.1　缝得好服装有限公司的采购单**

**Purchase Order**

cotton flannelette single-side

(1) XS-FLANNEL-01: 21*21, 64*54, 57/58 FOB QINGDAO USD1.3/Y, 5,000 yards

(2) XS-FLANNEL-03: 21*21, 80*60, 57/58 FOB QINGDAO USD1.8/Y, 10,000 yards

(3) XS-FLANNEL-09: 32*32, 80*68, 57/58 FOB QINGDAO USD1.6/Y, 12,000 yards

## Notes

1. purchase order 采购单
2. as to 关于
3. compromise *v.* 让步

   e.g. We won't compromise on the terms of payment.

我方不会在付款方式上让步。

4. long-term 长期的

相对应的：short-term（短期的）

5. 60 days L/C　60 天远期信用证

开证行在收到受益人的汇票和单据后的 60 天内付款。

6. document　*n.* 单据；文件

此处指国际贸易业务中卖方向买方提交的与货物有关的单据。在国际贸易中，卖方不但要向买方提交货物，并且，要同时向买方提交与货物有关的单据。尤其是在以信用证作为支付方式时，贸易可以被认为是单据的买卖。

7. commercial invoice 商业发票

商业发票指卖方开立的有关货物的票据，记载有关货物的详细信息。

8. packing list 装箱单

装箱单是记载商品包装情况的单据，用于海关检验货物或买方收货时清点货物的凭据。

9. certificate of origin 原产证

原产证指货物原产地证书，表明货物的生产国家或地区。原产证必须由政府授权的机构签发，在我国，由中国国际贸易促进委员会或中国海关总署签发。

10. test report 检验报告

检验报告是由权威的或买卖双方认可的检验机构签发的关于货物质量达到某种标准或等级的报告，常常作为交货时卖方必须提交的单据之一。

11. shipping advice 装运通知

装运通知是在货物装运后，由卖方向买方发出的通知，一般要求在货物装运后的三天内发出。

12. place an order with you 向你方下订单

place an order with sb. 向某人下订单

e.g. If your offer is reasonable, we are prepared to place an order with you.

如果你方的发盘合情合理，我方准备向你方下订单。

（四）还盘与接受（baoda-out 2）

From: Albert albert@163.com

To: Lisa lisa@stitchwell.com

Date: 2019.03.07

Subject: RE: RE: RE: counter-offer

Attachment: Sales Contract No. XS-2019001

Dear Lisa,

Thank you for your letter on March 3 about the cotton yarn-dyed fabrics.

We accept your offer mentioned in your letter.

Finally we have reached agreement on this deal through our mutual effort[1].

Now let's confirm the main trade terms as follows.

| Commodity | Item No. | Specifications | Quantity (yard) | Price (FOB QINGDAO) | Amount (USD) |
|---|---|---|---|---|---|
| Cotton yarn-dyed fabric | XS-FLANNEL-01 | 21*21, 64*54, 57/58 | 5,000 | USD1.3/yard | 6,500 |
| Cotton yarn-dyed fabric | XS-FLANNEL-03 | 21*21, 80*60, 57/58 | 10,000 | USD1.8/yard | 18,000 |
| Cotton yarn-dyed fabric | XS-FLANNEL-09 | 32*32, 80*68, 57/58 | 12,000 | USD1.6/yard | 19,200 |
| TOTAL | | | 27,000 | | 43,700 |

Shipment: 45 days after the seller receives the L/C in favor of the seller

Payment: letter of credit at 60 days after sight in favor of the seller

Packing: 100 yards per roll, one roll packed in a gunny bag

Inspection: by Guangzhou Fibre Product Testing Institute before shipment

Documents required:

(1) Signed Commercial Invoices in 3 copies

(2) Signed Packing List in 3 copies

(3) Full set of Bill of Lading

(4) Certificate of Origin issued by authorized institute of China

(5) Test Report issued by Guangzhou Fibre Product Testing Institute

(6) Shipping advice showing the name of the vessel, voyage No., date of shipment, marks, quantity, net and gross weight etc. to applicant within three days after the date of shipment

We are enclosing the Sales Contract[2], please check and sign it, and then return one copy for our file[3].

Look forward to hearing from you.

Yours sincerely

Albert

Sales Manager

Weifang Baoda Textiles Co., Ltd.

## Notes

1. mutual effort 共同努力
2. sales contract 销售合同

3. for our file 供我方存档

# CASE 2　Beijing Lucky Fibreboard Trading Co., Ltd.

## 一、信函的业务背景

北京幸运纤维板贸易有限公司采购部经理玲玲在收到澳大利亚松树纤维板工业有限公司比尔的发盘后，针对主要交易条件进行了还盘。

付款方式方面，玲玲不同意用信用证结算货款，因为信用证费用高、占用资金。玲玲想采用跟单托收的方式支付货款。

但卖方松树纤维板工业有限公司的比尔认为第一次交易就采用托收风险太大，提出采用 30%货款预付、70%货款见提单复印件后支付。

除了价格、付款方式、装运期等主要贸易条件外，本业务的交易磋商还涉及其他交易条件，如包装、检验、卖方向买方提供的单据等。

## 二、北京幸运纤维板贸易有限公司的业务信函

（一）还盘与接受（lucky-out 1）

From: Lingling lingling@163.com
To: Bill salesdepartment@pinetree.com.au
Date: 2019.06.01
Subject: counter-offer

Dear Bill,

Thank you for your offer and samples on May 25.

We are satisfied with[1] the samples you sent to us. However, we disagree with you about the payment terms you offer.

We propose to pay by Document against Payment[2] at sight (D/P at sight). As we feel that payment by L/C is costly for us, and we have to pay deposit[3] in the issuing bank[4], which will tie up[5] our fund.

Besides, if we place an order with you for 60 $M^3$ (two containers), can you give us 5% discount[6] on each item?

Hope you will agree to our proposal[7] for payment and discount.

Yours sincerely
Lingling
Purchasing Manager
Beijing Lucky Fibreboard Trading Co., Ltd.

## Notes

1. be satisfied with you 对你满意

   e.g. My boss is satisfied with my job.

   老板对我的工作感到满意。

2. Documents against Payment 付款交单

   付款交单是托收支付方式中的一种，简写为 D/P，指买方在付款时才能拿到货物的单据。托收支付方式中的另一种是承兑交单，简写为 D/A。D/A 方式下，买方只要承兑远期汇票，就可以从代收行拿到货物的单据提取货物。因此，对于卖方来说，D/A 支付方式的风险大于 D/P。

3. deposit *n.* 定金

4. the issuing bank 开证行

   开证行指接受开证申请人的委托而开立信用证的银行，承担付款责任。

5. tie up 占用

   e.g. Her money is tied up in securities and is not available to her at present.

   她的钱投入了证券，目前无法使用。

6. discount *n.* 折扣

   e.g. There is a discount store specializing in household goods near my school.

   在我学校附近有一家折扣商店，专门卖家居用品。

7. proposal *n.* 提议

（二）还盘与接受（lucky-in 1）

From: Bill salesdepartment@pinetree.com.au

To: Lingling lingling@163.com

Date: 2019.06.04

Subject: RE: counter-offer

Dear Lingling,

Referring to your counter-offer letter on June 1, we reply you as follows.

First, as to the payment terms, we can not agree with you on payment by D/P, because D/P is payment relying on business credit[1], which depends on[2] the credit of the buyer. We usually propose to pay by L/C or by T/T before shipment.

If you can not agree to pay us by L/C, we propose the following payment terms.

30% invoice value by T/T before production, 70% invoice value by T/T after we send you the copy of B/L by fax.

Second, regarding the 5% discount you mentioned, we can give you 2% discount at most[3] if you order two 40 foot containers[4]. We do you a favor[5] in order to establish long-term[6] business relations.

Hope to receive your order soon.

Yours sincerely
Bill
Sales Department
Pinetree Fibreboard Industries Co., Ltd.

## Notes

1. business credit 商业信用
   商业信用指货款或债务的偿还依赖于企业的信用。一般来说，商业信用的等级低于银行信用。
2. depend on 依赖于
3. at most 至多
   反义词：at least
4. 40 foot container 40 英尺集装箱（1 英尺=0.304 8 米）
   普通集装箱主要有 20 英尺和 40 英尺两种。
   20 英尺集装箱：（内长×宽×高）5.898 M×2.352 M×2.385 M
   40 英尺集装箱：（内长×宽×高）12.032 M×2.352 M×2.385 M
5. long-term 长期的
   e.g. All their money is tied up in long-term investments.
   他们所有的钱投入了长期投资。
6. do you a favor 帮你忙
   do sb. a favor
   e.g. Would you do me a favor and close the window?
   帮忙关上窗户，好吗？

（三）还盘与接受（lucky-out 2）

From: Lingling lingling@163.com
To: Bill salesdepartment@pinetree.com.au
Date: 2019.06.05
Subject: purchase order
Attachment: Purchase Order

Dear Bill,

In reply to your letter on June 4 about payment terms and discount, we agree on the terms you proposed.

Up to now[1], we have reached agreement on main trade terms.

To avoid subsequent dispute[2], we propose other trading terms which have not been mentioned before as follows.

1. Packing: according to our packing requirement (we will send you detailed packing requirement before shipment)

2. Inspection: be inspected by Australian authorized institute and issue Phytosanitary Certificate[3] before shipment

3. Documents required:

(1) Signed Commercial Invoice in 3 copies

(2) Signed Packing List in 3 copies

(3) Full set of clean on board Ocean Bills of Lading made out to order and blank endorsed and notify the buyer

(4) Certificate of Australian Origin issued by authorized institute of Australia

(5) Phytosanitary Certificate issued by Australian authorized institute

(6) Insurance Policy[4] in duplicate endorsed in blank for 110% invoice value, covering All Risks[5] as per ICC "A"[6] (1/1/2009)

If you agree with the above terms we propose, we will place an order with you for the premium panels.

Meanwhile, please send us the samples of the ordered fibreboard for test and later use.

Enclosed please find the Purchase Order for the premium panels for your reference.

Yours sincerely
Lingling
Purchasing Manager
Beijing Lucky Fibreboard Trading Co., Ltd.

附 3.2　北京幸运纤维板贸易有限公司的采购单

| Purchase Order | | | | | | | | |
|---|---|---|---|---|---|---|---|---|
| Commodity | Grade | Length (MM) | Width (MM) | Thickness (MM) | Unit Price USD/$M^3$ | Quantity $M^3$ | Quantity No. of Sheet | Amount (USD) |
| fibreboard | premium | 2,400 | 1,200 | 9 | 430 | 32 | 1235 | 13,760.00 |
| fibreboard | premium | 2,400 | 1,400 | 6 | 490 | 24.9 | 1235 | 12,201.00 |
| Total | | | | | | | | 25,961.00 |

## Notes

1. up to now 直到现在
2. subsequent dispute 后来的争议
3. phytosanitary certificate 植物检疫证书（简称植检证）
   为了避免植物病虫害的传播，政府对进出口的植物及其产品由政府指定机构进行强制性的检验，出具植检证。
4. insurance policy 保险单
   保险单是保险公司签发的承保单据。当卖方负责办理货物的运输保险时，保险单是卖方必须向买方提交的单据。
5. All Risks 一切险
   一切险是货物运输保险中的一种险别。保险公司负责赔偿除特殊外来风险，如罢工险、战争险等以外的所有风险造成的货物损失。
6. ICC "A" 英国伦敦保险业协会制定的《协会货物条款》A 险
   英国伦敦保险业协会制定的《协会货物条款》，在国际贸易中的货物运输保险业务中被广泛地采用。它主要包括 A、B、C 三种险别，其中，A 险的承保范围最广，相当于中国人民财产保险公司承保险别中的一切险。

（四）还盘与接受（lucky-in 2）

From: Bill salesdepartment@pinetree.com.au
To: Lingling lingling@163.com
Date: 2019.06.10
Subject: Re: purchase order

Dear Lingling,

With reference to[1] your letter of Purchase Order on June 5 for premium fibreboard, we accept the terms you proposed in the letter.

Now I would confirm the trade terms we have agreed upon:

| Commodity | Specification | | | | Price (USD/$M^3$) | Quantity | | Amount (USD) |
|---|---|---|---|---|---|---|---|---|
| | Grade | Length (MM) | Width (MM) | Thick-ness (MM) | CIF Xingang China | No. of Sheet | $M^3$ | |
| fibreboard | premium | 2,400 | 1,200 | 9 | 430 | 1,235 | 32 | 13,760.00 |
| fibreboard | premium | 2,400 | 1,400 | 6 | 490 | 1,235 | 24.90 | 12,201.00 |
| TOTAL | | | | | | 2,470 | 56.90 | 25,961.00 |

Shipment: within one month after receiving the deposit of 30% invoice value

Port of Loading: Melbourne, Australia

Port of Discharge: Xingang Port, China

Payment: 30% invoice value by T/T as deposit, 70% invoice value by T/T after we send you the copy of B/L by fax

Packing: according to the buyer's instruction

Inspection: be inspected by Australian authorized institute and issue Phytosanitary Certificate before shipment

Documents required:

(1) Signed Commercial Invoice in 3 copies

(2) Signed Packing List in 3 copies

(3) Full set of clean on board Ocean Bills of Lading made out to order and blank endorsed and notify the buyer

(4) Certificate of Australian Origin issued by authorized institute of Australia

(5) Phytosanitary Certificate issued by Australian authorized institute

(6) Insurance Policy in duplicate endorsed in blank for 110% invoice value, covering All Risks as per ICC "A" (1/1/2009)

I am very glad that we have reached agreement on this business through negotiation[2] and will send you the Sales Contract soon.

Please counter-sign[3] it and send one copy back for our file.

Yours sincerely

Bill

Sales Department

Pinetree Fibreboard Industries Co., Ltd.

## Notes

1. with reference to 关于

   "关于"的常见表示方式：as to，refer to，with reference to，regarding，with regard to。

2. negotiation *n.* 磋商；商谈

   e.g. The Doha Round Negotiations started in November 2001 and ended in July 2006.

   多哈回合谈判开始于 2001 年 11 月，结束于 2006 年 7 月。

3. counter-sign *v.* 会签

## 练习

**一、将下列句子译成中文。**

1. The price for XS-FLANNEL-03 is on the high side.
2. Please quote us the best price you can offer.
3. We cannot agree to the payment terms by T/T.
4. We propose to pay by L/C at 120 days.
5. Delivery in 60 days after contract date is rather long. Can you deliver the goods in 40 days after contract date?
6. Can you change the minimum quantity from 3,000 meters to 2,000 meters?
7. I noticed your Minimum Quantity is 500pcs, what is your quantity discount if we place a large order such as 3000pcs?
8. In reply to your counter-offer for car tire, asking for 10% discount, we can not accept it due to production cost.
9. We admit that our price is a little higher than other suppliers', but our quality is much better than others.
10. As the sum of advance payment is too large, we suggest paying by L/C.
11. We accept your offer mentioned in your letter.
12. We are enclosing the sales contract and please sign it and send one copy back.

**二、将下列句子译成英文。**

1. 关于激光打印机的价格，其他供应商可以以更低的价格向我方供货。请报出你方的最低价格。
2. 我方想通过即期付款交单的方式付款。
3. 通过信用证的方式付款对我方来说成本高。我方不得不向开证行支付押金，这样会占用我方的资金。
4. 如果我方订两个 40 英尺的货柜，你方能给我方 5%的折扣吗？
5. 由于人民币持续升值，我们没有降价的空间了。
6. 我抱歉地告诉你，由于这是一个小订单，我们不能接受你方使用跟单信用证进行付款的条件。
7. 我们接受你关于木刻品 5%折扣的还盘。
8. 遗憾地告诉你，我们无法接受承兑交单付款方式。
9. 在生产前支付发票金额 30%的定金，其余的 70%的货款在我方通过传真发给你方提单复印件时支付。
10. 由于该商品销售的季节性较强，你公司能否在 10 月份交货？
11. 最低起订量可以降低，但商品的价格需要相应提高。
12. 请在附件里找到我公司关于核桃的订单。

## 技能训练

### 根据业务情境和信息写信

（一）业务情境

大力神轮胎贸易公司的总经理大卫・桑德伯格在收到江苏通达轮胎有限公司的业务员李辉的发盘后，进行了还盘。

对于大卫・桑德伯格的还盘，李辉表示接受。

（二）信息

大卫・桑德伯格的还盘要点如下：

1. 发盘价格偏高，期望价格为 USD60/piece FOB 上海；
2. 付款方式：不接受即期信用证，改为 60 天的远期信用证；
   原因：公司流动资金有限；
3. 订货数量：360 条。

（三）任务

根据以上的业务情境和信息写信。

1. 大卫・桑德伯格针对李辉的发盘做出还盘。

信函应包括以下要点：

（1）提及李辉的发盘；

（2）针对发盘的内容，提出自己不同意的贸易条件，并说明原因；

（3）希望还盘被接受。

2. 李辉对大卫・桑德伯格的还盘表示接受。

信函应包括以下要点：

（1）提及大卫・桑德伯格的还盘；

（2）表示接受还盘；

（3）根据前面的交易磋商，列出主要的交易条件，供大卫・桑德伯格确认；

（4）表示近日会发出书面合同供大卫・桑德伯格签回。

## 补充阅读

信函 1：还盘

业务背景：法国的一家手工艺品贸易公司（优雅贸易有限公司）的总经理海伦对中国的一家草编工艺品生产企业（青岛兴旺手工艺品有限公司）的销售经理李华的发盘做出还盘。

From: helen1219@hotmail.com

To: lihua@handicraftschina.com
Date: 2019.03.20
Subject: counter-offer

Dear Lihua,

We are in receipt of your letter of offer on March 18 for straw knitting handicrafts.

We regret to inform you that we find your price higher than expected although we appreciate the quality of your products.

So we make the following counter-offer.

8,000 pieces of straw knitting handicrafts, at USD4.2 per piece, CIF Marseille, France.

As to other terms you mentioned, we agree with you on them as per your offer letter on March 18.

We are expecting your quick reply.

Yours sincerely
Helen Keller
General Manager
Elegance Trading Limited, France
Address: No. 1203 Garden Road, Paris, France
Tel: 33-1-8185678; Fax: 33-1-8185677

信函 2：接受

业务背景：中国的一家草编工艺品生产企业（青岛兴旺手工艺品有限公司）销售经理李华回复法国的一家手工艺品贸易公司（优雅贸易有限公司）总经理海伦的还盘，表示接受对方的还盘。

From: lihua@handicraftschina.com
To: helen1219@hotmail.com
Date: 2019.03.21
Subject: RE: counter-offer

Hi, Helen,

Thank you for your letter on March 20.

In reply to your request on price reduction, that is USD4.2 per piece, CIF Marseille, France.

We accept your offer in order to develop long-term business relations with you.

The following are the trading terms we have agreed upon.

Article: straw knitting handicrafts

Price: USD4.2/piece, CIF Marseille, France

Quantity: 8,000 pieces

Shipment: one month after receiving L/C

Packing: 25 pieces per carton

Payment: by irrevocable documentary Letter of Credit in favor of us

We are sending you the Sales Contract in the next few days by forwarder.

Regards

Li Hua

Sales Manager

Qingdao Xingwang Handicrafts Co., Ltd.

Address: No. 1251 Xingwang Road, Qingdao, Shandong, China

Tel: 86-0532-8745618; Fax: 86-0532-8745617

# 任务四

# 合同的签订

# Signing a Contract

## 学习目标

1. 了解销售合同（购货合同）的基本条款；
2. 掌握有关合同签订的信函的写作要点；
3. 熟悉有关合同签订的信函的常用词语和句子；
4. 能够阅读与撰写有关合同签订的信函。

## 背景知识

在国际贸易中，买卖双方通过交易磋商，在各项交易条件方面达成一致后，交易即成立，买卖双方就构成了合同关系。双方在磋商过程中的往来函电，即是合同成立的书面证明。

但根据国际贸易习惯，买卖双方还要签订书面的货物买卖合同，以此作为合同成立的证据和合同履行的依据。

书面合同的名称可以是销售合同（sales contract）、购货合同（purchase contract）、协议书（agreement）、订单（purchase order）等。

书面合同的内容一般包括三个部分：约首、正文和约尾。

约首，包括合同名称、编号、签订的日期和地点、买卖双方的名称和地址。

正文，包括各项交易条件的具体规定。

约尾，包括当事人的签字、盖章及附件等。

在实务中，合同可以由双方代表当面签字、盖章，也可以由买方或卖方签字、盖章后寄给对方，对方签字盖章后再寄回其中一份，买卖双方各保留一份。

## 写作提示

### 有关合同签订的信函内容及要点

（1）说明合同所涉及的商品；
（2）请对方在收到合同并审阅后签字；
（3）让对方在签字后寄回（传真回）一份。

## 示范信函

# CASE 1 Weifang Baoda Textiles Co., Ltd.

### 一、信函的业务背景

潍坊宝达纺织品有限公司在和缝得好服装有限公司就交易的各项条件进行磋商并达成一致后，按照自己公司的合同格式将合同拟定好并签字，然后寄给缝得好服装有限公司。

缝得好服装有限公司在审阅合同后签字，并寄回一份合同给潍坊宝达纺织品有限公司。

### 二、潍坊宝达纺织品有限公司的业务信函

（一）合同的签订（baoda-out 1）

From: Albert albert@163.com
To: Lisa lisa@stitchwell.com
Date: 2019.03.07
Subject: sales contract
Attachment: Sales Contract No. XS-2019001

Dear Lisa,

We are enclosing the Sales Contract[1] and sending you two original[2] Sales Contracts by DHL with its tracking No. SF33658974. Please check and sign it upon receipt of[3] it. Then please send one of the original Sales Contracts back to us.

The following is our address.

Weifang Baoda Textiles Co., Ltd.
No. 688 West Ring Road, Weifang, Shandong, China
Post Code: 261053

Meanwhile, please open the relevant L/C before May 8. We will prepare for your order upon receipt of the L/C.

Look forward to hearing from you.

Yours sincerely
Albert
Sales Manager
Weifang Baoda Textiles Co., Ltd.

### 附 4.1　销售合同 XS-2019001

### SALES CONTRACT

<table>
<tr><td rowspan="3">Seller:</td><td colspan="3" rowspan="3">Weifang Baoda Textiles Co., Ltd.<br>Address: No. 688 West Ring Road, Weifang, Shandong, China<br>Tel: 86-0536-8885678; Fax: 86-0536-8885677</td><td>NO.:</td><td>XS-2019001</td></tr>
<tr><td>DATE:</td><td>March 7, 2019</td></tr>
<tr><td rowspan="2">SIGNED IN:</td><td rowspan="2">WEIFANG, CHINA</td></tr>
<tr><td rowspan="2">Buyer:</td><td colspan="3" rowspan="2">Stitchwell Garments Co., Ltd.<br>456/1/A, Tejgaon Industrial Area, Dhaka 1208, Bangladesh<br>Tel: 880-2-9882934; Fax: 880-2-8891567</td></tr>
<tr><td></td><td></td></tr>
<tr><td colspan="6">This contract is made by and agreed between the BUYER and SELLER, in accordance with the terms and conditions stipulated below.</td></tr>
<tr><td colspan="3">Description of Goods</td><td rowspan="2">Quantity</td><td rowspan="2">Unit Price</td><td rowspan="2">Amount</td></tr>
<tr><td>Commodity</td><td>Style No.</td><td>Specification</td></tr>
<tr><td>Cotton Yarn-dyed Fabrics</td><td>XS-FLANNEL-01</td><td>21*21, 64*54, 57/58</td><td>5,000 yards</td><td>FOB QINGDAO<br>USD1.3/yard</td><td>USD6,500.00</td></tr>
<tr><td>Cotton Yarn-dyed Fabrics</td><td>XS-FLANNEL-03</td><td>21*21, 80*60, 57/58</td><td>10,000 yards</td><td>USD1.8/yard</td><td>USD18,000.00</td></tr>
<tr><td>Cotton Yarn-dyed Fabrics</td><td>XS-FLANNEL-09</td><td>32*32, 80*68, 57/58</td><td>12,000 yards</td><td>USD1.6/yard</td><td>USD19,200.00</td></tr>
<tr><td>TOTAL</td><td colspan="2"></td><td>27,000 yards</td><td></td><td>USD43,700.00</td></tr>
<tr><td>REMARKS:</td><td colspan="5">5% MORE OR LESS IN QUANTITY IS ALLOWED.</td></tr>
<tr><td>TOTAL:</td><td colspan="5">USD FORTY-THREE THOUSAND SEVEN HUNDRED ONLY.</td></tr>
</table>

续表

<table>
<tr><td>PACKING:</td><td>100 YARDS PER ROLL, ONE ROLL PACKED IN A GUNNY BAG.</td></tr>
<tr><td>SHIPPING MARKS:</td><td>ACCORDING TO THE BUYER’S OPTION.</td></tr>
<tr><td colspan="2">Transshipment: ALLOWED</td></tr>
<tr><td colspan="2">Partial Shipments: NOT ALLOWED</td></tr>
<tr><td colspan="2">Shipment:</td></tr>
<tr><td colspan="2">WITHIN 45 DAYS UPON RECEIPT OF THE L/C IN FAVOR OF THE SELLER, WHICH ACCORDS WITH THE RELEVANT CLAUSES OF THIS CONTRACT.<br>PORT OF LOADING: ANY PORT IN CHINA.<br>PORT OF DISCHARGE: CHITTAGONG BANGLADESH.</td></tr>
<tr><td colspan="2">Insurance:<br>to be covered by the <u>BUYER</u> .</td></tr>
<tr><td colspan="2">Terms of Payment:<br>☐The buyer shall issue an irrevocable L/C at 60 days after sight through <u>a bank acceptable to the seller</u> in favor of the seller prior to <u>MAY 8 2019</u> indicating L/C shall be valid in China through negotiation within <u>21</u> day after the shipment effected, and the L/C must mention the Contract Number.</td></tr>
<tr><td colspan="2"></td></tr>
<tr><td colspan="2">Shipping Advice:<br>The seller shall immediately, upon the completion of the loading of the goods, advise the buyer of the Contract No., names of commodities, loaded quantity, invoice values, gross weight, names of vessels and shipment date by TLX/FAX.</td></tr>
<tr><td colspan="2">Documents Required:<br>(1) Signed Commercial Invoices in 3 copies<br>(2) Signed Packing List in 3 copies<br>(3) Full set of Bills of Lading<br>(4) Certificate of Origin issued by authorized institute<br>(5) Test Report issued by Guangzhou Fibre Product Testing Institute<br>(6) Shipping Advice showing the name of the vessel, date of shipment, marks, quantity, net and gross weight etc. to applicant within three days after the date of shipment</td></tr>
<tr><td colspan="2">Inspection and Claims:<br>1. The buyer shall have the qualities of the goods carefully inspected by Guangzhou Fibre Product Testing Institute, which shall issue TEST REPORT before shipment.<br>2. The buyer shall have right to have the goods inspected by the local commodity inspection authority after the arrival of the goods at the port of destination if the goods are found damaged/short/their specifications and quantities not in compliance with that specified in the contract, and the buyer shall lodge claims against the seller based on the Inspection Certificate issued by the Commodity Inspection Authority within <u>30</u> days after the goods’ arrival at the destination.</td></tr>
<tr><td colspan="2">Force Majeure:<br>The seller shall not hold any responsibility for partial or total non-performance of this contract due to Force Majeure. But the seller shall advise the buyer on time of such occurrence.</td></tr>
</table>

续表

| | |
|---|---|
| Disputes Settlement:<br>All disputes in connection with this contract or arising in the execution thereof shall be amicably settled through negotiation. In case no amicable settlement can be reached between the two parties, the case under dispute shall be submitted to arbitration, which shall be held in the country where the defendant resides, or in third country agreed by both parties. The decision of the arbitration shall be accepted as final and binding upon both parties. The Arbitration Fees shall be borne by the losing party. | |
| This contract is in 2 copies, effective since being singed/sealed by both parties. | |
| The Buyer | The Seller |
| Stitchwell Garments Co., Ltd. | Weifang Baoda Textiles Co., Ltd. |

## Notes

1. sales contract 销售合同
   买卖双方签订的书面合同主要有以下几种形式：
   sales contract 销售合同 或 sales confirmation 销售确认书
   purchase order 采购订单 或 purchase contract 采购合同
2. original *n. & adj.* 正本（的）
3. upon receipt of 一旦收到

（二）合同的签订（baoda-in 1）

From: Lisa lisa@stitchwell.com
To: Albert albert@163.com
Date: 2019.03.15
Subject: RE: sales contract
Attachment: Sales Contract No. XS-2019001

Dear Albert,

After checking the Sales Contract sent on March 7, we have signed it and sent the original to your address through forwarder[1].

We will apply to open the L/C as stipulated[2] soon. Meanwhile, please make sure[3] that the goods can be produced and shipped on time[4].

Best regards
Lisa
Purchasing Manager

Stitchwell Garments Co., Ltd.

## Notes

1. forwarder *n.* 承运人
2. as stipulated 按照规定
3. make sure 确保
   e.g. Please make sure that the lights are turned off when you leave the office.
   离开办公室请随手关灯。
4. on time 准时
   e.g. The bus is never on time recently.
   最近公交车从不准时。

# CASE 2 Beijing Lucky Fibreboard Trading Co., Ltd.

## 一、信函的业务背景

北京幸运纤维板贸易有限公司和澳大利亚松树纤维板工业有限公司就密度板的买卖进行了多次磋商，在关于交易的各项条件达成一致后，澳大利亚松树纤维板工业有限公司依据自己的合同格式拟订了交易合同，并寄给北京幸运纤维板贸易有限公司签字。

北京幸运纤维板贸易有限公司对交易合同审阅并签字后，把两份正本合同中的一份寄给澳大利亚松树纤维板工业有限公司。

## 二、北京幸运纤维板贸易有限公司的业务信函

（一）合同的签订（lucky-in 1）

From: Bill salesdepartment@pinetree.com.au
To: Lingling lingling@163.com
Date: 2019.06.18
Subject: sales confirmation
Attachment: Sales Confirmation

Dear Lingling,

With reference[1] to your Purchase Order[2] of premium panel, we have made the Sales Confirmation (No. SC-PINE2019010) and are sending you signed Sales Confirmation by fax.

Please sign and fax one copy back upon receipt of the Sales Confirmation. At the same time, please remit us the deposit as early as possible so that we may process with the goods.

We appreciate your cooperation and expect your further orders in future.

Regards
Bill
Sales Department
Pinetree Fibreboard Industries Co., Ltd.
Address: No. 8 Pinetree Road, Melbourne, Australia
Tel: 61-3-85715322
Fax: 61-3-85715331
E-mail: salesdepartment@pinetree.com.au

## 附 4.2　销售合同 SC-PINE2019010
## SALES CONFIRMATION

| | | | |
|---|---|---|---|
| Seller: | Pinetree Fibreboard Industries Co., Ltd.<br>Address: No. 8 Pinetree Road, Melbourne, Australia<br>Tel: 61-3-85715322；Fax: 61-3-85715331 | NO.: | SC-PINE2019010 |
| | | DATE: | 2019.06.18 |
| Buyer: | Beijing Lucky Fibreboard Trading Co., Ltd.<br>Tel: 86-010-65771234; Fax: 86-010-65771233<br>Address: Room 801, International Trade Center, No. 92 Jianguo Road, Chaoyang, Beijing, China | SIGNED IN: | MELBOURNE, AUSTRALIA |

This contract is made by and agreed between the BUYER and SELLER, in accordance with the terms and conditions stipulated below.

| Commodity | Specification | | | | Unit Price | Quantity | | Amount |
|---|---|---|---|---|---|---|---|---|
| | Grade | Length | Width | Thickness | USD/$M^3$ CIF Xingang China | No. of Sheet | $M^3$ | USD |
| Fibreboard | premium | 2,400 MM | 1,200 MM | 9 MM | 430 | 1,235 | 32 | 13,760.00 |
| Fibreboard | premium | 2,400 MM | 1,400 MM | 6 MM | 490 | 1,235 | 24.90 | 12,201.00 |
| TOTAL | | | | | | 2,470 | 56.90 | 25,961.00 |

| | |
|---|---|
| REMARKS: | 1. QUALITY STANDARD APPLIED TO THE GOODS IS THE ENGLISH VERSION OF GB/T 11718-1999.<br>2. THE QUANTITY AND THE AMOUNT OF THIS CONTRACT IS ALLOWED TO BE 5% MORE OR LESS. |
| TOTAL: | USD TWENTY-FIVE THOUSAND NINE HUNDRED AND SIXTY-ONE ONLY. |
| PACKING: | ACCORDING TO THE BUYER'S INSTRUCTION. |
| Transshipment: ALLOWED | |
| Partial Shipments: NOT ALLOWED | |

续表

| |
|---|
| Shipment: within one month after receiving the deposit of 30% invoice value. |
| PORT OF LOADING: MELBOURNE, AUSTRALIA<br>PORT OF DISCHARGE: XINGANG PORT, CHINA |
| Insurance:<br>to be covered by the seller for 110% of invoice value covering All Risks as per ICC “A” (1/1/2009). |
| Terms of Payment:<br>☐ 30% invoice value by T/T as deposit, 70% invoice value by T/T after we send you the copy of B/L by fax. |
| Documents Required:<br>The seller shall present the following documents required for negotiation to the banks.<br>☐ Full set of Clean on Board Ocean Bills of Lading made out to order and blank endorsed and notify the buyer.<br>☐ Signed Commercial Invoice in 3 copies.<br>☐ Signed Packing List in 3 copies.<br>☐ Certificate of Australian Origin issued by authorized institute of Australia.<br>☐ Phytosanitary Certificate issued by Australian authorized institute.<br>☐ Insurance Policy in duplicate endorsed in blank. |
| Shipping Advice:<br>The seller shall immediately, upon the completion of the loading of the goods, advise the buyer of the Contract No., names of commodities, loaded quantity, invoice values, gross weight, names of vessels and shipment date by TLX/FAX. |
| Inspection and Claims:<br>1. Inspected by Australian authorized institute and issue Phytosanitary Certificate before shipment.<br>2. The buyer shall have right to have the goods inspected by the local commodity inspection authority after the arrival of the goods at the port of destination if the goods are found damaged/short/their specifications and quantities not in compliance with that specified in the contract, and the buyer shall lodge claims against the seller based on the Inspection Certificate issued by the Commodity Inspection Authority within 15 days after the goods' arrival at the destination. |
| Force Majeure:<br>The seller shall not hold any responsibility for partial or total non-performance of this contract due to Force Majeure. But the seller shall advise the buyer on time of such occurrence. |
| Disputes Settlement:<br>All disputes in connection with this contract or arising in the execution thereof shall be amicably settled through negotiation. In case no amicable settlement can be reached between the two parties, the case under dispute shall be submitted to arbitration, which shall be held in the country where the defendant resides, or in third country agreed by both parties. The decision of the arbitration shall be accepted as final and binding upon both parties. The Arbitration Fees shall be borne by the losing party. |
| This contract is in 2 copies, effective since being singed/sealed by both parties. |

| The Buyer | The Seller |
|---|---|
| Beijing Lucky Fibreboard Trading Co., Ltd. | Pinetree Fibreboard Industries Co., Ltd. |

## Notes

1. with reference to 关于，提及
2. purchase order 采购订单

（二）合同的签订（lucky-out 1）

From: Lingling lingling@163.com
To: Sales Department salesdepartment@pinetree.com.au
Date: 2019.06.20
Subject: RE: sales confirmation

Dear Bill,

As to the SALES CONFIRMATION No.SC-PINE2019010, we have signed and sent it to you by fax for your file.

We will pay the deposit[1] as arranged.

I expect to have more business with you in future.

Best regards,
Lingling
Purchase Manager
Beijing Lucky Fibreboard Trading Co., Ltd.

## Note

1. deposit *n.* 定金；存款

   e.g. (1) The buyer agrees to pay a 5,000 pound deposit.
   买方同意支付 5 000 英镑的定金。
   (2) A deposit is a sum of money which is in a bank account or savings account.
   存款是在银行账户或储蓄账户里的一笔钱。

## 练习

**一、将下列句子译成中文。**

1. Owing to our mutual efforts, we are able to bridge the gap and put the deal through.
2. We appreciate your Order No. 486 for 1,000 tons Dongbei rice, and agree the terms you proposed.
3. If you find everything is in order, please sign and return one copy to us for our file.
4. As the goods are urgently in need, we stress the importance of punctual shipment.
5. The sooner we get your L/C, the sooner shipment can be arranged.

6. We are sending the original Sales Contract by DHL with its tracking No. 12345.
7. Please countersign it and send one of the original Sales Contracts back to us upon receipt of it.
8. At your request, we are faxing you back the countersigned Sales Confirmation.

**二、将下列句子译成英文。**

1. 感谢我们的共同努力，终于达成了一致。
2. 我方将向你方寄出两份正本销售合同，运单号为 199875。
3. 请会签合同并传回一份供我方保存。
4. 请尽快安排我们所订购货物的装运。
5. 我们相信你方能在信用证有效期内交货。
6. 请及时开立信用证，以便我方安排你的订单。
7. 我们会在收到你方的定金后安排生产。
8. 如果产品质量令人满意，我方还会追加新订单。

## 技能训练

### 根据业务情境和信息写信

（一）业务情境

江苏通达轮胎有限公司的业务员李辉就大卫·桑德伯格的还盘向公司领导请示，公司领导同意了大卫·桑德伯格的还盘，于是李辉拟定了销售合同，并向大力神轮胎贸易公司的总经理大卫·桑德伯格发出接受信函及销售合同，让大卫·桑德伯格签后寄回。

（二）信息

1. 合同签订的日期：2019.06.30
2. 合同签订的地点：中国无锡
3. 合同编号：LLLT20190608
4. 运输标志：N/M
5. 溢短装：正负 5%可以接受
6. 信用证开立时间：2019 年 7 月 25 日前
7. 开证行：Bank of America, New York Branch
8. 装运时间：收到信用证后的 2 个月之内装运
9. 装运港：中国上海
10. 目的港：美国纽约
11. 允许转运
12. 禁止分批装运
13. 包装条款：根据买方的指示
14. 单据要求：

（1）发票一式三份；
（2）装箱单一式三份；
（3）全套（3 份）正本清洁已装船海运提单；
（4）由无锡海关出具的品质证书正本；
（5）原产地证明正本三份，由中国国际贸易促进委员会出具。

15. 江苏通达轮胎有限公司的销售确认书模板如表 4.1 所示。

**表 4.1　　销售确认书模板**

**SALES CONFIRMATION**

<table>
<tr><td rowspan="3">Seller:</td><td rowspan="3" colspan="2"></td><td>NO.:</td><td></td></tr>
<tr><td>DATE:</td><td></td></tr>
<tr><td rowspan="2">SIGNED IN:</td><td rowspan="2"></td></tr>
<tr><td rowspan="2">Buyer:</td><td rowspan="2" colspan="2"></td></tr>
<tr><td></td><td></td></tr>
<tr><td colspan="5">This contract is made by and agreed between the BUYER and SELLER, in accordance with the terms and conditions stipulated below.</td></tr>
<tr><td>Marks and Numbers</td><td>Description of Goods</td><td>Quantity</td><td>Unit Price</td><td>Amount</td></tr>
<tr><td></td><td></td><td></td><td></td><td></td></tr>
<tr><td>TOTAL</td><td></td><td></td><td></td><td></td></tr>
<tr><td>REMARKS:</td><td colspan="4"></td></tr>
<tr><td>TOTAL:</td><td colspan="4"></td></tr>
<tr><td>PACKING:</td><td colspan="4"></td></tr>
<tr><td colspan="5">Transshipment:</td></tr>
<tr><td colspan="5">Partial Shipments:</td></tr>
<tr><td colspan="5">Shipment:</td></tr>
<tr><td colspan="2">PORT OF LOADING:</td><td colspan="3">PORT OF DISCHARGE:</td></tr>
<tr><td colspan="5">Insurance:</td></tr>
<tr><td colspan="5">Terms of Payment:<br>☐ The buyer shall issue an irrevocable L/C at sight through ________________ in favor of the seller prior to ______________ indicating L/C shall be valid in China through negotiation within ______ day after the shipment effected, and the L/C must mention the Contract Number.</td></tr>
<tr><td colspan="5">Documents Required:<br>The seller shall present the following documents required for negotiation to the banks.<br>☐ Full set of Clean on Board Ocean Bills of Lading made out to order and blank endorsed and notify the buyer.<br>☐ Signed Commercial Invoice in ___ copies.<br>☐ Packing List/Weight Memo in ___ copies.<br>☐ Certificate of Inspection in ____ copies each issued by __________ .<br>☐ Certificate of Origin in ___ copies issued by ______________.</td></tr>
</table>

续表

<table>
<tr><td colspan="2">Shipping Advice:<br>The seller shall immediately, upon the completion of the loading of the goods, advise the buyer of the Contract No., names of commodities, loaded quantity, invoice values, gross weight, names of vessels and shipment date by TLX/FAX.</td></tr>
<tr><td colspan="2">Inspection and Claims:<br>1. The buyer shall have the qualities, specifications, quantities of the goods carefully inspected by ________________, which shall issue Inspection Certificate before shipment.<br>2. The buyer shall have right to have the goods inspected by the local commodity inspection authority after the arrival of the goods at the port of destination if the goods are found damaged/short/their specifications and quantities not in compliance with that specified in the contract, and the buyer shall lodge claims against the seller based on the Inspection Certificate issued by the Commodity Inspection Authority within ______ days after the goods' arrival at the destination.</td></tr>
<tr><td colspan="2">Force Majeure:<br>The seller shall not hold any responsibility for partial or total non-performance of this contract due to Force Majeure. But the seller shall advise the buyer on time of such occurrence.</td></tr>
<tr><td colspan="2">Disputes Settlement:<br>All disputes in connection with this contract or arising in the execution thereof shall be amicably settled through negotiation. In case no amicable settlement can be reached between the two parties, the case under dispute shall be submitted to arbitration, which shall be held in the country where the defendant resides, or in third country agreed by both parties. The decision of the arbitration shall be accepted as final and binding upon both parties. The Arbitration Fees shall be borne by the losing party.</td></tr>
<tr><td colspan="2">This contract is in 2 copies, effective since being singed/sealed by both parties.</td></tr>
<tr><td>The Buyer</td><td>The Seller</td></tr>
<tr><td></td><td></td></tr>
</table>

（三）任务

根据以上业务情境和信息完成以下任务。

1. 根据李辉与大卫·桑德伯格前面交易磋商中已经达成的贸易条件和给出的信息，依照江苏通达轮胎有限公司的销售合同模板拟定一份销售合同。

2. 江苏通达轮胎有限公司的业务员李辉写信给大卫·桑德伯格，让他签后寄回合同。

信函应包括以下要点：

（1）提及交易的货物；

（2）请大卫·桑德伯格在收到合同后审阅并签字、盖章；

（3）让大卫·桑德伯格在签字、盖章后寄送回一份合同；

（4）表示希望合作成功。

## 补充阅读

信函 1：签订合同

业务背景：中国的一家草编工艺品生产企业（青岛兴旺手工艺品有限公司）的销售经理李华与法国的一家手工艺品贸易公司（优雅贸易有限公司）总经理海伦通过交易磋

商达成了一致，李华向海伦发出签约函并附上电子销售合同。

From: lihua@handicraftschina.com
To: helen1219@hotmail.com
Date: 2019.03.23
Subject: sales contract
Attachment: Sales Contract

Dear Helen,

With reference to our recent exchange of e-mails, I am very happy for reaching agreement between us on 8,000 pieces of straw knitting handicrafts.

Enclosed please find the Sales Contract No. hc2019008, and please sign and return one copy to us by e-mail or fax.

If there is any problem, please contact me in time.

At the same time, please establish the relevant Letter of Credit in time in order for us to arrange the shipment for the ordered goods.

Regards
Li Hua
Sales Manager
Qingdao Xingwang Handicrafts Co., Ltd.
Address: No. 1251 Xingwang Road, Qingdao, Shandong, China
Tel: 86-0532-8745618; Fax: 86-0532-8745617

信函 2：采购单

业务背景：中国一家钢管生产企业（淄博海来特锥形钢管有限公司）销售经理大卫与印度的从事钢管贸易的公司（印度 API 钢管有限公司）总经理曼珠先生通过交易磋商达成了一笔商品交易。印度 API 钢管有限公司总经理曼珠先生通过电子邮件向淄博海来特锥形钢管有限公司销售经理大卫发出了锥形钢管的采购单。

From: mundra@indiapipe.com
To: davidli@steelpipechina.com
Date: 2019.04.12
Subject: purchase order for 500 pieces of tapered steel pipes

Dear David,

We are delighted to inform you that we have reached agreement on this deal through our negotiation. Now I am placing an order with you for tapered steel pipe. The following is our Purchase Order.

**Purchase Order**

Buyer: India API Steel Pipe Trading Limited

Seller: Zibo Highlight Tapered Steel Pipe Co., Ltd.

Date: April 12, 2019 PO Number: AT2019002

| Commodity | Quantity | Unit Price | Amount |
|---|---|---|---|
| tapered steel pipe XW091 | 3,000 pieces | USD300.00 per piece | USD900,000 |
| tapered steel pipe XW093 | 2,000 pieces | USD350.00 per piece | USD700,000 |
| Total Amount: CIF Mumbai, India | | | USD1600,000 |

Payment: 30% invoice value by T/T before production, 70% invoice value by T/T before shipment

Shipment: shipped before the end of May

Buyer (signature): Siddharth Mundra

Seller (signature):

Please fax the signed order to us after confirmation.

As our customers are in urgent need of the goods, please make sure that you can deliver the goods in time.

I look forward to hearing from you soon.

Regards

Siddharth Mundra

General Manager

India API Steel Pipe Trading Limited

Address: Bajaj Bhawan, 2nd Floor, Jamnalal Bajaj Marg, Nariman Point, Mumbai

Tel: 91-22023626; Fax: 91-22021174

信函 3：采购合同

业务背景：中国的一家贸易公司（青岛鱼山贸易有限公司）总经理爱丽斯与日本的一家智能玩具生产企业（三友智能玩具公司）销售经理呐呐先生通过交易磋商达成了关于智能玩具的进口协议。爱丽斯通过电子邮件向呐呐先生发送了拟定好的采购合同，要求其检查合同条款并在签字后传回一份合同。

From: alice0512@yushantrading.com

To: tunkis@smarttoy.com

Date: 2019.11.15

Subject: purchase contract

Attachment: Purchase Contract

Dear Mr. Okada Nana,

Thank you for your cooperation and finally we decide to place an order with you for 200 pieces of smart toys.

In the attachment, please see our Purchase Contract. If you have any disagreement with the terms and conditions of the Purchase Contract made out by us, please communicate with me through e-mail or phone call.

If there is no problem with the Purchase Contract, please countersign it and send one scanned copy back to us for our file.

I am anticipating your early reply.

Yours sincerely
Alice Chen
General Manager
Qingdao Yushan Trading Co., Ltd.
Address: No. 6381 Yushan Road, Qingdao, Shandong, China
Tel: 86-0532-8185678; Fax: 86-0532-8185677

# 情境二　合同的履行
# Fulfillment of Contract

# 任务五

# 信用证与付款

# L/C and Payment

## 学习目标

1. 了解国际贸易的主要支付方式;
2. 掌握信用证的开立和修改信函的写作要点;
3. 掌握货款预付信函的写作要点;
4. 熟悉信用证开立和修改信函的常用词语和句子;
5. 熟悉货款预付信函的常用词语和句子;
6. 能够阅读与撰写信用证的开立与修改的信函;
7. 能够阅读与撰写货款预付信函。

## 背景知识

在现代国际贸易中，主要的支付方式有信用证（L/C）、电汇（T/T）、托收（bank collection）。

在实务中，可以根据实际情况将不同的支付方式结合使用，如电汇与信用证相结合，电汇与托收相结合。

### 一、信用证

（一）信用证的特点

信用证是一种由银行依照客户的要求和指示开立的有条件的承诺付款的书面文件。

信用证支付方式的特点：

（1）信用证是一种银行信用，开证行承担第一付款责任。

根据《UCP600》的规定，信用证是一项约定，按此约定，根据规定的单据在符合信用证条件的情况下，开证银行向受益人或其指定人进行付款、承兑或议付。

（2）信用证是一种独立文件，它不依附于贸易合同而存在。

根据《UCP600》的规定，信用证与其可能依据的买卖合同或其他合同是相互独立的交易。即使信用证中提及该合同，银行也与该合同无关且不受其约束。

（3）信用证是一种单据的买卖。

根据《UCP600》的规定，在信用证业务中，各有关方面处理的是单据，而不是与单据有关的货物、服务及其他行为。只要受益人或其指定人提交的单据表面上符合信用证规定，开证行就应承担付款或承兑并支付的责任。

### （二）信用证的当事人

（1）开证申请人（applicant）。向银行申请开立信用证的人，一般是进口人，即货物的买方。

（2）开证行（opening/issuing bank）。接受开证申请人的委托开立信用证的银行，承担保证付款的责任。

（3）通知行（advising/notifying bank）。受开证行的委托，将信用证转交出口人的银行。它只证明信用证的真实性，并通知信用证的受益人，不承担其他义务。

（4）受益人（beneficiary）。信用证上所指定的提交单据并向付款银行索取款项的人，一般是出口人，即货物的卖方。

（5）议付行（negotiating bank）。买入受益人交来货物单据和（或）汇票的银行。

（6）付款行（paying/drawee bank）。信用证上指定付款的银行。在多数情况下，付款行就是开证行。

### （三）信用证的收付程序

（1）进口人与出口人签订商品的进出口合同。

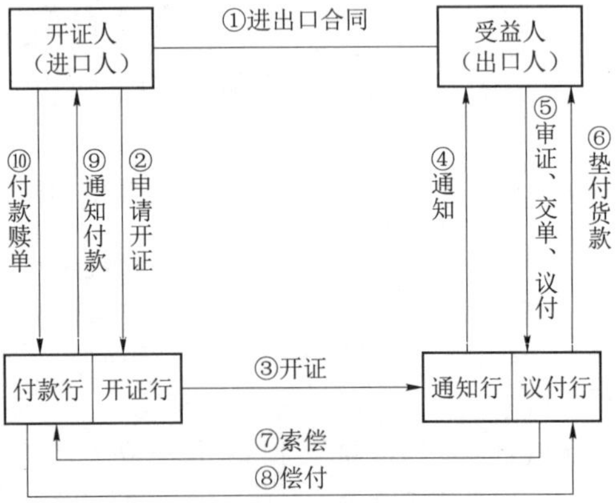


**图 5.1 信用证的收付程序**

（2）开证申请人根据合同填写开证申请书并交纳押金或提供其他保证，请开证行开证。

（3）开证行根据申请书内容，向受益人开出信用证并寄交出口人所在地通知行。

（4）通知行核对印鉴无误后，将信用证交受益人。

（5）受益人审核信用证内容与合同规定相符后，按信用证规定准备货物；备妥货物后，制作或取得信用证要求的单据，在信用证有效期内，送议付行议付。

（6）议付行按信用证条款审核单据无误后，把货款垫付给受益人。

（7）议付行将汇票和货运单据寄开证行或其特定的付款行索偿。

（8）开证行核对单据无误后，付款给议付行。

（9）开证行通知开证人付款赎单。

（10）开证人付款赎单。

### （四）信用证的主要内容

（1）对信用证本身的说明。如其种类、性质、有效期及到期地点。

（2）信用证的当事人。信用证的当事人包括开证申请人、开证行、通知行、受益人的名称及其地址。

（3）汇票条款。汇票条款包括汇票的金额、出票人、受票人、付款期限等。

（4）对运输的要求。它包括装运港（地）、卸货港（地）、装运期限、可否分批、可否转运等。

（5）货物的描述。根据合同进行货物的描述，包括货物的名称、规格、数量、包装、价格等。

（6）单据要求。具体说明提交单据的种类、份数、出证人等，通常包括发票、装箱单、运输单据（如海运提单）、保险单据、原产地证书、检验证书及其他有关单证。

（7）开证行对受益人及汇票持有人保证付款的责任文句。

（8）银行间电汇索偿条款（T/T Reimbursement Clause）。

SWIFT①信用证 MT700 格式说明如表 5.1 所示。

**表 5.1　　SWIFT 信用证的格式 MT700**

| M/O② | 代码（Tag） | 栏位名称（Field Name） |
|---|---|---|
| M | 27 | 合计次序（SEQUENCE OF TOTAL） |
| M | 40A | 跟单信用证类别（FORM OF DOCUMENTARY CREDIT） |
| M | 20 | 信用证编号（DOCUMENTARY CREDIT NUMBER） |
| O | 23 | 预先通知号码（REFERENCE TO PRE-ADVICE） |
| O | 31C | 开证日期（DATE OF ISSUE） |
| M | 31D | 信用证有效期和有效地点（DATE AND PLACE OF EXPIRY） |

① SWIFT 是环球银行金融电讯协会的英文简称，该组织是一个国际银行同业间非营利性的组织，专门从事各国之间金融电信业务的传递，如外汇买卖、证券交易、开立信用证、托收等。

② M/O 为 mandatory 与 optional 的缩写，前者是必要项目，后者为任意项目。

续表

| M/O | 代码（Tag） | 栏位名称（Field Name） |
| --- | --- | --- |
| O | 51A | 信用证开证的银行（APPLICANT BANK） |
| M | 50 | 申请人（APPLICATION） |
| M | 59 | 受益人（BENEFICIARY） |
| M | 32B | 币别代号、金额（CURRENCY CODE，AMOUNT） |
| O | 39A | 信用证金额加减百分率（PERCENTAGE CREDIT AMOUNT TOLERANCE） |
| O | 39B | 最高信用证金额（MAXIMUM CREDIT AMOUNT） |
| O | 39C | 可附加金额（ADDITIONAL AMOUNT COVERED） |
| M | 41A | 向……银行押汇，押汇方式为……（AVAILABLE WITH... BY...） |
| O | 42C | 汇票期限（DRAFTS AT...） |
| O | 42A | 付款人（DRAWEE） |
| O | 42M | 混合付款指示（MIXED PAYMENT DETAILS） |
| O | 42P | 延期付款指示（DEFERRED PAYMENT DETAILS） |
| O | 43P | 分运（PARTIAL SHIPMENTS） |
| O | 43T | 转运（TRANSHIPMENT） |
| O | 44A | 由……装船/发送/接管（LOADING ON BOARD/DISPATCH/TAKING IN CHARGE AT/FROM...） |
| O | 44B | 装运至……（FOR TRANSPORTATION TO...） |
| O | 44C | 最后装船日（LATEST DATE OF SHIPMENT） |
| O | 44D | 装运期（SHIPMENT PERIOD） |
| O | 45A | 货物描述与交易条件（DESCRIPTION OF GOODS AND/OR SERVICES） |
| O | 46A | 应具备单据（DOCUMENTS REQUIRED） |
| O | 47A | 附加条件（ADDITIONAL CONDITIONS） |
| O | 71B | 费用（CHARGES） |
| O | 48 | 提示期间（PERIOD FOR PRESENTATION） |
| M | 49 | 保兑指示（CONFIRMATION INSTRUCTIONS） |
| O | 53A | 清算银行（REIMBURSEMENT BANK） |
| O | 78 | 对付款/承兑/让购银行之指示（INSTRUCTIONS TO THE PAYING/ACCEPTING/NEGOTIATION BANK） |
| O | 57A | 收讯银行以外的通知银行（“ADVISE THROUGH” BANK） |
| O | 72 | 银行间的备注（SENDER TO RECEIVER INFORMATION） |

（五）信用证的修改

在收到信用证后，如果出口人（信用证的受益人）发现信用证的某些条款的规定与合同不相符或无法执行，可以向进口人（信用证的开证申请人）提出修改要求。

信用证的修改流程如图 5.2 所示。

**图 5.2 信用证修改流程**

（1）受益人（出口人）向开证人发出改证函，要求修改信用证。

（2）开证人（进口人）同意修改信用证，与开证行联系，向开证行提出改证申请。

（3）开证行将信用证修改书 MT707 发给通知行。

（4）通知行将信用证修改书交给受益人。

## 二、电汇

电汇是汇款人委托汇出银行将款项通过汇入银行付给指定收款人的付款方式。

电汇的当事人有四个：汇款人、汇款人开户银行、收款人开户银行、收款人。

电汇的业务程序如图 5.3 所示。

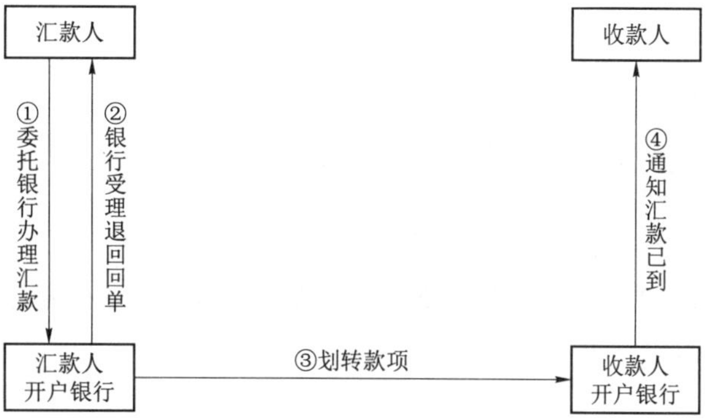


**图 5.3 电汇的业务程序**

国际贸易实务中，电汇的具体做法可分为预付货款、货到付款、先支付定金、发货后支付其余货款。其中，买方先支付定金、发货后支付其余货款是惯例做法。

卖方要求买方先支付定金，一方面为了防止买方悔约而不要货；另一方面，在订单量较大的情况下，买方需要一定的资金来购买原材料和进行生产。预付货款占总货款的比例，根据买卖双方的关系、市场行情等有所不同。一般情况下，预付货款占总货款的

30%左右。卖方可以通过信函告知买方自己的开户银行和账户，以便买方通过银行将预付货款转入卖方的账户。

## 三、托收

托收是出口人把货物的单据交给委托银行，由委托银行将货物的单据交给进口人并收取货款，然后将货款交给出口人。

托收的当事人有四个：委托人、托收行、代收行和付款人。

托收的业务程序如图 5.4 所示。

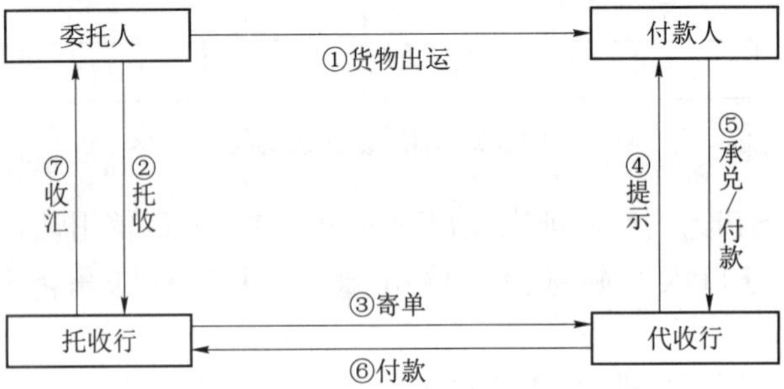


**图 5.4　托收的业务程序**

## 写作提示

## 一、信用证支付方式下有关信用证开立与修改的信函

它通常包括以下情境和要点：

（一）卖方催开信用证的信函

（1）提及合同号或订单号；

（2）说明合同中规定的关于开立信用证的时间；

（3）说明仍然没有收到信用证；

（4）提醒对方及时开立信用证，以免耽误交货期；

（5）其他事项，如信用证的内容要与合同保持一致，寄送信用证开立申请书供卖方核查，以免日后修改信用证等。

（二）买方告知卖方信用证已经开立的信函

（1）告知卖方信用证已经通过某银行开立；

（2）请卖方注意通知行的通知；

（3）请卖方及时准备货物并装运；

（4）表示感谢。

（三）卖方要求买方修改信用证的信函
（1）提及买方通过开证银行开出的信用证；
（2）告知买方信用证与合同的不符之处或信用证中提出的无法做到的要求；
（3）请买方及时与开证行联系并修改信用证；
（4）表示感谢。

（四）买方回复卖方提出的要求修改信用证的信函
（1）提及卖方关于修改信用证的信函；
（2）同意或拒绝卖方提出修改信用证条款的要求并说明原因；
（3）如果同意修改信用证，告知信用证修改书已经通过开证行寄给通知行；
（4）希望卖方立即准备货物并按时交货。

## 二、电汇支付方式下有关预付货款的信函

它通常包括以下情境和要点：
（一）卖方发给买方的关于预付货款的信函
（1）提及关于某合同或订单的预付货款；
（2）告知买方自己的开户银行和账户；
（3）请买方及时将预付货款汇到自己开户银行的账户；
（4）告知将在收到预付货款后开始准备货物；
（5）期待回信。

（二）买方回复卖方关于预付货款的信函
（1）表示收到关于支付某合同或订单的预付货款的信函；
（2）告知卖方已经将预付货款汇入卖方开户银行的账户；
（3）请卖方及时安排货物的生产或备货；
（4）表示感谢。

### 示范信函

# CASE 1　Weifang Baoda Textiles Co., Ltd.

## 一、信函的业务背景

潍坊宝达纺织品有限公司与缝得好服装有限公司签订了色织布的售货合同。根据合同约定，缝得好服装有限公司需要在 5 月 8 日前开立信用证，但直到信用证开立的最迟时间临近，潍坊宝达纺织品有限公司仍然没有收到信用证开立的通知。

于是，潍坊宝达纺织品有限公司的阿尔伯特向缝得好服装有限公司的丽莎发出了催开信用证的信函。

潍坊宝达纺织品有限公司在收到孟加拉国银行 Uttara Bank Ltd Badda Branch 开立的信用证后，对信用证的内容进行了仔细的核查，发现信用证的某些条款与合同的规定不符。于是，阿尔伯特向丽莎发出信函要求对信用证进行修改。

## 二、潍坊宝达纺织品有限公司的业务信函

（一）信用证的开立与修改（baoda-out 1）

From: Albert albert@163.com
To: Lisa lisa@stitchwell.com
Date: 2019.04.23
Subject: L/C establishment

Dear Lisa,

Regarding Contract No. XS-2019001 for cotton yarn-dyed fabrics, we would like to remind you that the relevant L/C shall be established before May 8, 2019 according to[1] our agreement.

Please open the relevant L/C on time so as not to delay[2] the shipment.

In order to[3] avoid any amendment[4] to the L/C, please fill the L/C Application Form[5] in conformity with[6] the stipulations[7] in the Sales Contract. And then send the copy of the Form to us for confirmation.

Look forward to receiving your quick response.

Yours sincerely
Albert
Sales Manager
Weifang Baoda Textiles Co., Ltd.
Address: No. 688 West Ring Road, Weifang, Shandong, China
Tel: 86-0536-8885678; Fax: 86-0536-8885677

### Notes

1. according to 依据

   e.g. Please fill up the form according to the instructions.
   请根据指示填写表格。

2. so as not to 以免

   e.g. Please be quiet so as not to disturb them.
   请保持安静以免打扰他们。

3. in order to 为了

e.g. In order to avoid any future dispute, we shall make the inspection term clear in the contract.

为了避免将来的争议，我们应该在合同里把检验条款写清楚。

4. amendment *n.* 修改

e.g. Amendment to the L/C is very troublesome to both parties.

信用证的修改对于双方都是非常麻烦的。

5. L/C Application Form 信用证开证申请书

信用证开证申请书是进口人向开证行递交的申请开立信用证的书面文件。

6. in conformity with 与……相符

e.g. The insurance item in the L/C is not in conformity with the contract.

信用证的保险条款与合同不相符。

其他表示与……相符（一致）的方式：according to、in accordance with、in compliance with。

7. stipulation *n.* 规定

e.g. There's no stipulation as to the amount you can invest.

关于你的投资金额，没有规定。

（二）信用证的开立与修改（baoda-in 1）

From: Lisa lisa@stitchwell.com

To: Albert albert@163.com

Date: 2019.04.26

Subject: RE: L/C establishment

Attachment: L/C Application Form

Dear Albert,

We received your letter on April 23, urging us to establish[1] the relevant L/C against Contract No. XS-2019001 for cotton yarn-dyed fabrics.

We have chosen Uttara Bank Ltd Badda Branch[2] as our issuing bank[3].

We are enclosing the filled L/C Application Form for you to check and confirm.

If any clauses[4] are not acceptable to you, please let us know.

We will open the relevant L/C through our bank upon receipt of your confirmation[5].

Regards

Lisa

Purchasing Manager

Stitchwell Garments Co., Ltd.

## 附 5.1 开证申请书（合同号 XS-2019001）

第一页：

<table>
<tr><td colspan="4">IRREVOCABLE DOCUMENTARY CREDIT APPLICATION</td></tr>
<tr><td colspan="2">TO: UTTARA BANK LTD - DHAKA, BAGLADESH</td><td>DATE:</td><td>APR 26，2019 CONTRACT NO. XS-2019001</td></tr>
<tr><td colspan="2">ISSUED BY TELETRANSMISSION</td><td colspan="2">IRREVOCABLE DOCUMENTARY CREDIT NO.</td></tr>
<tr><td colspan="2">APPLICANT</td><td colspan="2">DATE AND PLACE OF EXPIRY</td></tr>
<tr><td colspan="2" rowspan="3"><u>Stitchwell Garments Co., Ltd.</u><br><u>456/1/A, Tejgaon Industrial Area, Dhaka 1208 Bangladesh</u><br><u>Tel: 880-2-9882934; Fax: 880-2-8891567</u></td><td colspan="2">—</td></tr>
<tr><td colspan="2">BENEFICIARY</td></tr>
<tr><td colspan="2" rowspan="3"><u>Weifang Baoda Textiles Co., Ltd.</u><br><u>Address: No. 688 West Ring Road Weifang, Shandong, China</u><br><u>Tel: 86-0536-8885678; Fax: 86-0536-8885677</u></td></tr>
<tr><td colspan="2">ADVISING BANK</td></tr>
<tr><td colspan="2" rowspan="2"><u>BANK OF CHINA LIMITED, WEIFANG BRANCH</u></td></tr>
<tr><td colspan="2">AMOUNT</td></tr>
<tr><td colspan="2">PARTIAL SHIPMENTS</td><td colspan="2" rowspan="2"><u>USD43,700.00</u></td></tr>
<tr><td colspan="2"><u>ALLOWED</u></td></tr>
<tr><td colspan="2">TRANSHIPMENT</td><td colspan="2">CREDIT AVAILABLE WITH</td></tr>
<tr><td colspan="2"><u>NOT ALLOWED</u></td><td colspan="2"><u>ANY BANK IN CHINA</u></td></tr>
<tr><td colspan="2">LOADING ON BOARD/DISPATCH FROM</td><td colspan="2"><u>BY NEGOTIATION</u></td></tr>
<tr><td colspan="2"><u>QINGDAO PORT, CHINA</u></td><td colspan="2">AGAINST THE DOCUMENTS DETAILED HEREIN</td></tr>
<tr><td colspan="2">NOT LATER THAN</td><td colspan="2">AND BENEFICIARY’S DRAFT FOR</td></tr>
<tr><td colspan="2"><u>JUNE 15, 2019</u></td><td><u>100%</u></td><td>OF INVOICE VALUE</td></tr>
<tr><td colspan="2">FOR TRANSPORTATION TO</td><td>AT</td><td><u>60 DAYS SIGHT</u></td></tr>
<tr><td colspan="2"><u>CHITTAGONG SEA PORT, BANGLADESH</u></td><td colspan="2">DRAWN ON ISSUING BANK</td></tr>
<tr><td colspan="4">ADDITIONAL INSTRUCTIONS:</td></tr>
<tr><td>.</td><td colspan="3">ALL BANKING CHARGES OUTSIDE THE ISSUING BANK ARE FOR BENEFICIARY’S ACCOUNT.</td></tr>
<tr><td>.</td><td>DOCUMENTS MUST BE PRESENTED WITHIN</td><td><u>21</u></td><td>DAYS AFTER THE DATE OF ISSUANCE OF THE</td></tr>
<tr><td></td><td colspan="3">TRANSPORT DOCUMENTS BUT WITHIN THE VALIDITY OF THIS CREDIT.</td></tr>
<tr><td>.</td><td colspan="3">THIRD PARTY AS SHIPPER IS NOT ACCEPTABLE. SHORT FORM/BLANK BACK B/L IS NOT ACCEPTABLE.</td></tr>
<tr><td>.</td><td>BOTH QUANTITY AND AMOUNT</td><td><u>5%</u></td><td>MORE OR LESS ARE ALLOWED.</td></tr>
<tr><td>.</td><td colspan="3">PREPAID FREIGHT DRAWN IN EXCESS OF L/C AMOUNT IS ACCEPTABLE AGAINST PRESENTATION OF ORIGINAL CHARGES VOUCHER ISSUED BY SHIPPING CO./AIR LINE/OR ITS AGENT.</td></tr>
<tr><td>.</td><td colspan="3">ALL DOCUMENTS TO BE FORWARDED IN ONE COVER, UNLESS OTHERWISE STATED ABOVE.</td></tr>
<tr><td>.</td><td colspan="3">OTHER TERMS，IF ANY:</td></tr>
<tr><td></td><td colspan="3"><u>ALL DOCUMENTS MUST INDICATE THE L/C NO., DATE OF ISSUE AND THE NAME OF ISSUING BANK.</u></td></tr>
</table>

第二页：

| DOCUMENTS REQUIRED: (MARKED WITH X) | | | | | | |
|---|---|---|---|---|---|---|
| **X** | 1 | MANUALLY SIGNED COMMERCIAL INVOICE IN | | | **3** | COPIES |
| | | INDICATING THIS L/C NO. AND CONTRACT NO. | | | _ | |
| | | (PHOTO COPY AND CARBON COPY NOT ACCEPTABLE AS ORIGINAL.) | | | | |
| **X** | 2 | **FULL SET (INCLUDED** | **3** | ORIGINAL AND | **3** | NON-NEGOTIABLE COPIES) OF |
| | | CLEAN ON BOARD MARKED "FREIGHT | | **PREPAID**" | OCEAN BILLS OF LADING MADE OUT | |
| | | **TO ORDER AND BLANK ENDORSED** | | | | NOTIFYING |
| | | **THE APPLICANT** | | | | |
| _ | 3 | AIR WAYBILLS SHOWING "FREIGHT | | | _ | "AND CONSIGNED TO |
| | | _ | | | | |
| _ | 4 | **(PLS CHOOSE)** | _ | ORIGINAL AND | _ | COPIES) OF INSURANCE |
| | POLICY/CERTIFICATE FOR 110% OF THE INVOICE VALUE, SHOWING CLAIMS PAYABLE IN CHINA, | | | | | |
| | | IN CURRENCY OF THE DRAFT, BLANK ENDORSED, COVERING: | | | | |
| | | **(PLS CHOOSE)** | | | ALL RISKS AND WAR RISKS. | |
| **X** | 5 | PACKING LIST | **IN 3 COPIES** | | ISSUED BY | **BENEFICIARY** |
| | | INDICATING QUANTITY OF EACH PACKAGE AND PACKING | | | | |
| | | | | | | |
| **X** | 6 | CERTIFICATE OF QUALITY | | | **THREE (3)** | COPIES ISSUED BY |
| | | GUANGZHOU FIBRE PRODUCT TESTING INSTITUTE. | | | | |
| **X** | 7 | CERTIFICATE OF ORIGIN IN | | **3 COPIES** | ISSUED BY | **AUTHORIZED INSTITUTE OF CHINA** |
| **X** | 8 | SHIPPING ADVICE THROUGH FAX DISPATCHED TO THE APPLICANT WITHIN | | | | |
| | | **SEVEN DAYS** | AFTER SHIPMENT ADVISING | | | **NAME OF COMMODITY** |
| | | QUANTITY, WEIGHT AND SHIPPING MARKS, NAME OF VESSEL, SHIPMENT DATE AND ETA. | | | | |
| _ | 9 | OTHER DOCUMENTS, IF ANY: | | | | |
| COVERING | | **COMMODITY AND SPECIFICATION:**<br>**1) Cotton yarn-dyed fabric 21*21, 64*54, 57/58;**<br>**2) Cotton yarn-dyed fabric 21*21, 80*60, 57/58;**<br>**3) Cotton yarn-dyed fabric 32*32, 80*68, 57/58;**<br>**QUANTITY:**<br>**1) 5,000 yards; 2) 10,000 yards; 3) 12,000 yards;**<br>**UNIT PRICE:**<br>**1) USD1.3/yard; 2) USD1.8/yard; 3) USD1.6/yard FOB Qingdao, China**<br>**TOTAL AMOUNT:USD43,700.** | | | | |

## Notes

1. establish *v.* 开立
2. Uttara Bank Ltd Badda Branch 总部位于孟加拉国达卡的一家银行
3. issuing bank 开证行

   开证行指接受开证申请人（进口人）的申请，开立信用证的银行，承担第一付款责任。
4. clause *n.* 条款

   clauses 指开证申请书的各项条款。
5. confirmation *n.* 确认

   e.g. We shall begin to work on your order after receiving your confirmation of the samples.

   我方将在收到你方对样品的确认后着手处理你方的订单。

（三）信用证的开立与修改（baoda-out 2）

From: Albert albert@163.com
To: Lisa lisa@stitchwell.com
Date: 2019.04.28
Subject: RE: RE: L/C establishment

Dear Lisa,

Thank you for your letter on April 26 and the L/C Application Form.

We have checked the L/C Application Form and no mistakes were found in it.

Please open the L/C as soon as possible.

Look forward to receiving your L/C.

Yours sincerely
Albert
Sales Manager
Weifang Baoda Textiles Co., Ltd.

（四）信用证的开立与修改（baoda-in 2）

From: Lisa lisa@stitchwell.com
To: Albert albert@163.com
Date: 2019.05.03
Subject: RE: RE: RE: L/C establishment

Dear Albert,

The L/C against Contract No. XS-2019001 has been opened in your favor[1] for the amount of USD43,700.00 through Uttara Bank Ltd. – Dhaka, Bangladesh on May 2.

Please wait to be informed by the notifying bank[2].

Meanwhile, please prepare for our order immediately and ship the goods on time.

If you find any stipulation(s) unacceptable to you, please let us know.

Regards
Lisa
Purchasing Manager
Stitchwell Garments Co., Ltd.

## Notes

1. in your favor 以你方为受益人；对你方有利

   e.g. (1) We are opening an irrevocable L/C in your favor through Bank of China.
   我方将通过中国银行开立以你方为受益人的不可撤销信用证。

   (2) The appreciation of the dollar against the RMB is in your favor.
   美元对人民币的升值于你方有利。

2. notifying bank 通知行

   在信用证业务中，通知行是受开证行的委托，负责通知信用证受益人的银行。

（五）信用证的开立与修改（baoda-out 3）

From: Albert albert@163.com
To: Lisa lisa@stitchwell.com
Date: 2019.05.09
Subject: L/C amendment
Attachment: L/C issued by Uttara Bank Ltd. – Dhaka, Bangladesh

Dear Lisa,

The L/C issued by Uttara Bank Ltd. – Dhaka, Bangladesh against Contract No. XS-2019001 reached us yesterday, which is advised by[1] Bank of China, Weifang Branch.

However, we regret to say that[2] some stipulations are not in conformity with the terms in the contract after examination, therefore, they are not acceptable to us.

Please make the following amendments to the L/C NO. LC5TF90080073:

① Under field 59, BENEFICIARY[3] should be "WEIFANG BAODA TEXTILES CO., LTD." instead of[4] "SHANDONG BAODA TEXTILES CO., LTD.".

② Under field 31D, DATE AND PLACE OF EXPIRY[5] should be "date 190707 place in China" not "date 190630 place in China".

③ Under field 46A, BILL OF LADING, "FREIGHT PREPAID[6]" should be amended to "FREIGHT COLLECT[7]".

It is appreciated[8] if you make the above amendments upon receipt of this e-mail.

Yours sincerely
Albert
Sales Manager
Weifang Baoda Textiles Co., Ltd.

**附 5.2 信用证通知书**
**ADVICE OF A LETTER OF CREDIT**

致 TO: 日期 DATE: MAY 8, 2019
潍坊宝达纺织品有限公司
WEIFANG BAODA TEXTILES CO., LTD. 我行编号 OUR REF: 31079110015381
信用证编号（L/C No.）: LC5TF90080073
开证日期（Issuing Date）: MAY 2, 2019
信用证金额（Amount）: USD43,700.00
信用证效期（Date of Expiry）: JUNE 30, 2019
最后装船期（Latest Shipment Date）: JUNE 16, 2019
开证行（Issuing Bank）: UTTARA BANK LTD BADDA BRANCH – DHAKA, BAGLADESH

兹通知信用证一份，内容见附件。
WE HAVE PLEASURE IN ADVISING YOU A DOCUMENTARY CREDIT WHICH IS ATTACHED TO THIS ADVISING LETTER.
如贵公司发现本信用证有无法做到的条款和条件，或发现信用证存在错误，请直接与开证申请人联系，进行必要的修改，以避免在交单时产生困难。
IF YOU FIND ANY TERMS AND CONDITIONS IN THE L/C WHICH ARE UNABLE TO COMPLY WITH, OR IF YOU FIND ANY ERROR(S), IT IS SUGGESTED THAT YOU CONTACT THE APPLICANT DIRECTLY FOR NECESSARY AMENDMENT(S) SO AS TO AVOID ANY DIFFICULTIES WHICH MAY ARISE WHEN DOCUMENTS ARE PRESENTED.
本通知不构成我行其他任何责任和义务。
OUR ADVICE OF THE ABOVE L/C CONVEYS NO FURTHER ENGAGEMENT OR OBLIGATION ON OUR PART.
本信用证的通知依照国际商会《跟单信用证统一惯例》（2007 年修订版）第 600 号出版物。
THIS ADVICE IS SUBJECT TO UNIFORM CUSTOMS AND PRACTICE FOR DOCUMENTARY CREDITS (2007 REVISION) ICC PUBLICATION NO. 600.

中国银行股份有限公司
BANK OF CHINA LIMITED
签章
AUTHORIZED SIGNATURES

## 附 5.3　UTTARA 银行开立的信用证 LC5TF90080073

### L/C issued by UTTARA BANK LTD - DHAKA, BANGLADESH

MT 700　　　　　ISSUE OF A DOCUMENTARY CREDIT
SENDER:
UTBLBDDH
UTTARA BANK LTD BADDA BRANCH – DHAKA, BANGLADESH
RECEIVER:
BKCHCNBJ500
BANK OF CHINA LIMITED, WEIFANG BRANCH – WEIFANG, CHINA
L/C ARRIVAL DATE: MAY 5, 2019

27: SEQUENCE OF TOTAL
1 / 1
40A: FORM OF DOC. CREDIT
IRREVOCABLE
20: DOC. CREDIT NUMBER
LC5TF90080073
31C: DATE OF ISSUE
190502
40E: APPLICABLE RULES
UCP LATEST VERSION
31D: DATE AND PLACE OF EXPIRY
DATE 190630 PLACE IN CHINA
50: APPLICANT
STITCHWELL GARMENTS CO., LTD.
456/1/A, TEJGAON INDUSTRIAL AREA, DHAKA 1208, BANGLADESH
59: BENEFICIARY
SHANDONG BAODA TEXTILES CO., LTD.
NO. 688 WEST RING ROAD WEIFANG, SHANDONG, CHINA
32B: CURRENCY CODE, AMOUNT
USD43,700.00
41D: AVAILABLE WITH/BY
ANY BANK IN CHINA,
BY NEGOTIATION
42C: DRAFTS AT
60 DAYS AFTER SIGHT
42A: DRAWEE

UTTARA BANK LTD BADDA BRANCH – DHAKA, BANGLADESH
43P: PARTIAL SHIPMENT
PROHIBITED
43T: TRANSSHIPMENT
ALLOWED
44E: PORT OF LOADING/AIRPORT OF DEPARTURE
QINGDAO CHINA
44F: PORT OF DISCHARGE
CHITTAGONG SEA PORT, BANGLADESH
44C: LATEST DATE OF SHIPMENT
190616
45A: DESCRIPTION OF GOODS AND/OR SERVICES
COMMODITY AND SPECIFICATION:
1) Cotton yarn-dyed fabric 21*21, 64*54, 57/58;
2) Cotton yarn-dyed fabric 21*21, 80*60, 57/58;
3) Cotton yarn-dyed fabric 32*32, 80*60, 57/58
QUANTITY:
1) 5,000 yards; 2) 10,000 yards; 3) 12,000 yards
UNIT PRICE:
1) USD1.3/yard; 2) USD1.8/yard; 3) USD1.6/yard
FOB QINGDAO, CHINA
TOTAL AMOUNT: USD43,700.00
46A: DOCUMENTS REQUIRED
+ MANUALLY SIGNED COMMERCIAL INVOICE IN TRIPLICATE.
+ PACKING LIST IN TRIPLICATE ISSUED BY BENEFICIARY INDICATING QUANTITY OF EACH PACKAGE AND PACKING.
+ CERTIFICATE OF CHINESE ORIGIN CERTIFIED BY AUTHORIZED INSTITUTE OF CHINA IN TRIPLICATE.
+ FULL SET (3/3) OF CLEAN "ON BOARD" MARKED FREIGHT PREPAID OCEAN BILLS OF LADING MADE OUT TO ORDER AND BLANK ENDORSED NOTIFYING THE APPLICANT.
+ CERTIFICATE OF QUALITY IN TRIPLICATE ISSUED BY GUANGZHOU FIBRE PRODUCT TESTING INSTITUTE.
+ SHIPPING ADVICE THROUGH FAX DISPATCHED TO THE APPLICANT WITHIN SEVEN DAYS AFTER SHIPMENT ADVISING NAME OF COMMODDITY, QUANTITY, WEIGHT, SHIPPING MARKS, NAME OF VESSEL, SHIPMENT OF DATE AND ETA.
47A: ADDITIONAL CONDITIONS

+ DOCUMENTS DATED PRIOR TO THE DATE OF THIS CREDIT ARE NOT ACCEPTABLE.
+ THE NUMBER AND THE DATE OF THIS CREDIT AND THE NAME OF ISSUING BANK MUST BE QUOTED ON ALL DOCUMENTS.
+ TRANSSHIPMENT ALLOWED AT SINGAPORE ONLY.
+ 5% MORE OR LESS IN QUANTITY ACCEPTABLE.
+ SHORT FORM/CHARTER PARTY/THIRD PARTY BILL OF LADING ARE NOT ACCEPTABLE.
+ SHIPMENT MUST BE EFFECTED BY 1×40' FULL CONTAINER LOAD. B/L TO SHOW EVIDENCE OF THIS EFFECT IS REQUIRED.
+ ALL PRESENTATIONS CONTAINING DISCREPANCIES WILL ATTRACT A DISCREPANCY FEE OF USD100.00 PLUS TELEX COSTS OR OTHER CURRENCY EQUIVALENT. THIS CHARGE WILL BE DEDUCTED FROM THE BILL AMOUNT WHETHER OR NOT WE ELECT TO CONSULT THE APPLICANT FOR A WAIVER.

71B: CHARGES
ALL CHARGES AND COMMISSIONS ARE FOR ACCOUNT OF BENEFICIARY INCLUDING REIMBURSING FEE.

48: PERIOD FOR PRESENTATION
WITHIN 21 DAYS AFTER THE DATE OF SHIPMENT, BUT WITHIN THE VALIDITY OF THIS CREDIT.

49: CONFIRMATION INSTRUCTION
WITHOUT

78: INFORMATION TO PRESENTING BANK
ALL DOCUMENTS ARE TO BE REMITTED IN ONE LOT BY
COURIER TO UTTARA BANK LTD BADDA BRANCH – DHAKA, BAGLADESH,
JAHANARA PLAZA, HOLDING NO: F-15, MIDDLE BADDA,
PGOGATI SARANI, PO & PS: BADDA, DHAKA-1212, TEL: 88-02-9860645.

## Notes

1. advise *v.* 通知；建议

e.g. (1) We will advise you of our final decision as soon as possible.
我方会将最终决定尽快告知你方。
(2) I would like to advise you to attend the meeting in the afternoon.
我想通知你参加下午的会议。

2. regret to say that 抱歉地说

e.g. I regret to say that I can not agree with you on the price you offered.
很抱歉，我不能同意你的报价。

3. beneficiary *n.* 受益人
   受益人指信用证中有权向指定的银行索取价款的当事人，通常是出口人。
4. instead of 代替
   e.g. Look for ways to success instead of seeking excuses for failure.
   要寻找成功的方法，而不是为失败寻找理由。
5. date and place of expiry 到期时间与地点
   它是指信用证中规定的信用证的有效期和相应的地点。
6. freight prepaid 运费预付
7. freight collect 运费到付
8. appreciate *v.* 感激
   e.g. I really appreciate your great help through all these years.
   真心感激你这么多年来的帮助。

（六）信用证的开立与修改（baoda-in 3）

From: Lisa lisa@stitchwell.com
To: Albert albert@163.com
Date: 2019.05.11
Subject: RE: L/C amendment
Attachment: Amendment to the L/C No. LC5TF90080073

Dear Albert,

We received your letter on May 9 on amending the L/C against Contract No. XS-2019001.

We are sorry for the inconvenience caused and agree to amend the stipulations mentioned in your letter.

As requested, we are making the following amendments to the L/C through our issuing bank:

① Under field 59, BENEFICIARY should be "WEIFANG BAODA TEXTILES CO., LTD." instead of "SHANDONG BAODA TEXTILES CO., LTD.".

② Under field 31D, DATE AND PLACE OF EXPIRY should be "date 190707 place in China" not "date 190630 place in China".

③ Under field 46A, BILL OF LADING, "FREIGHT PREPAID" should be amended to "FREIGHT COLLECT".

The amendments of the L/C have been sent to the notifying bank (Bank of China, Weifang Branch) through the issuing bank[1] (Uttara Bank Ltd – Dhaka, Bangladesh), and it will reach you in due time[2].

Meanwhile, please prepare for our order immediately to ensure[3] shipping the goods on time.

Regards
Lisa
Purchasing Manager
Stitchwell Garments Co., Ltd.

**附 5.4　信用证 LC5TF90080073 修改书**

**Amendment to the L/C No. LC5TF90080073**

MESSAGE TYPE: MT707
SEND BANK:
UTBLBDDH
RECV BANK:
BKCHCNBJ500
PRINT TIMES: 1
PRINT DATE: 2019-05-11

20: SENDER'S REFERENCE
LC5TF90080073
21: RECEIVER'S REFERENCE
NON
31C: DATE OF ISSUE
20190502
30: DATE OF AMENDMENT
20190510
26E: NUMBER OF AMENDMENT
01
59: BENEFICIARY (BEFORE THIS AMENDMENT)
SHANDONG BAODA TEXTILES CO., LTD.
NO. 688 WEST RING ROAD WEIFANG, SHANDONG, CHINA
79: NARRATIVE
Please make the following amendments to the L/C:

① Under field 59, BENEFICIARY should be "WEIFANG BAODA TEXTILES CO., LTD." instead of "SHANDONG BAODA TEXTILES CO., LTD.".

② Under field 31D, DATE AND PLACE OF EXPIRY should be "date 190707 place in China" not "date 190630 place in China".

③ Under field 46A, BILL OF LADING, "FREIGHT PREPAID" should be amended to "FREIGHT COLLECT".

## Notes

1. issuing bank 开证行

   开证行指接受开证申请人（进口人）的申请，开立信用证的银行，承担第一付款责任。

2. in due time 按时地，及时地

   e.g. The samples will arrive in due time.

   样品将按时到达。

3. ensure *v.* 确保

   e.g. Please ensure every door is locked before you leave the office.

   请确保在离开办公室前锁上所有的门。

# CASE 2 Beijing Lucky Fibreboard Trading Co., Ltd.

## 一、信函的业务背景

在北京幸运纤维板贸易有限公司和澳大利亚松树纤维板工业有限公司签订的合同中，双方约定的付款条件如下：30%的货款预付，70%的货款见提单复印件后支付。

由于北京幸运纤维板贸易有限公司在合同签订后，一直没有向澳大利亚松树纤维板工业有限公司支付预付货款，澳大利亚松树纤维板工业有限公司的销售部经理比尔给北京幸运纤维板贸易有限公司的玲玲发出邮件，提醒对方尽快支付预付货款，以便为其订单进行生产。

玲玲在收到比尔催款的邮件后，于 2019 年 7 月 2 日将 30%的预付货款通过银行支付给澳大利亚松树纤维板工业有限公司。

## 二、北京幸运纤维板贸易有限公司的信函

（一）货款的预付（lucky-in 1）

From: Bill salesdepartment@pinetree.com.au

To: Lingling lingling@163.com

Date: 2019.06.30

Subject: deposit of the contract No. SC-PINE2019010

Dear Lingling,

With reference to deposit of the Contract No. SC-PINE2019010, I would like to remind you that you shall remit[1] 30% invoice value to us before the production of your order.

Will you please remit 30% invoice value to us soon in order for us to prepare for your order?

The following is our account[2] in HSBC[3] Bank Australia.

Bank Name: HSBC Bank Australia, South Melbourne Branch

Address: Shop G16-G17, 265 Clarendon Street, South Melbourne, VIC 3205

Account Name: Pinetree Fibreboard Industries Co., Ltd.

Account No.: 172314-258

Please remit the payment to the above account in HSBC Bank Australia as soon as possible.

We will prepare for your order upon receipt of the payment.

Look forward to receiving your quick response.

Best regards
Bill
Sales Department
Pinetree Fibreboard Industries Co., Ltd.

## Notes

1. remit　*v.* 汇款

   e.g. Please remit me the money in time.

   请及时给我汇款。

2. account　账户

   它是指在银行开立的存款账户。

3. HSBC 汇丰银行

   汇丰银行的中文全称：香港上海汇丰银行有限公司

   英文全称: The Hongkong and Shanghai Banking Corporation Limited

（二）货款的预付（lucky-out 1）

From: Lingling lingling@163.com
To: Bill salesdepartment@pinetree.com.au
Date: 2019.07.02
Subject: Re: Deposit of the contract No. SC-PINE2019010
Attachment: bank receipt

Dear Bill,

With reference to the deposit against the Sales Contract No.SC-PINE2019010, we have already remitted the amount of USD 7,788.30 by T/T to your account in HSBC Bank Australia through Bank of China Beijing Branch. You can see the bank receipt in the attachment.

Please check[1] your account in the next few days.

Meanwhile, please prepare for the goods as stipulated as soon as possible.

Thank you in advance[2].

Best regards
Lingling
Purchase Manager
Beijing Lucky Fibreboard Trading Co., Ltd.

## Notes

1. check *v.* 查看
   e.g. Please check your answers carefully after you finish the test paper.
   请在完成测试卷后仔细地检查所有的答案。
2. Thank you in advance. 提前表示感谢。

## 练习

一、将下列句子译成中文。

（一）信用证支付方式下的练习

1. The relevant L/C shall be established before January 16, 2019 according to the contract.
2. We would like to remind you that you should open the relevant L/C on time in case of delaying the shipment on March.
3. In order to avoid any amendment to the L/C, please fill and send the copy of the L/C Application Form to us for confirmation.
4. We are enclosing the filled L/C Application Form for you to check and confirm.
5. We will open and send the relevant L/C through our bank upon receipt of your confirmation.
6. The L/C of Contract No. SD-2019006 for 100 MT rice has been issued in your favor for the amount of USD41,000.00 through BANK OF CHINA QINGDAO BRANCH on May 10.
7. I regret to say that some items do not comply with the stipulations of the Contract.
8. Under field 59, BENEFICIARY should be "WEIFANG XINTONG STEEL CO., LTD." instead of "SHANDONG XINTONG STEEL CO., LTD.".
9. Under field 46A, BILL OF LADING, "FREIGHT TO COLLECT" should be amended to "FREIGHT PREPAID".
10. Please extend the shipment date to October 20 and the expiry date of the L/C to November 10 respectively.

（二）电汇支付方式下的练习

1. Please remit 30% invoice value to us in order for us to prepare for your order.
2. Please remit the amount USD15,600.00 to the above account No. in HSBC Bank Australia.

3. We will prepare for your order upon receipt of the payment.

**二、将下列句子译成英文。**

（一）信用证支付方式下的练习

1. 请尽快开立信用证以免延迟交货日期。
2. 请按照合同的条款开立信用证，以免以后修改信用证。
3. 合同 LUCKY-2019-01 项下的信用证，已经由中国银行于 5 月 15 日开立，请注意通知行——纽约银行的通知。
4. 我方已经收到合同 LUCKY-2019-01 项下由中国银行开立的信用证，但遗憾地发现其中的某些条款无法接受。
5. 受益人应为“北京幸运纤维板贸易有限公司”，而不是“中国幸运纤维板贸易有限公司”。
6. 请将信用证的到期时间修改为“2019 年 6 月 21 日在中国到期”。
7. 请把信用证的最迟装运期由“6 月 20 日”修改为“7 月 10 日”。
8. 第 46A 项，提单中的“运费预付”修改为“运费到付”。
9. 第 46A 项，提单的收货人不是“开证申请人”而是“根据指示”。
10. 请把装运期和信用证有效期分别延长至 8 月 15 日和 9 月 5 日。

（二）电汇支付方式下的练习

1. 请汇付 18 356 美元到我公司在中国银行开立的账户。
2. 一旦收到你方的货款，我方会立即安排你方订单的生产。
3. 我方已经向你公司在中国交通银行潍坊分行的账户汇出了 15 475 美元。

## 技能训练

### 根据业务情境和信息写信

（一）业务情境

1. 江苏通达轮胎有限公司与大力神轮胎贸易公司签订了销售合同。根据合同规定，大力神轮胎贸易公司必须在 2019 年 7 月 25 日前开出信用证。但到了 7 月 15 日，江苏通达轮胎有限公司仍然没有收到大力神轮胎贸易公司开立信用证的信息。为此，江苏通达轮胎有限公司的李辉写信给大力神轮胎贸易公司的大卫 • 桑德伯格，催其尽快开立信用证。

2. 大卫 • 桑德伯格收到李辉催开信用证的信函后，于 7 月 17 日通过美国银行纽约分行开立了以江苏通达轮胎有限公司为受益人的信用证。

3. 李辉收到通知行中国银行无锡分行通知的信用证，审查后发现信用证的一些条款与合同不符，不能接受。于是，写信给大卫 • 桑德伯格要求修改信用证。

4. 大卫·桑德伯格收到李辉要求修改信用证的信函后，同意李辉修改信用证的要求，与开证行美国银行纽约分行联系，对信用证进行了修改。

（二）信息

1. 合同中的支付条款规定：买方在 2019 年 7 月 25 日前开立以卖方为受益人的不可撤销 60 天远期信用证。

2. 7 月 17 日，大卫·桑德伯格通过美国银行纽约分行开立了以江苏通达轮胎有限公司为受益人的信用证。

3. 信用证金额：USD21 600。

4. 信用证与合同不符的条款：

（1）45A，货物描述中的货物名称应为“TRUCK TIRE D928”，而不是“TRUCK TIRE O928”；

（2）最迟装运期应为“Sept 18, 2019”而不是“Sept 8, 2019”。

（三）任务

根据以上的业务情境和信息写信。

1. 李辉写信催大卫·桑德伯格尽快开立信用证。

信函应包括以下要点：

（1）提及合同号；

（2）合同规定信用证开立的时间；

（3）表示仍然没有收到大卫·桑德伯格开立信用证的消息；

（4）提醒大卫·桑德伯格及时开立信用证；

（5）提醒信用证的内容与合同保持一致，以免日后修改。

2. 大卫·桑德伯格回复李辉：信用证已经开出。

信函应包括以下要点：

（1）告知李辉信用证已经通过美国银行纽约分行开出；

（2）请李辉注意通知行中国银行无锡分行的通知；

（3）请卖方立即准备货物的生产；

（4）表示感谢。

3. 李辉在收到信用证后，写信要求大卫·桑德伯格修改信用证。

信函应包括以下要点：

（1）提及合同号 LLLT20190608 项下的信用证已经收到；

（2）告知信用证条款与合同不相符的内容；

（3）要求大卫·桑德伯格与开证行美国银行纽约分行联系修改信用证；

（4）表示感谢。

4. 大卫·桑德伯格回复李辉：信用证已经按照要求修改。

信函应包括以下要点：

（1）提及李辉发出的关于要求修改信用证的信函；

（2）同意李辉关于修改信用证的要求；

（3）告知信用证修改书已经通过开证行（美国银行纽约分行）寄给通知行（中国银行无锡分行）；

（4）希望李辉立即准备货物并按时交货。

## 补充阅读

信函 1：信用证的开立

业务背景：法国的优雅贸易有限公司总经理海伦按照合同中的约定，通过银行向青岛兴旺手工艺品有限公司开立信用证。

From: helen1219@hotmail.com

To: lihua@handicraftschina.com

Date: 2019.04.16

Subject: L/C against the Sales Contract No. 2019-025

Dear Lihua,

We would inform you that the L/C for USD33,600.00 in your favor has been opened through Societe Generale, Paris, France.

All bills drawn under this credit must be marked "Drawn under Societe Generale, Paris, France Credit No. 3843" and must be accompanied by the following documents:

(1) Full set of Clean on Board Bills of Lading, made out to order and endorsed in blank

(2) Signed Commercial Invoice in triplicate

(3) Signed Packing List in triplicate

(4) Certificate of Origin by CCPIT

(5) Insurance Policy or Certificate for the CIF value plus 10%

Please fax us confirming that the order has been accepted and the goods can be delivered within one month.

Yours faithfully

Helen Keller

General Manager

Elegance Trading Limited, France

Address: No. 1203 Garden Road, Paris, France

Tel: 33-1-8185678; Fax: 33-1-8185677

信函 2：信用证的展期

业务背景：青岛兴旺手工艺品有限公司由于无法在信用证规定的交货期内交货，要求法国的优雅贸易有限公司对信用证中的交货时间和信用证到期时间展期。

From: lihua@handicraftschina.com
To: helen1219@hotmail.com
Date: 2019.05.10
Subject: L/C extension

Dear Helen,

Refer to the L/C No. 3843 covering your order for 8,000 pieces of straw knitting handicrafts.

We regret to say that we are unable to get the goods ready by the middle of this month due to heavy commitments. The earliest shipment we can arrange is before May 30.

For the above reason, we ask you to extend the latest date of shipment to May 30 and the expiring date of the L/C to June 20.

We are sorry for the inconvenience caused by us and will appreciate if you accept our request.

Yours sincerely
Li Hua
Sales Manager
Qingdao Xingwang Handicrafts Co., Ltd.
Address: No. 1251 Xingwang Road, Qingdao, Shandong, China
Tel: 86-0532-8745618; Fax: 86-0532-8745617

信函 3：预付款

业务背景：青岛鱼山贸易有限公司与日本的三友智能玩具公司签订了智能玩具的买卖合同。合同中规定由买方先向卖方支付预付款 30%。青岛鱼山贸易有限公司的总经理爱丽斯在向三友智能玩具公司的银行账户汇款后，写信给三友智能玩具公司的销售经理呐呐先生，告知预付款已汇出。

From: alice0512@yushantrading.com
To: tunkis@smarttoy.com
Date: 2019.11.26
Subject: deposit for Contract No. SMART2019006

Dear Nana,

The amount of the 30% invoice value of the goods under Contract No. SMART2019006, that is, USD12,000 has been remitted to your account in Fuji Bank, Tokyo through Bank of China, Weifang.

Please confirm it by e-mail upon receiving the payment.

Meanwhile, please prepare for our order as soon as possible and deliver the goods on time.

Yours sincerely
Alice Chen
General Manager
Qingdao Yushan Trading Co., Ltd.
Address: No. 6381 Yushan Road, Qingdao, Shandong, China
Tel: 86-0532-8185678; Fax: 86-0532-8185677

# 任务六

# 样品与货物的检验

# Samples and Inspection of Goods

## 学习目标

1. 了解样品与货物检验的相关知识;
2. 掌握有关样品与货物检验的信函的写作要点;
3. 熟悉有关样品与货物检验的信函的常用词语和句子;
4. 能够阅读与撰写有关样品与货物检验的信函。

## 背景知识

### 一、样品

样品是代表或反映商品品质的少量实物，是交易双方交接货物的质量依据。

许多商品的贸易是凭样品表示货物的品质的，样品既是卖方生产的依据，也是买方验货和索赔的依据。在合同签订前，需要进行样品的寄送。买卖双方通过对样品的确认，对交易货物的品质达成协议。在许多实际业务中，在合同签订后仍然需要样品的寄送，买方对样品进行检验，以确认货物的品质是否符合合同的要求。

有关样品的信函分散于货物交易的各个阶段，包括市场开发阶段、交易磋商阶段、合同的履行阶段[①]。

在不同行业的贸易中，由于交易货物的特点不同，使用的样品类型各不相同，常见的样品类型有推销样、确认样、产前样、船样（大货样）等。

### 二、货物的检验

货物的品质是否符合合同的规定是货物的买方所关注的重点，买方可以在卖方交货

---

① 出于阅读的方便，关于样品的信函集中放在本任务中。

前派人自行对货物进行检验或委托检验机构对货物进行检验，在货物到达目的港或目的地后，买方还有最终检验权。

为了避免买卖双方可能出现的争议，通过有资格的、权威的、独立于买卖双方的商品检验机构对交易的商品进行检验并出具检验报告或证书，这是国际贸易中通用的方法。

无论是交货前的检验还是交货后的检验，都是通过对货物抽取样品进行的。

商品检验机构对商品的样品进行检验时，要以某一标准为依据进行，对需要检验的项目按一定的方法进行检验并出具检验报告或检验证书。每个行业都有对产品的检验标准，包括行业标准、国家标准、国际标准等。合同中应该事先规定产品的检验所适用的标准，以及产品要达到的等级。

另外，为了保护人类健康和安全、动物或者植物的生命和健康、环境等，国家对法律规定的某些进出口商品通过法定检验机构实施强制性的检验或检疫。

### （一）检验的方式

在出口国检验、在进口国复验是国际贸易中通常采用的检验方式。货物在装运前由双方约定的检验机构或买方进行检验，其检验证书或检验报告作为卖方要求买方或要求银行支付货款的单据之一。

在货物运抵目的港或目的地后的一定时间内，买方有权对货物进行复验。如果复验时货物不符合合同的规定，买方可以凭买卖双方认可的检验机构出具检验证书或检测报告，向卖方或其他机构进行索赔。

### （二）检验机构

1. 国外的检验机构

表 6.1 列出了部分国际著名的检验认证机构。

**表 6.1　国际著名检验认证机构**

| 中文名称 | 英文名称或简称 |
|---|---|
| 美国食品药物管理局 | FDA |
| 法国国际检验局 | Bureau Veritas |
| 瑞士日内瓦通用鉴定公司 | SGS |
| 美国保险人实验室 | UL |
| 英国劳合氏公证行 | Lloyd’s Surveyor |
| 英国英之杰检验集团 | IITS |
| 日本海事鉴定协会 | NKKK |

2. 我国的检验检疫机构

我国官方的检验检疫机构是各地海关，主要负责法定检验检疫（强制性检验或检疫）的进出口商品检验检疫，也接受进出口企业或机构的委托，办理进出口商品的检验鉴定业务，签发检验鉴定证书。

除了官方的检验检疫机构，有许多中资或外资的第三方检验认证机构从事商品检验鉴定、认证、测试业务。有的检验认证机构是综合性的，从事多个行业商品的检验认证，有的检验认证机构则从事某一行业商品的检验认证。

表 6.2 列出了在我国从事商品检验认证业务的部分检验认证机构。

**表 6.2　我国部分检验认证机构**

| 中资检验认证机构 | 外资检验认证机构 |
|---|---|
| 中国海关总署 | Intertek 天祥集团 |
| 中国检验认证集团（CCIC） | UL 集团 |
| 国家纺织品服装服饰产品质量监督检验中心 | 德国莱茵 TÜV 集团 |
| 北京中联海陆商品检验有限公司 | SGS 集团 |
| PONY 谱尼测试集团公司 | BUREAU VERITAS 集团 |
| 上海市毛麻纺织科学技术研究所 | |

（三）检验证书

表 6.3 列出了常见的检验证书。

**表 6.3　常见的检验证书**

| 证书名称 | 适用范围/作用 |
|---|---|
| 品质检验证书 | 证明货物品质是否符合合同规定 |
| 数量/重量检验证书 | 证明货物的数量/重量是否符合合同规定 |
| 兽医检验证书 | 适用于出入境动物产品，证明货物符合输出国或输入国的检疫规定 |
| 动物卫生证书 | 适用于出入境动物，证明货物符合输出国或输入国的检疫规定 |
| 植物检疫证书 | 适用于出入境植物或植物产品，证明货物符合输出国或输入国的检疫规定 |
| 卫生/健康检验证书 | 适用于出入境的食品，证明货物符合输出国或输入国的食品卫生规定 |
| 消毒/熏蒸检验证书 | 适用于出入境的动植物及其产品、包装材料等，证明货物或包装材料符合输出国或输入国的相关规定 |
| 原产地证书 | 证明货物的原产地，包括一般原产地证书和普惠制原产地证书等 |

## 写作提示

样品与货物的检验密切相关，所以把关于样品与货物检验的信函放在一起。有关样品与货物检验的信函通常包括以下情境和要点：

## 一、产前样品的寄送与确认：买方要求卖方寄送样品

（1）提及所订购货物或合同号；
（2）要求卖方寄送样品；
（3）说明对样品的具体要求；
（4）说明样品费用和运费由哪方承担；
（5）表示感谢。

## 二、产前样品的寄送与确认：卖方向买方寄送样品

（1）提及买方所订购货物或合同号；
（2）告知买方要求寄送的样品已经寄出，并附上运单号码；
（3）希望对方在收到样品后及时反馈和确认。

## 三、产前样品的寄送与确认：买方对样品的确认或意见

（1）提及卖方寄送的样品；
（2）确认样品或对样品提出意见；
（3）（如果提出意见）希望卖方根据提出的意见修改后再次寄送样品供确认。

## 四、交货前样品的寄送与检验：买方要求卖方在交货前检验货物

（1）提及合同号；
（2）a. 要求卖方在交货前将货物的样品交给指定的检验机构进行检验并出具检验证书；
　　b. 要求卖方寄送货物的样品供买方检验；
（3）表示感谢。

## 五、交货前样品的寄送与检验：卖方的回复信函

（1）提及合同号；
（2）a. 告知货物的样品已经交给指定的检验机构进行检验；
　　b. 告知货物的样品已经寄送给买方，请注意查收；
（3）a. 告知买方将及时寄送检验结果；
　　b. 请买方收到样品后进行检验并及时反馈检验结果。

## 示范信函

# CASE 1　Weifang Baoda Textiles Co., Ltd.

## 一、信函的业务背景

缝得好服装有限公司要求潍坊宝达纺织品有限公司在大货生产开始前提供产前样

品，由其制成产前样衣后提供给它的客户确认。

另外，双方约定，在交货前对大货进行抽样，提供样品（船样）给缝得好服装有限公司和指定的检验机构（广州纤维产品检验所）检验，由广州纤维产品检验所出具检验报告。

图 6.1 是潍坊宝达纺织品有限公司在广交会上展出的部分样品。

**图 6.1**　潍坊宝达纺织品有限公司的样品

## 二、潍坊宝达纺织品有限公司的业务信函

（一）样品与货物的检验（baoda-in 1）

From: Lisa lisa@stitchwell.com

To: Albert albert@163.com

Date: 2019.05.12

Subject: samples

Dear Albert,

With reference to Contract No. XS-2019001, we would like you to send us samples of the yarn-dyed fabric we ordered before mass production[1].

The size of the samples will be 20 yards each and please send them to our address below for us to make buyers' samples for fits[2] and PP[3].

The delivery time for our order is very pressing[4], so please prepare and send the samples quickly.

Thank you for your cooperation.

Address:

Stitchwell Garments Co., Ltd.

456/1/A Tejgaon Industrial Area, Dhaka 1208, Bangladesh

Receiver: Lisa Ramsey

Best wishes
Lisa
Purchasing Manager
Stitchwell Garments Co., Ltd.

## Notes

1. mass production 大货生产
   亦称 bulk production，指进行批量生产。
2. fit *n.* 尺码样
   亦可写作 fit sample，尺码样用于观察真人模特穿起的效果以及存在的尺寸问题。服装贸易中，卖方往往在大货生产前向买方提供尺码样。
3. PP 产前样
   全称 pre-production sample，是在大货生产前的样品。服装贸易中，产前样主要用于客人确认大货所要做的产品及辅料等，是做大货的参照样。买方可能要求产前样做一定的修改，所以可能会多次做。
4. pressing *adj.* 紧急的
   e.g. Pressing business matters prevented him from taking a holiday.
   紧急的业务使他无法休假。

（二）样品与货物的检验（baoda-out 1）

From: Albert albert@163.com
To: Lisa lisa@stitchwell.com
Date: 2019.05.13
Subject: RE: samples

Dear Lisa,

In reply to your letter on May 12 about the samples of Contract No.XS-2019001, I regret to say that[1] we can not afford[2] the charges of the samples and freight because it is against my company's policy[3].

As you know, the whole industry is a low profit industry[4] and our profit is very marginal[5]. It will cost us much if we send samples free of charge to customers.

If you agree to pay for the samples required I will send them to you by forwarder[6].

Look forward to hearing from you.

Sincerely
Albert
Sales Manager
Weifang Baoda Textiles Co., Ltd.

## Notes

1. regret to say that 抱歉地说

   e.g. I regret to say that we can't agree on payment by T/T.

   抱歉，我们不能同意使用电汇作为支付方式。

2. afford *v.* 承担

   e.g. Her family can not afford the tuition for Lining's schooling.

   她的家庭不能负担李宁学业上的学费。

3. policy *n.* 政策

4. low profit industry 低利润的行业

   e.g. Once, car industry is a high profit industry in developed countries, but now it is a low profit industry.

   在发达国家，汽车工业曾经是高利润的行业，但是现在是一个低利润的行业。

5. marginal *adj.* 微不足道的

   e.g. The profit is quite marginal for factories in weaving industry.

   纺织行业中工厂的利润非常低。

6. forwarder *n.* 快递公司；承运人（公司）

（三）样品与货物的检验（baoda-in 2）

From: Lisa lisa@stitchwell.com

To: Albert albert@163.com

Date: 2019.05.14

Subject: RE: RE: samples

Dear Albert,

As to the freight, we agree to afford it by freight collect upon receipt of the samples. But we hope the charges of the samples will be paid together with the goods ordered because recently we are busily engaged in[1] orders from our customers and it takes a lot of time for us to remit the charges through bank.

Meanwhile, please make sure[2] that the samples you are sending match[3] the confirmed samples.

Thank you for your cooperation.

Best wishes

Lisa

Purchasing Manager

Stitchwell Garments Co., Ltd.

## Notes

1. be engaged in 忙于……

   e.g. I am engaged in preparing my lessons.

   我正忙于准备功课。

2. make sure 确保

   e.g. Make sure that the door is locked before leaving the office.

   请确保在离开办公室时锁上门。

3. match *v.* 与……相匹配

   e.g. The colour of the shoes she is wearing does not match the colour of her skirt.

   她穿的鞋的颜色与裙子的颜色不匹配。

（四）样品与货物的检验（baoda-out 2）

From: Albert albert@163.com

To: Lisa lisa@stitchwell.com

Date: 2019.05.15

Subject: RE: RE: RE: samples

Dear Lisa,

Regarding the sample charges of Contract No. XS-2019001, we agree with you on paying the charges of the samples with the mass production.

The samples① (No. BD-YD57848, BD-YD57849, BD-YD57850) have been sent to you on May 16 by FedEx, the tracking No. is FD156987546.

Please confirm the samples or send your feedback[1] when receiving them.

Sincerely

Albert

Sales Manager

Weifang Baoda Textiles Co., Ltd.

**图 6.2　潍坊宝达纺织品有限公司寄送的产前样**

① 潍坊宝达纺织品有限公司寄送的产前样见图 6.2。

## Note

1. feedback　*n.* 反馈

   e.g. The students' feedback is crucial for teachers to improve teaching effect.

   学生的反馈对于教师提高教学效果非常关键。

（五）样品与货物的检验（baoda-in 3）

From: Lisa lisa@stitchwell.com

To: Albert albert@163.com

Date: 2019.05.20

Subject: comments on sample BD-YD57849

Dear Albert,

We have just received your samples under Contract No. XS-2019001.

As to the samples, we have confirmed the samples BD-YD57848, BD-YD57850. But for BD-YD57849, we would give our comments[1].

1. The color of the red yarn should be darker than the sample. So please change the color of the red yarn to Poppy Red 17-1664[2] in the PANTONE Textile Numbering System[3].

2. The handfeel[4] is not good. The handfeel of the fabric should be softer than the sample.

Please amend the above points for BD-YD57849 and send the sample BD-YD57849 again for us to confirm.

Best regards

Lisa

Purchasing Manager

Stitchwell Garments Co., Ltd.

## Notes

1. comment　*n.* & *v.* 评价，评论

   e.g. (1) He made his comments at a news conference in Beijing.

   在北京的新闻会议上他做出了自己的评论。

   (2) The discovery is commented widely by the press.

   此发现被媒体广泛地评论。

2. Poppy Red 17-1664　罂粟红 17-1664

3. PANTONE Textile Numbering System PANTONE 纺织品编号系统

   它是由 PANTONE 公司开发的。PANTONE 公司是 X-Rite, Incorporated 的全资子公司，是一家以专门开发和研究色彩而闻名全球的权威机构，也是色彩系统和领先技术的供应商，提供许多行业专业的色彩选择和精确的交流语言。

4. handfeel *n.* 手感

（六）样品与货物的检验（baoda-in 4）

From: Lisa lisa@stitchwell.com
To: Albert albert@163.com
Date: 2019.05.25
Subject: test report
Attachment: Kmart Textile Testing Requirement

Dear Albert,

With reference to Contract No. XS-2019001, we would like to remind you that you shall have the goods inspected[1] before shipment and the Test Report[2] is a necessary document for payment.

Please send the samples of the ordered fabric in mass production to the designated[3] testing institute and show us the copy of the Test Report before shipment.

As to the requirement of the items inspected, please see the attachment.

At the same time, please send us the duplicate sample[4] tested by the designated testing institute for our reference.

Best wishes
Lisa
Purchasing Manager
Stitchwell Garments Co., Ltd.

## Notes

1. have the goods inspected 检验货物
   have sth. done 让某物被……
   e.g. I had better have my hair cut to look in good spirit.
   为了看上去精神，我最好理发。
2. test report 检测报告
3. designated *adj.* 指定的
   e.g. The vessel must land the goods at designated ports.
   船只必须在指定的港口卸货。
4. duplicate sample 复样，留样
   e.g. A duplicate sample shall be sealed after inspection.
   在检验后留样应该被封好。

（七）样品与货物的检验（baoda-out 3）
From: Albert albert@163.com
To: Lisa lisa@stitchwell.com
Date: 2019.05.26
Subject: RE: test report

Dear Lisa,

As to the inspection and Test Report for the samples mentioned in your letter on May 25, we have sent the samples to Guangzhou Fibre Product Testing Institute[1] and the copy of the Test Report will be sent to you when we get it.

The duplicate samples[2] which are tested by the testing institute were sent to your address yesterday by FedEx[3] and the tracking No. is FD65879256.

Yours sincerely
Albert
Sales Manager
Weifang Baoda Textiles Co., Ltd.

### Notes

1. Guangzhou Fibre Product Testing Institute 广州纤维产品检验所
2. duplicate sample 复样，留样
   复样或留样一般指卖方向买方提供样品时自己留存的一份同样的样品，用于进行生产及交货时核对。在此指与检验样品相同的样品。
3. FedEx 联邦快递
   FedEx 是一家知名国际性速递集团，总部设于美国田纳西州。

## CASE 2　Beijing Lucky Fibreboard Trading Co., Ltd.

### 一、信函的业务背景

北京幸运纤维板贸易有限公司和澳大利亚松树纤维板工业有限公司签订了纤维板的买卖合同。

在开始生产前，北京幸运纤维板贸易有限公司要求澳大利亚松树纤维板工业有限公司把订购货物的样品寄来供检验、确认，并作为收货时检验货物的依据。

图 6.3 是澳大利亚松树纤维板工业有限公司生产的产品图片。

图 6.3　澳大利亚松树纤维板工业有限公司的产品

## 二、北京幸运纤维板贸易有限公司的信函

### （一）样品与货物的检验（lucky-out 1）

From: Lingling lingling@163.com
To: Bill salesdepartment@pinetree.com.au
Date: 2019.06.05
Subject: samples

Dear Bill,

With reference to the purchase of Premium Panel, please send us the samples of the following articles to our address below, which we will keep for test and reference.

Grade: premium.

Specifications:

1. length 2,400 mm, width 1,200 mm, thickness 9 mm;
2. length 2,400 mm, width 1,400 mm, thickness 6 mm.

Address: Beijing Lucky Fibreboard Trading Co., Ltd.

Room 801, International Trade Center, Chaoyang, Beijing, China

Receiver: Lingling

The item which we especially pay attention to is the Formaldehyde Emission[1], E0[2] (Ultra low emission) standard for the resin type[3] is the requirement of this item for the goods ordered.

As to other inspection items, please refer to the English Version of GB/T 11718 (1999 edition)[4] we sent you.

Look forward to your quick response.

Best wishes
Lingling
Purchasing Manager
Beijing Lucky Fibreboard Trading Co., Ltd.

## Notes

1. formaldehyde emission 甲醛释放量
   甲醛释放量是建筑材料的一项质量指标，甲醛释放量越低，建筑材料的环保指标越好。
2. E0 甲醛释放量的标准之一
   E0 是等级最高的甲醛释放量标准，优于 E1 和 E2 标准。
3. resin type 树脂类型
   它指用于黏合密度板的树脂类型。
4. GB/T 11718（1999 edition）密度板的国家标准（1999 年版本）

（二）样品与货物的检验（lucky-in 1）

From: Bill salesdepartment@pinetree.com.au
To: Lingling lingling@163.com
Date: 2019.06.10
Subject: RE: samples

Dear Lingling,

In reply to your letter on June 5, the samples[①] of the ordered goods have been sent to you by DHL on June 9 at your request, and the tracking No. is AM134856.

Please confirm the samples upon receipt of them.

Look forward to receiving your response.

Best regards
Bill
Sales Department
Pinetree Fibreboard Industries Co., Ltd.

图 6.4　澳大利亚松树纤维板工业有限公司寄送的密度板样品

① 澳大利亚松树纤维板工业有限公司寄送的密度板样品见图 6.4。

## 练习

一、将下列句子译成中文。

1. We would like you to send us samples of the yarn-dyed fabric we order.
2. Please send the samples to the following address.
3. The freight will be for your account.
4. I regret to say that we can not afford the charges of the samples and freight.
5. The samples have been sent to you by DHL on May 26 at your request, and the tracking No. is AM134856.
6. Please give your comment when you receive the samples.
7. As to the sample yh-2019021, please amend it according to the comment in the attachment.
8. Please send the samples to the designated testing institute and get the test report before shipment.
9. We especially pay attention to the item of colorfastness. Please make sure that the colorfastness of the fabric meets the requirement.
10. I am sorry to inform you that we failed in the final inspection. Please find the inspection report issued by SGS in the attachment.

二、将下列句子译成英文。

1. 请寄送我方所订购的纤维板的样品。
2. 请把样品发往如下地址。
3. 按照我公司的惯例，样品快递费由买方承担。
4. 你方所需的样品已经发往你方地址，请注意查收。
5. 关于你方样品 JK-2019306 的修改意见，请见附件。
6. 希望你方能尽快确认样品，以便我们安排生产。
7. 请在发货前从大货中抽取样品送官方检验机构进行检验并出具检验报告。
8. 商品的甲醛含量是我们关注的一项重要指标。
9. 取得检验报告后，我方会及时把检验报告的复件发给你方。
10. 测试报告应由 SGS 公司出具，并在发货前寄给我们。

## 技能训练

### 根据业务情境和信息写信

（一）业务情境

1. 轮胎输入美国市场要经过认证（DOT 认证）。大卫·桑德伯格要求江苏通达轮胎有限公司提供样品。

2. 江苏通达轮胎有限公司的李辉回复了大卫·桑德伯格要求提供样品的信函。

（二）信息

1. 样品：TRUCK TIRE D928，规格 10.00R20（见图 6.5）。

2. 样品费用和运费：大卫·桑德伯格要求样品费用和运费由江苏通达轮胎有限公司承担。

3. 样品要求：轮胎的样品必须有 DOT 认证标志和工厂代码。

**图 6.5　样品**

（三）任务

根据以上的业务情境和信息写信。

1. 大卫·桑德伯格要求江苏通达轮胎有限公司提供所订购轮胎的样品，以供检验。

信函应包括以下要点：

（1）提及要订购的商品的名称和规格；

（2）要求李辉寄送轮胎样品；

（3）轮胎的样品必须有 DOT 认证标志和工厂代码；

（4）大卫·桑德伯格要求样品费用和运费由江苏通达轮胎有限公司承担；

（5）表示感谢。

2. 李辉回复大卫·桑德伯格要求提供样品的信函。

信函应包括以下要点：

（1）提及大卫·桑德伯格关于要求寄送样品的信函；

（2）不同意样品费用和运费由江苏通达轮胎有限公司承担，原因是样品费用和运费较高；

（3）希望对方同意自己的意见。

## 补充阅读

信函 1：订货前，买方要求卖方寄样品

业务背景：法国的一家手工艺品贸易公司（优雅贸易有限公司）的总经理海伦对中国的一家草编工艺品生产企业（青岛兴旺手工艺品有限公司）的某些产品感兴趣，写信给青岛兴旺手工艺品有限公司的销售经理李华，要求寄送样品。

From: helen1219@hotmail.com
To: lihua@handicraftschina.com
Date: 2019.03.19
Subject: samples for article Nos. SK201-2 and SK201-5

Dear Lihua,

We have looked through the catalogue sent to us and are interested in article Nos. SK201-2 and SK201-5.

Please send the samples of the above articles to us.

Our address is as follows.

Elegance Trading Limited, France
No. 1203 Garden Road, Paris, France
Receiver: Helen Keller

Your kind cooperation will be much appreciated.

Yours sincerely
Helen Keller
General Manager
Elegance Trading Limited, France
Address: No. 1203 Garden Road, Paris, France
Tel: 33-1-8185678; Fax: 33-1-8185677

信函 2：货物装运前，卖方向买方寄出样品供确认

业务背景：法国的优雅贸易有限公司与中国的青岛兴旺手工艺品有限公司签订了订货合同。在交货前，青岛兴旺手工艺品有限公司的销售经理李华向优雅贸易有限公司的总经理海伦寄出样品供确认。

From: lihua@handicraftschina.com
To: helen1219@hotmail.com
Date: 2019.05.08
Subject: shipment samples for article Nos. SK201-2 and SK201-5

Dear Helen,

With reference to the goods under Sales Contract No. HC2019008, we have finished half of the goods ordered.

We are sending you the shipment samples for article Nos. SK201-2 and SK201-5 through forwarder.

The samples will reach you in due time. Please give your comment about the samples upon receipt of them.

Yours sincerely
Li Hua
Sales Manager
Qingdao Xingwang Handicrafts Co., Ltd.
Address: No. 1251 Xingwang Road, Qingdao, Shandong, China
Tel: 86-0532-8745618; Fax: 86-0532-8745617

# 任务七

# 货物的包装及运输标志

# Packing and Shipping Marks

## 学习目标

1. 了解货物的包装及运输标志的有关知识；
2. 掌握有关货物包装及运输标志的信函的写作要点；
3. 熟悉货物的包装及运输标志的常用词语和句子；
4. 能够阅读与撰写有关货物包装及运输标志的信函。

## 背景知识

### 一、货物的包装

包装是国际贸易业务中的一个必要环节。包装的目的在于使商品在运输的过程中保持完好的状况，避免运输过程中的损坏，同时，可以提升商品的市场价值。

#### （一）包装的类型

包装可以分为两种类型：外包装和内包装。

外包装，也称运输包装，主要用来在运输过程中保护商品的完好。外包装适合长距离的运输，并且容易装卸。

内包装，也称为销售包装，用来使消费者识别商品的信息及美化商品，从而促进商品的销售。

无论是外包装还是内包装，都要根据商品的性质和运输的类型来确定包装种类和包装材料，并通常由买方给出具体的包装要求①。

① 在合同中，包装条款对货物的包装有大概的说明。在合同履行的过程中，买方往往再给出具体的包装要求。

（二）常用包装容器的种类

袋（bag）：由结实的纸、亚麻布、帆布、塑料、橡胶等制成（见图 7.1a）。常用来装粉状、颗粒状、块状的货物，如粮食、化肥。

麻袋（sack）：通常是用黄麻制成（见图 7.1b）。它常用来装农产品等。

图 7.1a　纸袋

图 7.1b　麻袋

纸箱（carton）：用轻而结实的硬纸板或纤维板制成，有双盖和双底，用胶水、胶带、金属带或骑马钉缝合（见图 7.1c）。应用广泛，常用来包装日用消费品。

木箱（case）：用木板制成的结实容器，可有横档加固。有时用薄木板和铁皮或铁丝绕扎，箱内可衬各种材料例如防潮纸、锡纸等以防水、空气或昆虫损坏箱内的货物（见图 7.1d）。它常用于包装价值较高、易损的货物，如家电、家具。

图 7.1c　纸箱

图 7.1d　木箱

盒（box）：用木板、硬纸板或金属制成（见图 7.1e）。

板条箱（crate）：这是一种箱，但不是全封闭的，它有一底板和框架，通常顶部敞开（见图 7.1f）。板条箱常用来装机器设备等。

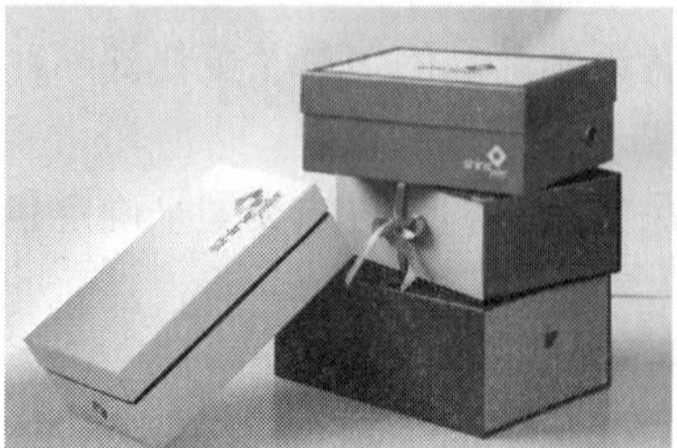

图 7.1e　纸盒

图 7.1f　板条箱

桶（drum）：圆筒形的容器，通常由金属、木头或纸板等制成（见图 7.1g 和图 7.1h）。它用于装液体、粉状或颗粒状货物，某些化学品、油漆等。

图 7.1g　木桶

图 7.1h　铁桶

罐头（can，tin）：由金属制成。它用于装少量的油漆、油或某种食品的小金属容器（见图 7.1i）。

瓶子（bottle）：由玻璃或塑料制成（见图 7.1j）。它用于装液体商品，如饮料。

图 7.1i　罐头

图 7.1j　玻璃瓶

货盘（pallet）：由木头或塑料等材料制成，按一定规格制成的单层或双层平板载货工具（见图 7.1k）。托盘包装是将许多单件包装组合起来，成为一个运输单位，便于在运输过程中使用机械进行装卸、搬运和堆放。

图 7.1k　托盘

集装箱（container）：用于公路、铁路、海运或空运货物的金属大箱（见图 7.11）。货物装在集装箱的优点在于方便运输时的起吊或搬动，因而节省时间。常用规格有 20 英尺和 40 英尺两种。集装箱运输已经成为国际上普遍采用的运输方式。

**图 7.11 集装箱**

## 二、包装标志

在商品的外包装上往往要刷上包装标志，以方便货物的交接及海关的查验等。包装标志主要有运输标志（唛头）（shipping marks）、指示性标志（indicative marks）和警告性标志（warming marks）几种类型。

在实际业务中，运输标志可以根据买方的要求在外包装上标识；如果没有要求，卖方可以不刷唛或根据自己的习惯做法在外包装上刷唛。

通常，运输标志包括以下内容：

（1）收货人或发货人的代号名称；

（2）参考号：合同号码或信用证号码；

（3）目的港或目的地；

（4）包装的件号、序号。

另外，外包装常常带有侧唛（side mark），标记货物的型号、毛重、净重、体积等。

运输标志使得货物易于识别，方便运输。

图 7.2a 和图 7.2b 分别是外包装箱上的主唛和侧唛。

指示性标志是针对一些易碎、易损、易变质的商品用醒目的图形和简单的文字提醒有关人员在装卸、搬运和存储时应注意的事项。

警告性标志是对一些易燃易爆、有毒等危险品在其包装上清楚而明显地刷制的标志，以示警告。

图 7.3 和图 7.4 分别是外包装上的指示性标志和警告性标志的部分示例。

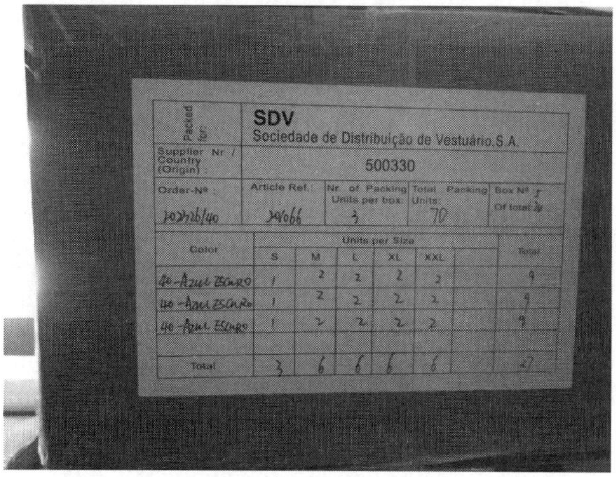


图 7.2a　外包装上的运输标志（唛头）——主唛

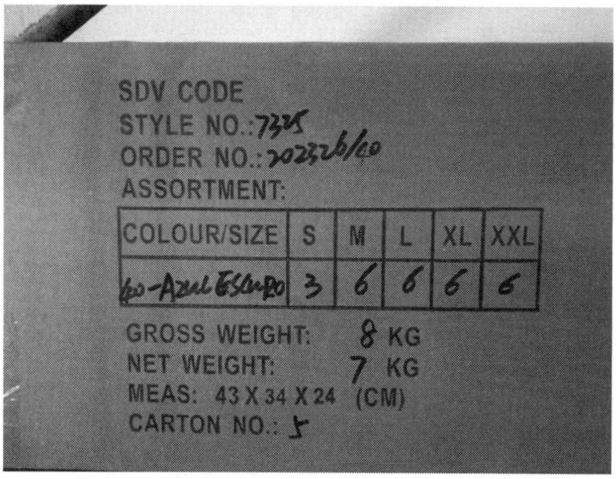


图 7.2b　外包装上的运输标志（唛头）——侧唛

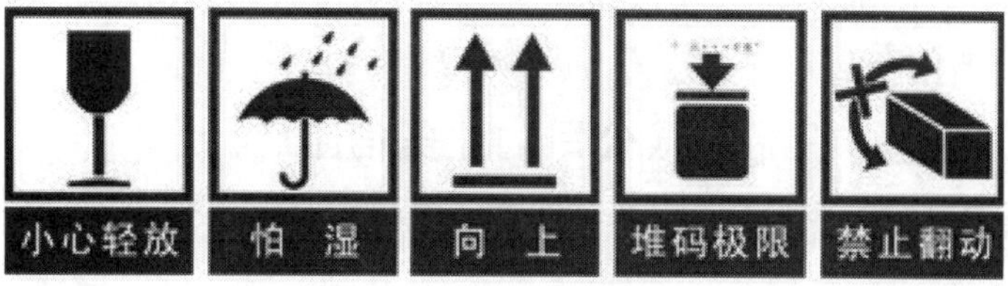


图 7.3　外包装上的指示性标志

A　　B　　C　　D

图 7.4　外包装上的警告性标志

## 写作提示

有关货物包装的信函通常包括以下情境和要点：

### 一、买方发出的包装要求信函

（1）提及合同号，提出包装要求；
（2）具体的包装要求；
（3）提出包装费用由谁承担（合同签订前一般已经确定）；
（4）希望卖方同意提出的包装要求；
（5）表示感谢。

### 二、卖方对买方包装要求的回复信函

（1）提及买方的包装要求；
（2）回复是否同意对方的包装要求；
（3）说明对样品包装完毕后，发照片给买方确认。

## 示范信函

## CASE 1　Weifang Baoda Textiles Co., Ltd.

### 一、信函的业务背景

缝得好服装有限公司向潍坊宝达纺织品有限公司给出了具体的包装要求及运输标志的内容。潍坊宝达纺织品有限公司按照缝得好服装有限公司的包装要求和运输标志的内容包装、打印运输标志。

### 二、潍坊宝达纺织品有限公司的业务信函

（一）货物的包装（baoda-in 1）

From: Lisa lisa@stitchwell.com
To: Albert albert@163.com
Date: 2019.05.28.
Subject: packing instruction[1]
Attachment: packing example graph; illustration of shipping marks[2]

Dear Albert,

I would like to give you the detailed packing instruction in order to avoid any future trouble.

The goods should be wrapped by[3] plastic bags to avoid dampness[4] and then be packed in[5] gunny bags[6] as outer packing[7]. Every 100 yards are in one gunny bag. Straps[8] should be used to tighten the gunny bags. Please see the example packing graph[9] in the attachment.

As to shipping marks, the requirement is as follows.

The main mark[10] should be read[11] in four lines. The first line is the abbreviation[12] of our company which should be "STITCHWELL", the second line is the Contract No. which should be "XS-2019001", the third line should be the destination port which is "CHITTAGONG BANGLADESH", and the fourth line is the package No. of outer packing.

The side mark[13] should include item No., quantity, G.W. and N.W. [14], measurement[15].

Please also see the illustration[16] of shipping marks which includes main mark and side mark in the attachment.

If you have any problems about our packing requirement, please let us know.

Regards
Lisa
Purchasing Manager
Stitchwell Garments Co., Ltd.

**附 7.1　孟加拉国缝得好服装有限公司的外包装图示**
**Packing Example Graph**

附 7.2 孟加拉国缝得好服装有限公司的外包装唛头

**Illustration of Shipping Marks**

**MAIN MARK**

CONSIGNEE: STITCHWELL

CONTRACT NO.: XS-2019001

DESTINATION: CHITTAGONG BANGLADESH

PACKAGE NO.: 1-UP

**SIDE MARK**

ITEM NO.: XS-FLANNEL-01

QUANTITY: 100 YARDS

NET WEIGHT: 50 KGS

GROSS WEIGHT: 52 KGS

MEASUREMENT: 2.54 CBM

## Notes

1. packing instruction 包装指示

   包装指示指买方对于包装的具体要求。

2. shipping marks 运输标志，唛头

   运输标志或唛头指外包装上印的关于货物及运输的信息，用于买方识别货物，往往有收货人简称、目的港（地）、参考号、箱号、重量、体积等信息。

3. be wrapped by 由……包裹

   e.g. Each television should be wrapped by plastic bag as inner packing.

   每台电视机应该用塑料袋包裹作为内包装。

4. avoid dampness 避免受潮

5. be packed in 包装在……

   e.g. Each television should be packed in one carton.

   每台电视机应该装入一个纸箱。

6. gunny bag 麻袋

7. outer packing 外包装

   外包装与内包装相对。内包装是对商品的初次包装，用来使消费者识别商品的信息及美化商品，从而促进商品的销售；外包装是在内包装的基础上对货物的再次包装，用来保护运输过程中商品的完好。

8. strap *n.* 带子

   e.g. A strap is a narrow piece of leather, cloth, or other material. Straps are used to carry things, or fasten things together.

   一条带子是由皮革或布料或其他材料做成的窄条状物。带子用来提东西或把东西紧固。

9. example packing graph 示范包装图
10. main mark 主唛
    主唛是印在外包装正面的运输标志。
11. read *v.* 写作
12. abbreviation *n.* 缩写
13. side mark 侧唛
    侧唛是印在外包装侧面的运输标志。
14. G.W. and N.W. 毛重和净重
    G.W.的全称：gross weight；N.W.的全称：net weight。
15. measurement *n.* 体积；尺寸
16. illustration *n.* 图示
    e.g. The illustration shows the procedure of L/C.
    此图示表示信用证的使用流程。

# CASE 2　Beijing Lucky Fibreboard Trading Co., Ltd.

## 一、信函的业务背景

在北京幸运纤维板贸易有限公司和澳大利亚松树纤维板工业有限公司签订的合同中，双方约定的货物包装条款如下：ACCORDING TO THE BUYER'S INSTRUCTION（根据买方的指示）。

在交货前，北京幸运纤维板贸易有限公司向澳大利亚松树纤维板工业有限公司给出具体的包装要求，澳大利亚松树纤维板工业有限公司根据给出的包装要求对货物进行包装。

## 二、北京幸运纤维板贸易有限公司的信函

货物的包装（lucky-out 1）

From: Lingling lingling@163.com

To: Bill salesdepartment@pinetree.com.au

Date: 2019.06.08

Subject: packing requirement[1]

Attachment: illustration of the packing requirement

Dear Bill,

Regarding Sales Confirmation No. SC-PINE2019010, I would like to give you the specific packing requirement for our ordered goods.

The panels shall be wrapped by plastic bags to avoid dampness, and protection boards[2] should be put around every side. Then iron wrap belts[3] should be used to fasten[4] the panels. Every 90 sheets for 9 mm are in one pack and every 120 sheets for 6 mm panel are in one pack respectively[5]. And a wood pallet[6] should be put at the bottom of[7] each pack.

Finally, every 12 packs are for one container[8].

We hope you can meet the packing requirement and packing charges shall be afforded by you[9] as arranged.

Enclosed please find the illustration[10] of the packing requirement.

If you have any question about the packing, please contact me in time.

Thank you in advance.

Sincerely
Lingling
Purchasing Manager
Beijing Lucky Fibreboard Trading Co., Ltd.

附 7.3　北京幸运纤维板贸易有限公司的包装要求图示

**Illustration of the Packing Requirement**

## Notes

1. packing requirement 包装要求
   packing requirement 与 packing instruction 的含义相同。
2. protection board 保护板
3. iron wrap belt 铁包裹带
4. fasten *v.* 紧固
5. respectively *adj.* 各自地，分别地
   e.g. My two kids, Adam and Bill, are ten and thirteen respectively.
   我的两个孩子——10 岁的亚当和 13 岁的比尔。

6. wood pallet 木托盘

   托盘是一种集装工具，托盘的图示见图 7.1 k。

7. at the bottom of 在……的底部

   e.g. The correct answers can be found at the bottom of page 195.

   正确答案可以在 195 页的底部找到。

8. container *n.* 集装箱

   集装箱是一种大型装货容器。使用集装箱转运货物，中途转运时无须将货物从箱内取出换装，是一种集装运输方式。集装箱分为干货集装箱、散货集装箱、液体集装箱、冷藏集装箱等。

9. be afforded by you 费用由你方负担

   类似的说法：be for your account

10. illustration *n.* 图示

## 练习

**一、将下列句子译成中文。**

1. I would like to give you the packing instruction in order to avoid any future trouble.
2. The goods should be packed in roll and every 150 metres per roll.
3. Each roll is wrapped by plastic bag with a gunny bag as outer packing.
4. Each pill must be put in one small box sealed with wax.
5. Each carton should be protected from being crushed by putting foamed plastics inside.
6. The measurements of each carton must not exceed 50cm x 60cm x 40cm.
7. The main mark should be read in four lines.
8. The side mark should include item No., quantity, G.W. and N.W., measurement.
9. Please mark the country of origin, the destination port, consignee and the carton No. on the outer packing.
10. The panels shall be wrapped by plastic bags to avoid dampness, then use wooden cases as outer packing.

**二、将下列句子译成英文。**

1. 对于合同 SC-08539，我公司对订购商品的包装要求如下。
2. 商品应该由塑料袋包装以免受潮，外包装用纸箱包装。
3. 每 10 个托盘装一个集装箱。
4. 请在外包装上标明“易碎”和“小心轻放”。
5. 包装费用由你方负担。
6. 我们的包装方式被客户广泛认可，到目前为止还没有接到投诉。
7. 请放心所有的纸箱内附有塑料片，因此可以防水。
8. 该种包装成本低，并且可以有效防止货物在搬动时被损坏。

9. 希望你方能够满足我方关于商品包装的要求。
10. 在完成对货物的包装后，我方会发给你方包装的照片。如果有不满意的地方请及时提出。

## 技能训练

### 根据业务情境和信息写信

（一）业务情境

1. 大卫·桑德伯格要求轮胎必须用塑料编织袋进行包装。
2. 江苏通达轮胎有限公司的李辉回复了大卫·桑德伯格提出的包装要求。

（二）信息

1. 包装材料：塑料编织袋。

2. 包装方式：每个轮胎用塑料编织袋缠绕作为销售包装（见图 7.5）；用布袋作为运输包装，每 10 个轮胎装入一个布袋。

3. 运输标志：

收货人：HTTC

合同号：HTTC-20190608

目的港：NEW YORK, USA

包装号：1-UP

图 7.5　江苏通达轮胎有限公司的轮胎出口包装

（三）任务

根据以上的业务情境和信息写信。

信函应包括以下要点：

1. 提及合同号；

2. 提出包装要求；
3. 请参照附件里的包装示例进行包装；
4. 表示感谢。

## 补充阅读

信函 1：货物的包装指示

业务背景：青岛鱼山贸易有限公司的总经理爱丽斯向日本的供货商三友智能玩具公司的销售经理呐呐先生发出包装指示的信函。

From: alice0512@yushantrading.com
To: tunkis@smarttoy.com
Date: 2019.11.14
Subject: packing instruction
Attachment: Packing Illustration

Dear Mr. Okada Nana,

Thank you for your letter on November 10 informing us of the shipment date and enquiring for packing requirement.

Now we are giving packing instruction as follows.

Each item should be packed in a plastic bag, then in a paper box. 10 boxes are packed in one carton with cushions in each side of the carton. The cartons should be strong enough to bear rough handling and long-distance ocean transportation.

Please see the attachment for detailed packing requirement.

Regards
Alice Chen
General Manager
Qingdao Yushan Trading Co., Ltd.
Address: No. 6381 Yushan Road, Qingdao, Shandong, China
Tel: 86-0532-8185678; Fax: 86-0532-8185677

信函 2：运输标志

业务背景：青岛鱼山贸易有限公司的总经理爱丽斯向日本的供货商三友智能玩具公司的销售经理呐呐先生写信，说明外包装的运输标志和内包装上需要打印内容的具体要求。

From: alice0512@yushantrading.com
To: tunkis@smarttoy.com
Date: 2019.11.18

Subject: shipping marks

Hi, Mr. Okada Nana,

Thank you for your letter enquiring about the Shipping Marks on outer packing of our goods.

Please put the Shipping Marks on outer packing as follows.

Manufacturer: Smart Toy Company Ltd.

Origin: Japan

Destination: Qingdao, China

Carton No.: 1-up

As to the inner packing, please put the following items on as arranged.

Article No., commodity, quantity, measurement, weight and etc.

Please send me the photo of one sample carton after finishing the packing and Shipping Marks.

Regards

Alice Chen

General Manager

Qingdao Yushan Trading Co., Ltd.

Address: No. 6381 Yushan Road, Qingdao, Shandong, China

Tel: 86-0532-8185678; Fax: 86-0532-8185677

# 任务八

# 货物的装运

# Shipment

## 学习目标

1. 了解货物装运的有关知识;
2. 掌握有关货物装运的信函的写作要点;
3. 熟悉有关货物装运的信函的常用词语和句子;
4. 能够阅读与撰写有关货物装运的信函。

## 背景知识

### 一、国际贸易的主要运输方式

在国际贸易中，货物可以通过多种方式进行运输，如海洋运输、航空运输、铁路运输、公路运输、管道运输等。其中，海洋运输是国际贸易最主要的运输方式。

（一）海洋运输

海洋运输具有运量大、不受道路限制的优点，可以降低商品运输的单位商品运费，因此成为国际贸易最主要的运输方式。

集装箱班轮运输是海洋运输方式中最常用的运输方式。班轮运输中，船公司按固定航线、固定停靠港口、固定的航行时间表航行，按相对固定的运费率收取运费。

表 8.1 列出了世界著名船公司的名称及其缩写。

**表 8.1　　世界著名船公司**

| 全　称 | 简称 | 英文缩写 |
|---|---|---|
| 澳大利亚国家航运公司<br>ANL CONTAINER LINE PTY LIMITED | 澳国航运 | ANL |

续表

| 全　　称 | 简称 | 英文缩写 |
| --- | --- | --- |
| 美国总统轮船私人有限公司<br>AMERICAN PRESIDENT LINES LTD. | 美国总统 | APL |
| 中国远洋集装箱运输有限公司<br>COSCO CONTAINER LINES CO., LTD. | 中远集运 | COSCO |
| 长荣海运股份有限公司<br>EVERGREEN MARINE LTD. | 长荣海运 | EVERGREEN |
| 汉堡南美航运公司<br>HAMBURG SUD GROUP | 汉堡南美 | HAMBURG SUD |
| 韩进海运有限公司<br>HANJIN SHIPPING CO., LTD. | 韩进海运 | HANJIN |
| 现代商船有限公司<br>HYUNDAI MERCHANT MARINE LTD. | 现代商船 | HYUNDAI |
| 川崎汽船株式会社<br>K-LINE KAWASAKI KISEN KAISHA, LTD. | 川崎汽船 | K-LINE |
| 地中海航运公司<br>MEDITERRANEAN SHIPPING COMPANY | 地中海航运 | MSC |
| 马士基航运有限公司<br>MAERSK SHIPPING CO., LTD. | 马士基 | MAERSK LINE |
| 日本邮船株式会社<br>NIPPON YUSEN KAISHA LINE | 日本邮船 | NYK |
| 中外运集团总公司<br>SINOTRANS CONTAINER LINES CO., LTD. | 中外运 | SINOTRANS |
| 阿拉伯联合国家轮船公司<br>UNITED ARAB SHIPPING COMPANY | 阿拉伯轮船 | UASC |

### （二）航空运输

与海洋运输相比，航空运输的优点是交货迅速，缺点是运量小、运输费用较高。航空运输适合于鲜活商品、急需商品以及价值高而体积、重量较小的商品。

班机运输是航空运输最常用的运输方式。航空运输的承运人是航空运输公司或航空货运代理公司。

### （三）铁路运输

铁路运输也是国际贸易的主要运输方式之一。

铁路运输的特点是运量大、安全可靠，但仅限于有陆路相连接的国家。

我国的国际铁路运输路线主要有两条：一是西伯利亚大陆桥；二是新亚欧大陆桥，由江苏连云港经过新疆与哈萨克斯坦铁路连接，贯通俄罗斯、波兰、德国至荷兰的鹿特丹（又称新丝绸之路）。

## 二、货物的装运

在卖方将货物准备好后，就要在合同或信用证规定的时间内将货物装运。装运涉及的工作环节有托运、订舱、投保、报关、装运货物和发装运通知等。

采用不同的贸易术语时，卖方和买方承担不同的运输责任。在采用 FOB 术语或其他 F 组术语时，由买方安排运输工具；而采用 CIF、CFR 术语或其他 C 组术语时，由卖方安排运输工具并将货物装运。

装运过程中，买卖双方要及时进行沟通[①]，保证货物按时装运并到达目的地。

## 写作提示

对卖方来说，有关货物装运的信函通常包括要求买方发装运指示，告知买方货物已经装运等；对买方来说，通常包括向卖方发送装运指示，催卖方及时装运货物等。

写作内容的要点通常如下：

### 一、卖方要求买方发装运指示

（1）告诉买方某合同项下的货物已经准备好；
（2）请买方发装运指示：告知船名、航次、买方在装运港的货运代理的联系方式；
（3）表示感谢。

### 二、买方向卖方发装运指示

（1）感谢卖方已经准备好货物；
（2）告知卖方选择的承运人及船名、航次；
（3）告知卖方在装运港指定的货运代理的联系方式；
（4）请卖方及时联系指定的货运代理；
（5）表示感谢。

### 三、买方催卖方及时装运货物

（1）提及某合同项下的货物，并提醒卖方交货时间已经临近；
（2）表示没有收到卖方关于货物的装运信息；
（3）请卖方告知货物的准备情况及具体的装运信息；
（4）表示感谢。

### 四、卖方告知买方货物已经装运

（1）提及某合同项下的货物；
（2）告知买方货物已经装上指定的船只或运输工具；

---

① 在本环节，涉及的商务函电主要有催运、装运指示、装运通知等。

（3）告知买方货物离开启运港（启运地）的时间和预计到目的港（目的地）的时间；
（4）附上“装运通知”；
（5）告知买方在收货后，如果发现货物有损坏或其他问题，及时提出。

## 示范信函

# CASE 1 Weifang Baoda Textiles Co., Ltd.

## 一、信函的业务背景

潍坊宝达纺织品有限公司的外贸业务员阿尔伯特在货物生产完毕后，通过信函告知孟加拉国缝得好服装有限公司的丽莎货物已经准备好，等待对方给出装运指示。

在丽莎发出装运指示后，阿尔伯特及时联系船公司在装运港的货运代理进行订舱、报关、装运，并在货物装运后及时发出了装运通知。

## 二、潍坊宝达纺织品有限公司的业务信函

（一）货物的装运（baoda-out 1）

From: Albert albert@163.com
To: Lisa lisa@stitchwell.com
Date: 2019.05.30
Subject: shipment for Contract No. XS-2019001

Dear Lisa,

With reference to Contract No. XS-2019001 for yarn-dyed fabric 27,000 yards, the goods are ready for shipment now. The goods are packed in 270 gunny bags and shall be shipped with a 40 foot container.

Please send the Shipping Instruction[1] for us to ship the goods in time[2]. The Shipping Instruction shall include vessel name[3], voyage No. [4], the estimated time of arrival[5] etc. In addition[6], please give us the contact information of the shipping agent[7] at the loading port (Qingdao Port) in order for us to contact them in time.

Thank you for your cooperation.

Yours sincerely
Albert
Sales Manager
Weifang Baoda Textiles Co., Ltd.

## Notes

1. shipping instruction 装运指示
   装运指示一般是在 F 组术语（如 FOB、FCA）的条件下由买方向卖方发出，说明使用的装运工具和到达装运港或装运地的时间，以便卖方将货物送到指定地点。
2. in time 及时
   e.g. Fortunately, the policemen arrived in time and avoided more injuries.
   幸运的是，警察及时赶到，避免了更多的伤害。
3. vessel name 船名
4. voyage No. 航次
5. estimated time of arrival 预计到达时间（缩写 ETA）
6. in addition 另外
   e.g. In addition to my salary, I earn more by doing part-time job.
   在我的工资以外，我通过做兼职赚更多的钱。
7. shipping agent 货运代理
   货运代理简称货代，为出口人或进口人办理货物运输业务的企业。

（二）货物的装运（baoda-in 1）

From: Lisa lisa@stitchwell.com
To: Albert albert@163.com
Date: 2019.05.31
Subject: RE: shipment for Contract No. XS-2019001

Dear Albert,

Thank you for your information covering[1] the readiness of our goods under Contract No. XS-2019001.

We have chosen COSCO SURABAYA① as the shipping vessel and the voyage No. is 019S. The estimated time of arrival at Qingdao Port for the vessel is June 10.

As to our forwarder, please contact the following shipping agent.

Contact person: Wang Qiang
Company: Qingdao Ocean & Great Asia Logistics Co., Ltd.
Phone: 86-536-8221588
Fax: 86-536-8221599
E-mail: wangyaqian@163.com

Please contact the above person to book the shipping space[2] 10 days prior to[3] shipment to

① 中国远洋集装箱有限公司的货船见图 8.1。

ensure the goods delivery.

Best regards
Lisa
Purchasing Manager
Stitchwell Garments Co., Ltd.

图 8.1　中国远洋集装箱有限公司的货船

## Notes

1. cover　*v.* 涉及

   e.g. The course covers all aspects of business and law.
   
   此课程涉及商业和法律的所有方面。

2. shipping space 装运空间

   shipping space 这里指舱位。
   
   e.g. For bulk goods, it's very convenient for sellers to arrange the shipping space.
   
   对于散货，卖方订舱是很方便的。

3. prior to　先于

   prior to 相当于 before。
   
   e.g. Prior to his Japan trip, he went to New York.
   
   在去日本旅行前，他去了纽约。

（三）货物的装运（baoda-out 2）

From: Albert albert@163.com
To: Lisa lisa@stitchwell.com
Date: 2019.06.03
Subject: shipment for goods under Contract No. XS-2019001

Dear Lisa,

Thank you for your kind information about your forwarder. I have contacted the forwarder and booked[1] the shipping space[2].

The vessel COSCO SURABAYA will depart[3] from Qingdao Port on June 12 and we will send the goods to container yard[4] in time to ship the goods.

Once the goods are loaded on board[5] I will send you Shipping Advice[6] immediately.

Yours sincerely
Albert
Sales Manager
Weifang Baoda Textiles Co., Ltd.

## Notes

1. book *v.* 预订
   e.g. She had booked herself a flight home last night.
   她昨晚已经订好了回家的机票。
2. shipping space 舱位
3. depart *v.* 离开
   e.g. Lisa is planning to depart from the company she founded.
   丽莎打算离开她创立的公司。
4. container yard 集装箱场站（堆场）
   container yard 简称 CY，办理集装箱重箱或空箱装卸、转运、保管、交接的场所。
5. load on board 装上船
6. shipping advice 装运通知
   装运通知指国际贸易中，卖方将货物装运后，通过电传、邮件等方式向买方发出的有关货物装运信息的通知。装运通知的作用在于便于买方做好接货准备，尤其在货物运输保险由买方办理的情况下更为重要。

（四）货物的装运（baoda-out 3）

From: Albert albert@163.com
To: Lisa lisa@stitchwell.com
Date: 2019.06.10
Subject: shipping advice
Attachment: Shipping Advice

Dear Lisa,

The goods under Contract No. XS-2019001 have been loaded on the liner COSCO SURABAYA, which is expected to leave Qingdao on June 12 and arrives at Singapore on June 30.

The goods then will be transshipped[1] on the vessel “THARSTREAM” to Chittagong Port[2] and the estimated time of arrival at Chittagong is July 6.

Please find the Shipping Advice in the attachment for the detailed shipping information.

Any complaints[3] or claims[4] should be made within 30 days upon receipt of the goods.

Have a nice day.

Yours sincerely
Albert
Sales Manager
Weifang Baoda Textiles Co., Ltd.

附 8.1　潍坊宝达纺织品有限公司发出的装运通知

**Weifang Baoda Textiles Co., Ltd.**
**Address: No. 688 West Ring Road Weifang, Shandong, China**
Tel: 86-0536-8885678; Fax: 86-0536-8885677

**SHIPPING ADVICE**

| | | | |
|---|---|---|---|
| **TO:** | Stitchwell Garments Co., Ltd.<br>456/1/A Tejgaon Industrial Area, Dhaka 1208, Bangladesh<br>Tel: 880-2-9882934; Fax: 880-2-8891567 | **ISSUE DATE:** | June 12, 2019 |
| | | **Sales Contract No.:** | XS-2019001 |
| | | **L/C No.:** | LC5TF90080073 |
| | | **Invoice No.:** | 2019XS009 |

**Dear Sir or Madam:**

We are pleased to advise you that the following mentioned goods have been shipped out, and full details were shown as follows:

| | |
|---|---|
| **Bill of Loading No.:** | COSU6066092540 |
| **Ocean Vessel:** | COSCO SURABAYA |
| **Voyage No.:** | 019S |
| **Port of Loading:** | Qingdao, China |
| **Date of Shipment:** | June 12, 2019 |
| **Port of Destination:** | Chittagong, Bangladesh |
| **Estimated Date of Arrival:** | July 6, 2019 |
| **Container/Seal No.:** | CRLU1812690/P14591 |
| **Description of Goods:** | Cotton Yarn-dyed Fabrics |
| **Shipping Marks:** | STITCHWELL<br>XS-2019001<br>CHITTAGONG BANGLADESH<br>Carton No.1-270 |

续表

| | |
|---|---|
| **Quantity:** | 27,000 yards, packed in 270 bags |
| **Gross Weight:** | 1.4 MT |
| **Net Weight:** | 1.3 MT |
| Thank you for your patronage. We look forward to the pleasure of receiving your valuable repeat orders.<br><br>Sincerely yours | |
| Weifang Baoda Textiles Co., Ltd. | |

## Notes

1. transship　*v.* 转运
2. Chittagong Port 吉大港
   吉大港是孟加拉国的主要港口之一。
3. complaint　*n.* & *v.* 投诉
   e.g. The company received a lot of complaints from customers because of the design defects of its products.
   公司接到了客户许多投诉，原因是产品设计存在缺陷。
4. claim　*n.* & *v.* 索赔
   e.g. They raise a claim on the insurance for the stolen luggage.
   他们向保险公司提出了索赔，事由是行李被偷。

# CASE 2　Beijing Lucky Fibreboard Trading Co., Ltd.

## 一、信函的业务背景

在北京幸运纤维板贸易有限公司和澳大利亚松树纤维板工业有限公司签订的合同中，双方约定的货物装运条款如下：收到30%货款后的一个月之内交货（within one month after receiving the deposit of 30% invoice value）。

7月3日，澳大利亚松树纤维板工业有限公司收到了北京幸运纤维板贸易有限公司电汇的30%货款。

7月25日，交货时间临近，但北京幸运纤维板贸易有限公司仍然没有收到澳大利亚松树纤维板工业有限公司的货物装运信息，玲玲写信催问对方货物的准备情况。

7月28日，澳大利亚松树纤维板工业有限公司写信告知北京幸运纤维板贸易有限公司货物已经准备好并委托货运公司发货。

## 二、北京幸运纤维板贸易有限公司的信函

（一）货物的装运（lucky-out 1）

From: Lingling lingling@163.com
To: Bill salesdepartment@pinetree.com.au
Date: 2019.07.25
Subject: inquiry about shipment

Dear Bill,

Regarding Contract No. SC-PINE2019010, I would like to remind you that the shipment deadline[1] is approaching[2] and I have not received any information about the shipment of the ordered goods.

Will you please advise the production schedule[3] of the goods ordered and the specific shipment information?

Hope to receive your quick response.

Sincerely
Lingling
Purchasing Manager
Beijing Lucky Fibreboard Trading Co., Ltd.

### Notes

1. shipment deadline 最迟装运日
   shipment deadline 相当于 latest date of shipment。
2. approach *v.* 临近，接近
   与 approach 类似的说法：draw near。
   e.g. (1) The Christmas is approaching.
   圣诞节临近了。
   (2) When I approached, they grew silent.
   当我走近时，他们变得安静了。
3. production schedule 生产日程表

（二）货物的装运（lucky-in 1）

From: Bill salesdepartment@pinetree.com.au
To: Lingling lingling@163.com
Date: 2019.07.28
Subject: RE: inquiry about shipment

Dear Lingling,

In reply to your letter on July 25 about shipment of the goods under Contract No. SC-PINE2019010, the goods you ordered have just been finished on July 26 and we have booked space for your goods.

We have chosen Hamburg Sud[1]① as the carrier[2] and the name of the ocean vessel is Maersk Virginia with the voyage No. 530E.

The estimated time for departure[3] from Melbourne is August 1 and the estimated time for arrival to Xingang is August 24.

We will send you Shipping Advice and the copy of the Bill of Lading when the goods are shipped.

Have a pleasant day!

Best regards
Bill
Sales Department
Pinetree Fibreboard Industries Co., Ltd.

**图 8.2　Hamburg Sud 公司的货船**

## Notes

1. Hamburg Sud 汉堡南美航运公司
   德国历史最悠久、规模最大的私有海运企业，是世界二十大班轮公司之一。
2. carrier　*n.* 承运人
   与 carrier 类似的说法：forwarder。
3. estimated time for departure（ETD）预计离港时间

---

① 汉堡南美航远公司（Hamburg Sud）的货船见图 8.2。

（三）货物的装运（lucky-in 2）

From: Bill salesdepartment@pinetree.com.au
To: Lingling lingling@163.com
Date: 2019.08.03
Subject: shipping advice
Attachment: SHIPPING ADVICE

Dear Lingling,

The goods under Contract No. SC-PINE2019010 have been shipped on board the vessel Maersk Virginia with the voyage No. 530E on August 1.

Please see the attached Shipping Advice for detailed shipping information.

If any damage is found upon the arrival of the goods, please notify[1] us immediately.

Best regards
Bill
Sales Department
Pinetree Fibreboard Industries Co., Ltd.

附 8.2　松树纤维板工业有限公司发出的装运通知

<table>
<tr><td colspan="4">PINETREE FIBREBOARD INDUSTRIES CO., LTD.<br>Address: No. 8 Pinetree Road, Melbourne, Australia<br>Tel: 61-3-85715322；Fax: 61-3-85715331</td></tr>
<tr><td colspan="4">SHIPPING ADVICE</td></tr>
<tr><td rowspan="4">TO:</td><td rowspan="4">Beijing Lucky Fibreboard Trading Co., Ltd.<br>Room 801, International Trade Center, Chaoyang, Beijing, China</td><td>ISSUE DATE:</td><td>AUG 2, 2019</td></tr>
<tr><td>Sales Contract No.:</td><td>SC-PINE2019010</td></tr>
<tr><td>L/C No.:</td><td>N/A</td></tr>
<tr><td>Invoice No.:</td><td>PINE20190610</td></tr>
<tr><td colspan="4">Dear Sir or Madam:</td></tr>
<tr><td colspan="4">We are pleased to advise you that the following mentioned goods have been shipped out, and full details were shown as follows:</td></tr>
<tr><td colspan="2">Bill of Loading No.:</td><td colspan="2">SUDU393501955096</td></tr>
<tr><td colspan="2">Ocean Vessel/ Voyage No.:</td><td colspan="2">Maersk Virginia/530E</td></tr>
<tr><td colspan="2">Port of Loading:</td><td colspan="2">Melbourne, Australia</td></tr>
<tr><td colspan="2">Date of Shipment:</td><td colspan="2">AUG 1, 2019</td></tr>
<tr><td colspan="2">Port of Destination:</td><td colspan="2">Xingang, China</td></tr>
</table>

续表

| | |
|---|---|
| **Estimated Date of Arrival:** | AUG 24, 2019 |
| **Container/Seal No.:** | SUDU5981109/0134842<br>SUDU5978109/0134803 |
| **Description of Goods:** | Fibreboard, 25 Packages |
| **Shipping Marks:** | NM |
| **Quantity:** | 58.06 CBM |
| **Gross Weight:** | 49.5 MT |
| **Net Weight:** | 48.28 MT |
| Thank you for your order. We look forward to the pleasure of receiving your repeat orders.<br>Sincerely yours | |

## Note

1. notify　*v.* 通知

与 notify 意义相近的词：inform, advise。

e.g. Wanglin will notify us where we are to meet.

王林将通知我们在哪里聚会。

## 练习

### 一、将下列句子译成中文。

（一）海运方式下的练习

1. With reference to Contract No. YB-2019001 for 12 MT steel, the goods are ready for shipment now.
2. The goods shall be shipped with two 40 foot containers.
3. Please send the Shipping Instruction for us to ship the goods in time.
4. Please give us the information of the shipping agent at the loading port for us to contact them in time.
5. Please ship the first lot under Contract No. XS-2019-13 by Ruby scheduled to sail on or about May 10.
6. As our customers are in urgent need of the goods, please make sure that the goods shall be dispatched within the stipulated time.
7. The estimated time of arrival at Melbourne Port for the vessel is Jan 12.
8. Please book the shipping space 10 days prior to shipment to ensure the shipping space.

（二）空运方式下的练习

1. With reference to Order No. NB-20190601 for 100 KG medicine, the goods are now ready for shipment.
2. We have chosen AIR CHINA as our carrier and the flight No. is CA 2304.
3. We will send you Shipping Advice once the goods are shipped by air.
4. The goods under Order No. NB-20190601 have been shipped by flight CA2304 and the Airway Bill No. is 999-1099 1588.

**二、将下列句子译成英文。**

（一）海运方式下的练习

1. 你方所订购的合同号 NB-19501 项下的 120 吨大米已经准备发货了。
2. 请给我方寄送装运指示，以便我方及时发货。
3. 请告诉我方装运港货运代理的联系方式，以便我方与他们联系。
4. 请你方将货物分两批分别在 11 月和 12 月装运。
5. 我们很高兴地通知你方货物已经于 10 月 12 日装上了中远公司的黎明号货船。
6. 到达纽约港的预计时间是 5 月 30 日。
7. 请于发货前 10 天订舱以保证能订上舱位。
8. 附件里是提单的复印件以及装运通知。

（二）空运方式下的练习

1. 提及合同号 HG-20190254 项下的 100 千克西红柿种子，货物已经准备好了。
2. 我方已经选择了美国联合航空公司作为承运人，航班号为 UA5437。
3. 货物装运后，我方会以传真的方式立即向你方发送装运通知。
4. 合同号 HG-20190254 项下的货物已经通过美国联合航空公司的航班 UA5437 发运，空运单号为 016-6895 2635。

## 技能训练

### 根据业务情境和信息写信

（一）业务情境

1. 江苏通达轮胎有限公司将大力神轮胎贸易公司订购的货物准备好后，李辉写信告知大卫·桑德伯格货物已经准备好，请对方发出装运指示，以便及时发货。

2. 大卫·桑德伯格收到李辉货物准备好的信函后，向李辉发出了装运指示，告知船名、航次，并让李辉及时联系指定船公司在装运港——上海港的货运代理进行订舱、报关、装运。

3. 李辉根据装运指示联系了承运人 APL 船公司的代理——上海琪邦（Kbans）国际货运代理的联系人王均益，办理了订舱、报关等手续。在货物装船后，及时向大卫·桑德伯格发出装运通知。

（二）信息

1. 大卫・桑德伯格指定的船公司：APL

2. 承运人的代理：

上海琪邦（Kbans）国际货运代理

联系人：王均益

Tel: 86-021-52656285

Fax: 86-021-62573231

E-mail: Janice@kbans.com

地址：上海市杨浦眉州路 381 号 1005 室

3. 船名、航次：APL Korea/191，APL Oman/042（见图 8.3 和图 8.4）；

4. 到达上海港时间：2019.09.06，从上海港开船时间：2019.09.08；

5. 预计到达纽约港时间：2019.10.11。

图 8.3　APL 船公司的货船

**Customizable Schedule Details**

| | | | |
|---|---|---|---|
| **Origin :** | Shanghai, SH, CN | **Departure Date :** | Tue, 08-Sep-15 |
| **Destination :** | New York Container Terminal, NY, US | **Arrival Date :** | Sun, 11-Oct-15 |
| **Transit Time :** | 33 days | **Cutoff :** | |

**Routing**

| Dep Port | Dep Date | Arr Port | Arr Date | Mode / Vessel | Voyage | Service |
|---|---|---|---|---|---|---|
| Shanghai, SH, CN | Tue, 08-Sep | Busan-Pnit, KR | Thu, 10-Sep | Apl Korea | 191 | CC3 |
| Busan-Pnit, KR | Fri, 11-Sep | Busan-Hpnt, KR | Fri, 11-Sep | Dummy Feeder - P6h/p2h | 139 | P6H |
| Busan-Hpnt, KR | Sun, 13-Sep | Maher Terminal, NJ, US | Sun, 11-Oct | Apl Oman | 042 | PA2 |

**Equipment Specifications**

| Location | Equipment(ft) | | | | | Cargo | | | | Restrictions | |
|---|---|---|---|---|---|---|---|---|---|---|---|
| | 20 | 40 | 45 | CY | CF | RY | RF | SD | Crane | 20ft Over The Road | 40ft Over The Road |
| Shanghai, SH, CN | Y | Y | Y | Y | Y | Y | N | N | 50 L/T | 22.7 KT | 21 KT |

图 8.4　APL 船公司的货船 APL Oman/042 的船期

（三）任务

根据以上的业务情境和信息写信。

1. 李辉写信告知大卫·桑德伯格货物已经准备好，请对方发出装运指示。
信函应包括以下要点：
（1）提及合同号 LLLT20190608 项下的货物已经准备好；
（2）请大卫·桑德伯格告知指定的船公司、船名、航次等信息；
（3）请大卫·桑德伯格告知船公司的货运代理的联系方式；
（4）表示感谢。
2. 大卫·桑德伯格回复李辉：向李辉发出了装运指示。
信函应包括以下要点：
（1）感谢李辉已经准备好货物；
（2）告知李辉指定 APL 船公司为承运人，以及船名、航次；
（3）告知李辉船公司的货运代理的联系方式；
（4）请李辉及时与货运代理联系，进行订舱；
（5）表示感谢。
3. 李辉在货物装上指定船只后，立即向大卫·桑德伯格发出装运通知。
信函应包括以下要点：
（1）提及合同号 LLLT20190608 项下的货物已经装上指定的船只；
（2）告知开船时间和预计到达目的港的时间；
（3）告知“装运通知”在附件里（见表 8.2）；
（4）请大卫·桑德伯格在收货后，如果发现货物存在问题及时告知。

**表 8.2　　装运通知模板**

<table>
<tr><td colspan="4">SHIPPING ADVICE</td></tr>
<tr><td colspan="4"></td></tr>
<tr><td rowspan="4">TO:</td><td rowspan="4"></td><td>ISSUE DATE:</td><td></td></tr>
<tr><td>Sales Contract No.:</td><td></td></tr>
<tr><td>L/C NO.:</td><td></td></tr>
<tr><td>Invoice No.:</td><td></td></tr>
<tr><td colspan="4">Dear Sir or Madam:</td></tr>
<tr><td colspan="4">We advise you that the following mentioned goods have been shipped out, and full details were shown as follows:</td></tr>
<tr><td colspan="2">Bill of Loading No.:</td><td colspan="2"></td></tr>
<tr><td colspan="2">Ocean Vessel:</td><td colspan="2"></td></tr>
<tr><td colspan="2">Voyage No.:</td><td colspan="2"></td></tr>
<tr><td colspan="2">Port of Loading:</td><td colspan="2"></td></tr>
<tr><td colspan="2">Date of Shipment:</td><td colspan="2"></td></tr>
<tr><td colspan="2">Port of Destination:</td><td colspan="2"></td></tr>
</table>

续表

| | |
|---|---|
| **Estimated Date of Arrival:** | |
| **Container/Seal No.:** | |
| **Description of Goods:** | |
| **Shipping Marks:** | |
| **Quantity:** | |
| **Gross Weight:** | |
| **Net Weight:** | |
| Thank you for your order. We look forward to receiving your repeat orders.<br>Sincerely yours | |

## 补充阅读

信函 1：装运通知

业务背景：青岛兴旺手工艺品有限公司销售经理李华在将货物装船后，及时向法国的优雅贸易有限公司的总经理海伦发出了装运通知。

From: lihua@handicraftschina.com

To: helen1219@hotmail.com

Date: 2019.05.28

Subject: shipping advice

Attachment: Shipping Advice

Dear Helen,

I am pleased to inform you that the 8,000 pieces of straw knitting handicrafts under Contract No. hc2019008 have been shipped by COSCO ITALY 0008W on June 9 from Qingdao Port, China to Le Havre, France. The goods will be transshipped in Singapore by HANJIN BUDDHA 0009W.

Please see the attachment for detailed shipping information.

Any complaints to the ordered goods should be notified to us within 10 days upon arrival.

Yours sincerely

Li Hua

Sales Manager

Qingdao Xingwang Handicrafts Co., Ltd.

Address: No. 1251 Xingwang Road, Qingdao, Shandong, China

Tel: 86-0532-8745618; Fax: 86-0532-8745617

信函 2：卖方提出分批装运

业务背景：淄博海来特锥形钢管有限公司与印度 API 钢管有限公司签订了购销合同。该合同数量较大，由于订单任务重以及运输旺季的来临，淄博海来特锥形钢管有限公司销售经理大卫向印度 API 钢管有限公司提出分批装运，以免耽误交货。

From: davidli@steelpipechina.com

To: mundra@indiapipe.com

Date: 2019.05.03

Subject: asking for partial shipment

Dear Mr. Mundra,

Regarding your Order No. AT2019002 for 5,000 pieces of tapered steel pipes, we have finished 2,000 pieces of the goods now. We are considering having these finished goods shipped to you now in order to avoid any possible delay of the shipment.

We propose this due to the following reasons.

First, we are heavily committed at present. We can hardly ship the whole lot of the goods ordered by the end of May as arranged.

Second, the shipping space is getting harder to get because the boom season for shipment is coming.

If you agree with us on our proposal, we will book the shipping space immediately.

Look forward to hearing your quick response.

Regards

David Li

Sales Manager

Zibo Highlight Tapered Steel Pipe Co., Ltd.

Address: No. 1251 Nanshan Road, Zibo, Shandong, China

Tel: 86-0533-8265184; Fax: 86-0533-8265173

# 任务九

# 交单与付款

# Documents Presentation and Payment

## 学习目标

1. 了解交单与付款的有关知识；
2. 掌握交单与付款信函的写作要点；
3. 熟悉交单与付款信函的常用词语和句子；
4. 能够阅读和撰写有关交单与付款的信函。

## 背景知识

现代国际贸易中，主要的支付方式有电汇、托收和信用证。

在实务中，可以根据实际情况将不同的支付方式结合使用，如电汇与信用证相结合，电汇与托收相结合。

无论何种支付方式，卖方向买方交付有关货物的单据都是卖方应有的义务。

常用的单据有发票、装箱单、检验证书、原产地证明、提单、保险单、汇票等。

卖方提交有关货物的单据的几个基本要求：正确、完整、及时、规范、整洁。

1. 正确

可以概括为三个一致：单证或单约一致、单单一致、单货一致。单据要与信用证的要求或合同保持一致。另外，单据与单据之间，各个项目的内容要保持一致，不能出现相互矛盾的地方。单据与货物也要保持一致，以正确地反映货物的实际情况。

2. 完整

完整指信用证或合同要求的各种单据不能短缺，单据的种类、份数和单据的必要项目内容，以及签字、盖章都必须完整。

3. 及时

必须在规定的时间内（信用证的交单期限或合同规定的交单期限）制作或取得相应的单据；并且，各种单据的制作或取得的时间必须符合逻辑。

4. 规范

单据的格式和项目内容必须符合单据的惯例要求，不能遗漏必要的项目。

5. 整洁

单据的布局要美观，字迹要清楚。单据表面一般不能有更改（尤其是重要的单据如汇票、提单，或单据的重要项目如金额、数量等），如果有更改，要加盖校对章。

## 一、信用证支付方式下的交单与付款

卖方在发运货物后，应在信用证规定的时间内，将信用证要求提交的全部单据提交开证行指定的银行或开证行，要求付款。

### （一）议付行或开证行对单据的处理

（1）如果单据符合信用证的要求，且单据与单据之间一致，则议付行或开证行向受益人（出口人）议付货款。

（2）如果议付行发现单据有不符点，可以凭保函议付、电提不符点、托收寄单、退单。

（3）如果开证行发现单据有不符点，可以在规定的期限内提出不符点，并将不符点通知交单者，或退回单据。

### （二）当单据存在不符点时，出口人对单据的处理方式

（1）若不符点成立，且条件允许，可补交相符单据。

（2）若不符点成立，且无法补交相符单据，出口人要及时与开证申请人沟通。

## 二、电汇支付方式下的交单与付款

（1）前 T/T 结算方式。出口人在货物装运前已收到进口人通过电汇支付的全部货款，在货物装运后，把合同要求的全部单据寄给进口人。

（2）后 T/T 结算方式。出口人在货物装运后把合同要求的全部单据寄给进口人，进口人在收到货物后，再用电汇方式把全部货款支付给出口人。

（3）生产前用电汇支付定金，发货后用电汇支付其余货款[①]。生产前，进口人通过电汇支付定金；货物生产完毕、发货后，出口人把海运提单或运单的复印件或传真件交给进口人，进口人通过电汇支付其余货款。出口人收到全部货款后，再把合同要求的全部单据寄给进口人。

① 该方式是采用电汇支付方式时的惯例做法。

## 三、托收支付方式下的交单与付款

托收支付方式下的交单与付款一般流程：
（1）出口人在装运货物后，及时将全部单据交托收行办理托收。
（2）托收行将单据寄给进口人所在国的代收行。
（3）代收行收到单据后，通知进口人付款赎单。
（4）进口人付款后，代收行将货款汇入托收行，托收行将货款支付给出口人。

# 写作提示

## 一、信用证支付方式下的交单与付款信函

（一）开证行提示单据存在不符点时，出口商与进口商的沟通
（1）提及单据对应的合同或信用证；
（2）说明单据存在不符点；
（3）具体说明单据存在的不符点及原因；
（4）请求买方与开证行联系，让开证行接受不符点；
（5）表示感谢。

（二）进口商接受或不接受不符点交单
（1）提到对方关于交单不符点的来信；
（2）同意或拒绝接受卖方提出的要求；
（3）如果同意卖方的要求，告知卖方已经与开证行联系并告知结果；
（4）如果拒绝卖方的要求，说明原因。

## 二、电汇支付方式下的交单与付款信函

（一）出口商告知进口商货物已经发出并要求进口商付款
（1）告知进口商某合同项下的货物已经发出，并提供提单复印件；
（2）要求进口商付款；
（3）告知进口商货物的单据将在付款后寄出。

（二）进口商付款后告知出口商，并要求出口商寄送单据
（1）告知出口商货款已经汇出，请出口商注意查收并反馈收款信息；
（2）要求出口商将单据尽快寄出，以方便提货；
（3）表示感谢。

（三）出口商收到货款后，告知进口商单据已经寄出
（1）告知进口商货款已经收到；

（2）告知进口商货物的单据已经寄出，并告知快递的运单号；

（3）列出货物单据的明细。

示范信函

# CASE 1 Weifang Baoda Textiles Co., Ltd.

## 一、信函的业务背景

潍坊宝达纺织品有限公司的阿尔伯特在将合同 XS-2019001 项下的货物装运完毕后，制作和取得包括海运提单在内的信用证要求的所有单据，在信用证有效期内向议付行——中国银行潍坊分行交单结汇。

但交单后的第三天，收到了议付行——中国银行潍坊分行的通知，内容是开证行——Uttara Bank Ltd Badda Branch 提出了信用证项下提交的单据有不符点，并发出了拒付通知。

潍坊宝达纺织品有限公司在确认了提交的单据中的确存在不符点后，由于无法在信用证的有效期内提交正确的单据，向开证申请人孟加拉国缝得好服装有限公司的丽莎发出信函，请求对方同意接受单据不符点。

缝得好服装有限公司的丽莎做出了怎样的答复呢？

## 二、潍坊宝达纺织品有限公司的业务信函

（一）交单与付款（baoda-out 1）

From: Albert albert@163.com

To: Lisa lisa@stitchwell.com

Date: 2019.06.25

Subject: discrepancies[1] between documents and L/C stipulations

Attachment: Advice of Refusal by Uttara Bank Ltd Badda Branch

Dear Lisa,

With reference to the documents under L/C No. LC5TF90080073, last week we submitted[2] all the required documents to our negotiating bank[3], but several discrepancies were found by the negotiating bank. Then, our bank approached[4] the issuing bank[5] to inform the discrepancies of the documents required. Unfortunately, the issuing bank refused to pay due to the discrepancies (See the attachment for the Advice of Refusal[6] sent by the issuing bank.). The discrepancies are as follows.

1. Bill of Lading: According to the field 47A of the L/C, THE NUMBER AND THE DATE OF THIS CREDIT AND THE NAME OF ISSUING BANK MUST BE QUOTED[7] ON

ALL DOCUMENTS. But there is no “THE NUMBER AND THE DATE OF THIS CREDIT AND THE NAME OF ISSUING BANK” shown on the B/L.

2. Late shipment: the date of shipment on B/L is later than the latest date of shipment (field 44c) on L/C. The actual date of shipment is June 12 and the date of shipment on the B/L presented is June 22. This is a printing error[8] made by the shipping company[9].

We can not correct[10] the above discrepancies of the documents because the deadline for documents presentation[11] is approaching[12].

Will you please accept the above discrepancies and approach the issuing bank to let it accept the above discrepancies?

It is greatly appreciated if you agree to do so.

Thank you.

Yours sincerely
Albert
Sales Manager
Weifang Baoda Textiles Co., Ltd.

**附 9.1　Uttara Bank Ltd Badda Branch 发出的拒付电传**

………………………………………**Message Header**………………………………………

Swift Output: FIN 734 Advice of Refusal
Sender: UTBLBDDH
Receiver: BKCHCNBJ500

………………………………………**Message Text**………………………………………

20 Sender's TRN
LC5TF90080073
21 Presenting Bank's Reference
LX11757/5188
32A Date and Amount of Utilisation
Date 190621
Amount USD43,700.00
72 Sender to Receiver Information
LC5TF90080187
77J Discrepancies
① THE NUMBER AND THE DATE OF THIS CREDIT
AND THE NAME OF ISSUING BANK ARE NOT
SHOWN ON THE B/L, WHICH DOES NOT COMPLY
WITH THE FIELD 47A.

② LATE SHIPMENT
77B Disposal of Documents
WE WILL RELEASE DOCS TO APPLICANT
AGAINST THEIR PMT/ACCEPTANCE
WITHOUT FURTHER NOTICE.

……………………………………**Message Trailer**……………………………………

## Notes

1. discrepancies *n.* 不相符的地方
   e.g. Discrepancies of the documents presented might cause delay or refusal of payment.
   提交的单据有不符点，可能引起延迟或拒绝付款。
2. submit *v.* 提交
   e.g. Please submit your final version of the thesis to your tutor before July 30.
   请在 7 月 30 日前向你的导师提交你最终版论文。
3. negotiating bank 议付行
   议付行指根据开证行的授权买入受益人开立的汇票和提交的符合信用证的单据的银行。
4. approach *v.* 联系
   e.g. (1) Andy approached several universities and finally decided to apply for Havard University.
   安迪联系了几个大学，最终决定申请哈佛大学。
   (2) I have approached several steel suppliers.
   我已经联系了几家钢材供应商。
5. issuing bank 开证行
   开证行指接受开证申请人的委托开立信用证的银行，接受受益人提交的单据并承担保证付款的责任。
6. advice of refusal 拒绝（付款）通知
   拒绝（付款）通知指开证行由于单据与信用证要求不相符或单据提交的日期超出了信用证的有效期而发出的拒绝付款的通知。
7. quote *v.* 引用
   e.g. She quoted a great line from *Bible*.
   她引用了《圣经》上一大段话。
8. printing error 打印错误
9. shipping company 运输公司
   运输公司即承运人。
10. correct *v.* 纠正
    e.g. The teacher corrected my errors in my paper.
    老师纠正了我论文中的错误。

11. documents presentation　提交单据
    此处指向议付行或开证行提交信用证要求的单据。
12. approach　*v.* 临近
    e.g. The date for the final exam is approaching.
    期终考试时间临近了。

（二）交单与付款（baoda-in 1）

From: Lisa lisa@stitchwell.com
To: Albert albert@163.com
Date: 2019.06.26
Subject: RE: discrepancies between documents and L/C stipulations

Dear Albert,

In reply to your letter on June 25 about documents discrepancies, we have approached the issuing bank and the bank agrees to accept the discrepancies.

But you still have to pay the charges for discrepancies to the issuing bank and the amount is USD120.00. The charges will be deducted[1] from the remittance[2] by the issuing bank.

This is the best we can do and hope you will be satisfied with this solution[3].

Regards
Lisa
Purchasing Manager
Stitchwell Garments Co., Ltd.

## Notes

1. deduct　*v.* 减去，扣除
   e.g. Commission will be deducted from the invoice value.
   佣金会在发票金额里扣除。
2. remittance　*n.* 汇款
3. solution　*n.* 解决方案
   e.g. China and Russia are seeking a diplomatic solution to the frontier issue.
   中国和俄罗斯正在寻求通过外交途径解决边境问题。

（三）交单与付款（baoda-out 2）

From: Albert albert@163.com
To: Lisa lisa@stitchwell.com
Date: 2019.06.27

Subject: RE: RE: discrepancies between documents and L/C stipulations

Dear Lisa,

Thank you for your quick action and cooperation[1].

The documents required by the L/C No. LC5TF90080073 along with the draft[2] have been sent to the issuing bank—Uttara Bank Ltd Badda Branch on June 27 by DHL with the tracking No. 957134568.

You can track the documents on line[3] and contact the issuing bank in time upon their arrival.

The following is the list of the documents required.

(1) Signed Commercial Invoice in 3 copies

(2) Signed Packing List in 3 copies

(3) Bill of Lading in 3 originals

(4) Certificate of Origin issued by China Council for the Promotion of International Trade

(5) Test Report issued by Guangzhou Fibre Product Testing Institute

(6) Shipping Advice

Thank you and look forward to receiving your repeat order[4].

Yours sincerely

Albert

Sales Manager

Weifang Baoda Textiles Co., Ltd.

**附 9.2a　潍坊宝达纺织品有限公司出具的商业发票（合同 XS–2019001）**

<table>
<tr><td colspan="6">Weifang Baoda Textiles Co., Ltd.<br>Address: No. 688 West Ring Road, Weifang, Shandong, China<br>Tel: 86-0536-8885678; Fax: 86-0536-8885677</td></tr>
<tr><td colspan="6">COMMERCIAL INVOICE</td></tr>
<tr><td rowspan="4">To:</td><td rowspan="4" colspan="3">Stitchwell Garments Co., Ltd.<br>456/1/A Tejgaon Industrial Area, Dhaka 1208, Bangladesh<br>Tel: 880-2-9882934; Fax: 880-2-8891567</td><td>Invoice No.:</td><td>2019XS009</td></tr>
<tr><td>Invoice Date:</td><td>June 1, 2019</td></tr>
<tr><td>S/C No.:</td><td>XS-2019001</td></tr>
<tr><td>S/C Date:</td><td>March 7, 2019</td></tr>
<tr><td>From:</td><td colspan="2">QINGDAO, CHINA</td><td>To:</td><td colspan="2">CHITTAGONG, BANGLADESH</td></tr>
<tr><td>Letter of Credit No.:</td><td colspan="2">LC5TF90080073</td><td>Issued By:</td><td colspan="2">UTTARA BANK LTD BADDA BRANCH – DHAKA , BANGLADESH</td></tr>
<tr><td></td><td colspan="2"></td><td></td><td colspan="2"></td></tr>
<tr><td>Marks and Numbers</td><td>Description of Goods</td><td>Quantity</td><td colspan="2">Unit Price</td><td>Amount</td></tr>
<tr><td rowspan="4">STITCHWELL<br>XS-2019001<br>CHITTAGONG BANGLADESH<br>Carton No.<br>1-270</td><td colspan="5"></td></tr>
<tr><td>Cotton Yarn-dyed Fabrics<br>21*21, 64*54, 57/58</td><td>5,000 yards</td><td colspan="2">FOB QINGDAO<br>USD1.3/yard</td><td>USD6,500.00</td></tr>
<tr><td>21*21, 80*60, 57/58</td><td>10,000 yards</td><td colspan="2">USD1.8/yard</td><td>USD18,000.00</td></tr>
<tr><td>32*32, 80*68, 57/58</td><td>12,000 yards</td><td colspan="2">USD1.6/yard</td><td>USD19,200.00</td></tr>
<tr><td colspan="2">TOTAL:</td><td colspan="3">27,000 yards</td><td>USD43,700.00</td></tr>
<tr><td>SAY TOTAL:</td><td colspan="5">USD FORTY-THREE THOUSAND AND SEVEN HUNDRED ONLY.</td></tr>
<tr><td colspan="6">Weifang Baoda Textiles Co., Ltd.<br>Signature: Albert</td></tr>
</table>

附 9.2b 潍坊宝达纺织品有限公司出具的包装单（合同 XS-2019001）

<table>
<tr><td colspan="7">Weifang Baoda Textiles Co., Ltd.<br>Address: No. 688 West Ring Road, Weifang, Shandong, China<br>Tel: 86-0536-8885678; Fax: 86-0536-8885677</td></tr>
<tr><td colspan="7">PACKING LIST</td></tr>
<tr><td rowspan="4">To:</td><td rowspan="4" colspan="2">Stitchwell Garments Co., Ltd.<br>456/1/A Tejgaon Industrial Area, Dhaka 1208, Bangladesh<br>Tel: 880-2-9882934; Fax: 880-2-8891567</td><td colspan="2">Invoice No.:</td><td colspan="2">2019XS009</td></tr>
<tr><td colspan="2">Invoice Date:</td><td colspan="2">June 1, 2019</td></tr>
<tr><td colspan="2">S/C No.:</td><td colspan="2">XS-2019001</td></tr>
<tr><td colspan="2">S/C Date:</td><td colspan="2">March 7, 2019</td></tr>
<tr><td>From:</td><td colspan="2">QINGDAO, CHINA</td><td colspan="2">To:</td><td colspan="2">CHITTAGONG, BANGLADESH</td></tr>
<tr><td colspan="2">Letter of Credit No.:</td><td>LC5TF90080073</td><td colspan="2">Date of Shipment:</td><td colspan="2">June 14, 2019</td></tr>
<tr><td colspan="2"></td><td></td><td colspan="2"></td><td colspan="2"></td></tr>
<tr><td>Marks and Numbers</td><td>Number and Kind of Package Description of Goods</td><td>Quantity</td><td>Package</td><td>G.W.</td><td>N.W.</td><td>Meas.</td></tr>
<tr><td rowspan="3">STITCHWELL<br>XS-2019001<br>CHITTAGONG BANGLADESH<br>Carton No. 1-270</td><td>Cotton Yarn-dyed Fabrics<br>21*21, 64*54, 57/58</td><td>5,000 YARDS</td><td>50 BAGS</td><td>260 KGS</td><td>240 KGS</td><td>5.81 M³</td></tr>
<tr><td>21*21, 80*60, 57/58</td><td>10,000 YARDS</td><td>100 BAGS</td><td>520 KGS</td><td>480 KGS</td><td>11.63 M³</td></tr>
<tr><td>32*32, 80*68, 57/58</td><td>12,000 YARDS</td><td>120 BAGS</td><td>620 KGS</td><td>480 KGS</td><td>13.96 M³</td></tr>
<tr><td colspan="2">TOTAL:</td><td>27,000 yards</td><td>270 BAGS</td><td>1,400 KGS</td><td>1,300 KGS</td><td>31.4 M³</td></tr>
<tr><td>SAY TOTAL:</td><td colspan="6">TWO HUNDRED AND SEVENTY BAGS ONLY.</td></tr>
<tr><td colspan="7">Weifang Baoda Textiles Co., Ltd.<br>Signature: Albert</td></tr>
</table>

## 附 9.2c 中国远洋集装箱运输有限公司出具的海运提单

| | |
|---|---|
| Shipper Insert Name, Address and Phone | B/L No. |
| Weifang Baoda Textiles Co., Ltd.<br>Address: No. 688 West Ring Road, Weifang, Shandong, China<br>Tel: 86-0536-8885678; Fax: 86-0536-8885677 | **COSU6066092540** |
| Consignee Insert Name, Address and Phone | 中国远洋集装箱运输有限公司<br>**COSCO CONTAINER LINES**<br>TLX: 33057 COSCO CN<br>FAX: +86(021) 6545 8984<br>**ORIGINAL** |
| Stitchwell Garments Co., Ltd.<br>456/1/A Tejgaon Industrial Area, Dhaka 1208, Bangladesh<br>Tel: 880-2-9882934 ; Fax: 880-2-8891567 | |
| Notify Party Insert Name, Address and Phone<br>(It is agreed that no responsibility shall attach to the Carrier or his agents for failure to notify.) | Port-to-Port or Combined Transport<br>**BILL OF LADING** |
| TO ORDER OF SHIPPER | |

| | | | |
|---|---|---|---|
| Combined Transport * | | Combined Transport* | |
| Pre-carriage by | | Place of Receipt | |
| Ocean Vessel Voy. No. | | Port of Loading | |
| COSCO SURABAYA /019S | | Qingdao, China | |
| Port of Discharge | | Combined Transport * | |
| Singapore, Singapore | | Place of Delivery | Chittagong Bangladesh |

RECEIVED in external apparent good order and condition except as otherwise noted. The total number of packages or unites stuffed in the container, the description of the goods and the weights shown in this Bill of Lading are furnished by the Merchants, and the carrier has no reasonable means of checking and is not a part of this Bill of Lading contract. The carrier has issued the number of Bills of Lading stated below, all of this tenor and date, one of the original Bills of Lading must be surrendered and endorsed or signed against the delivery of the shipment and whereupon any other original Bills of Lading shall be void. The Merchants agree to be bound by the terms and conditions of this Bill of Lading as if each had personally signed this Bill of Lading.
SEE clause 4 on the back of this Bill of Lading (Terms continued on the back hereof, please read carefully).
*Applicable Only When Document Used as a Combined Transport Bill of Lading.

| Marks & Nos. Container/Seal No. | No. of Containers or Packages | Description of Goods (If Dangerous Goods, See Clause 20) | Gross Weight Kgs | Measurement |
|---|---|---|---|---|
| STITCHWELL<br>XS-2019001<br>CHITTAGONG<br>BANGLADESH<br>Carton No. 1-270<br><br>**CRLU1812690/P14591** | 1 CONTAINER<br>270 BAGS | Cotton Yarn-dyed Fabrics | 1,400 KGS | 31.4 CBM |
| | | Description of Contents for Shipper's Use Only<br>(Not Part of This B/L Contract) | | |

Total Number of Containers and/or Packages (in Words) **TWO HUNDRED AND SEVENTY BAGS ONLY.**

| | | | | | |
|---|---|---|---|---|---|
| Subject to Clause 7 Limitation | | | | | |
| Freight & Charges | Revenue Tons | Rate | Per | Prepaid | Collect |
| FREIGHT COLLECT | | | | | |
| Declared Value Charge | | | | | |

| | | | |
|---|---|---|---|
| Ex. Rate: | Prepaid at | Payable at | Place and Date of Issue |
| | | Chittagong, Bangladesh | **Qingdao, China June 22, 2019** |
| | Total Prepaid | No. of Original B (s)/L | Signed for the Carrier, COSCO CONTAINER LINES |
| | | THREE (3) | 魏金顺 |

| | | | |
|---|---|---|---|
| LADEN ON BOARD THE VESSEL | | | |
| DATE | JUNE 22, 2019 | BY | COSCO CONTAINER LINES |

## 附 9.2d 中国国际贸易促进委员会签发的原产地证书

**ORIGINAL**

| | |
|---|---|
| Exporter | Certificate No. 365426789 |
| Weifang Baoda Textiles Co., Ltd.<br>Address: No. 688 West Ring Road, Weifang, Shandong, China<br>Tel: 86-0536-8885678; Fax: 86-0536-8885677 | **CERTIFICATE OF ORIGIN**<br>**of**<br>**THE PEOPLE'S REPUBLIC OF CHINA** |
| Consignee | |
| Stitchwell Garments Co., Ltd.<br>456/1/A Tejgaon Industrial Area, Dhaka 1208, Bangladesh<br>Tel: 880-2-9882934 ; Fax: 880-2-8891567 | |
| Means of Transport and Route | For Certifying Authority Use Only |
| BY SEAFREIGHT<br>FROM QINGDAO, CHINA TO CHITTAGONG, BANGLADESH | *CHINA COUNCIL FOR THE PROMOTION OF INTERNATIONAL TRADE IS CHINA CHAMBER OF INTERNATIONAL COMMERCE* |
| Country/Region of Destination | |
| BANGLADESH | |

| Marks and Numbers | Number and Kind of Packages; Description of Goods | H.S.Code | Quantity | Number and Date of Invoices |
|---|---|---|---|---|
| STITCHWELL<br>XS-2019001<br>CHITTAGONG<br>BANGLADESH<br>Carton No. 1-270 | 1 CONTAINER（270 BAGS）OF<br>Cotton Yarn-dyed Fabrics | 5,208.420,0 | 1,400 KGS<br>G.W. | 2019XS009 |

*****************************************************************************************************************

| | |
|---|---|
| Declaration by the Exporter<br>The undersigned hereby declares that the above details and statements are correct, that all the goods were produced in China and that they comply with the Rules of Origin of the People's Republic of China. | Certification<br>It is hereby certified that the declaration by the exporter is correct. |
| **Weifang Baoda Textiles Co., Ltd.**<br>Albert | 薛国涛 |
| WEIFANG, SHANDONG, CHINA<br>JUNE 3, 2019 | WEIFANG, SHANDONG, CHINA<br>JUNE 3, 2019 |
| ----------------------------------------------------------------<br>Place and date, signature and stamp of authorized signatory | ----------------------------------------------------------------<br>Place and date, signature and stamp of certifying authority |

## 附 9.2e　广州市纤维产品检测院签发的检验报告（页 7–3）

**Test Report Issued by Guangzhou Fibre Product Testing Institute (page 7-3)**

# TEST REPORT

No:140066142

**PILLING**
**起球**

(GB/T 4802.1-2008, CIRCULAR LOCUS METHOD 圆轨迹法, PILLING 起球:600 CYCS 600次, PRESSURE 压力:780 cN)

3 GRADE 级 — REQUIREMENT 要求 ≥3 GRADE 级 (FZ/T 73045-2013)

**FIBRE COMPOSITION**
**纤维成分含量**

(FZ/T 01057-2007)

COTTON 棉　100%

**pH VALUE[INCLUDING PRINT]**
**pH值[含印花部位]**

(GB/T 7573-2009, KCl EXTRACTING SOLUTION 0.1mol/L KCl溶液萃取)
(GB/T 7573-2009 MOD修改采用 ISO 3071: 2005)

7.0 — REQUIREMENT 要求 4.0~8.5 B类 (GB 18401-2010)

**FORMALDEHYDE CONTENT[INCLUDING PRINT]**
**甲醛含量[含印花部位]**

(GB/T 2912.1-2009, WATER EXTRACTION METHOD 水萃取法)
(GB/T 2912.1-2009 MOD修改采用 ISO 14184-1:1998)

NOT DETECTED 未检出 — REQUIREMENT 要求 ≤75 mg/kg B类 (GB 18401-2010)

REMARK注: DETECTION LIMITS 检出限 20mg/kg

**DETERMINATION OF ODOURS[INCLUDING PRINT]**
**异味[含印花部位]**

(GB 18401-2010 6.7)

NO ABNORMAL ODOUR 无异味 — REQUIREMENT 要求 NO ABNORMAL ODOUR 无异味 (GB 18401-2010)

**COLOUR FASTNESS TO WASHING WITH SOAP OR SOAP AND SODA(GRADE)[INCLUDING PRINT]**
**耐皂洗色牢度(级)[含印花部位]**

(GB/T 3921-2008, A(1), 40℃)
(GB/T 3921-2008 MOD修改采用 ISO 105-C10:2006)

| | | |
|---|---|---|
| COLOUR CHANGE 变色 | 4 | |
| COLOUR STAINING 沾色 | | |
| - COTTON 棉 | 4-5 | |
| - WOOL 羊毛 | 4-5 | |

REQUIREMENT 要求
≥3
≥3
(FZ/T 73045-2013)

**COLOUR FASTNESS TO PERSPIRATION(GRADE)[INCLUDING PRINT]**
**耐汗渍色牢度(级)[含印花部位]**

(GB/T 3922-1995)
(GB/T 3922-1995 EQV等效采用 ISO 105-E04: 1994)

| | ACID 酸 | ALKALINE 碱 |
|---|---|---|
| COLOUR CHANGE 变色 | 4 | 4 |
| COLOUR STAINING 沾色 | | |
| - COTTON 棉 | 4-5 | 4-5 |
| - WOOL 羊毛 | 4-5 | 4-5 |

REQUIREMENT 要求
≥3-4
≥3-4
(FZ/T 73045-2013)

PAGE 3 of 7

附 9.2f 装运通知

<table>
<tr><td colspan="5">Weifang Baoda Textiles Co., Ltd.<br>Address: No. 688 West Ring Road, Weifang, Shandong, China<br>Tel: 86-0536-8885678; Fax: 86-0536-8885677</td></tr>
<tr><td colspan="5">SHIPPING ADVICE</td></tr>
<tr><td rowspan="4">TO:</td><td rowspan="4">Stitchwell Garments Co., Ltd.<br>456/1/A Tejgaon Industrial Area, Dhaka 1208, Bangladesh<br>Tel: 880-2-9882934; Fax: 880-2-8891567</td><td>ISSUE DATE:</td><td>June 12, 2019</td></tr>
<tr><td>Sales Contract No.:</td><td>XS-2019001</td></tr>
<tr><td>L/C NO.:</td><td>LC5TF90080073</td></tr>
<tr><td>Invoice No.:</td><td>2019XS009</td></tr>
<tr><td colspan="5">Dear Sir or Madam:</td></tr>
<tr><td colspan="5">We are pleased to advise you that the following mentioned goods have been shipped out, and full details were shown as follows:</td></tr>
<tr><td colspan="5"></td></tr>
<tr><td colspan="2">Contract No.:</td><td colspan="3">XS-2019001</td></tr>
<tr><td colspan="2">Bill of Loading No.:</td><td colspan="3">COSU6066092540</td></tr>
<tr><td colspan="2">Ocean Vessel:</td><td colspan="3">COSCO SURABAYA</td></tr>
<tr><td colspan="2">Voyage No.:</td><td colspan="3">019S</td></tr>
<tr><td colspan="2">Port of Loading:</td><td colspan="3">Qingdao, China</td></tr>
<tr><td colspan="2">Date of Shipment:</td><td colspan="3">June 12, 2019</td></tr>
<tr><td colspan="2">Port of Destination:</td><td colspan="3">Chittagong, Bangladesh</td></tr>
<tr><td colspan="2">Estimated Date of Arrival:</td><td colspan="3">July 6, 2019</td></tr>
<tr><td colspan="2">Container/Seal No.:</td><td colspan="3">CRLU1812690/P14591</td></tr>
<tr><td colspan="2">Description of Goods:</td><td colspan="3">Cotton Yarn-dyed Fabrics</td></tr>
<tr><td colspan="2">Shipping Marks:</td><td colspan="3">STITCHWELL<br>XS-2019001<br>CHITTAGONG BANGLADESH<br>Carton No.1-270</td></tr>
<tr><td colspan="2">Quantity:</td><td colspan="3">27,000 yards, PACKED IN 270 BAGS</td></tr>
<tr><td colspan="2">Gross Weight:</td><td colspan="3">1.4 MT</td></tr>
<tr><td colspan="2">Net Weight:</td><td colspan="3">1.3 MT</td></tr>
<tr><td colspan="5">Thank you for your patronage. We look forward to the pleasure of receiving your valuable repeat orders.<br>Sincerely yours</td></tr>
<tr><td colspan="5">Weifang Baoda Textiles Co., Ltd.</td></tr>
</table>

附 9.2g　潍坊宝达纺织品有限公司开具的汇票

**BILL OF EXCHANGE**

NO. 2019XS009　WEIFANG　JUNE 15, 2019

EXCHANGE FOR USD43,700.00

AT 60 DAYS SIGHT　OF THIS *FIRST* OF

EXCHANGE (SECOND OF THE SAME TENOR AND DATE UNPAID)

PAY TO THE ORDER OF BANK OF CHINA, WEIFANG BRANCH

THE SUM OF U.S. DOLLAR FORTY-THREE THOUSAND SEVEN HUNDRED ONLY.

VALUE RECEIVED

DRAWN UNDER UTTARA BANK LTD, BADDA BRANCH

L/C NO. LC5TF90080073　DATED MAY 2, 2019

TO

BKCHCNBJ500

*(2-1)*　*AUTHORISED SIGNATURE(S) Albert*

## Notes

1. cooperation　*n.* 合作

   e.g. Cooperation is a vital factor in business success.

   合作对于商业成功是一项关键因素。

2. draft　*n.* 汇票

   draft 也常用 bill of exchange 表示。根据出票人的不同，汇票分为银行汇票和商业汇票；根据付款期限的不同，分为即期汇票和远期汇票；根据承兑人的不同，分为银行承兑汇票和商业承兑汇票；根据是否附有单据，分为光票和跟单汇票。

3. on line 在线

4. repeat order 返单

   返单指再次订购同样或类似的商品。

# CASE 2　Beijing Lucky Fibreboard Trading Co., Ltd.

## 一、信函的业务背景

澳大利亚松树纤维板工业有限公司比尔在将货物装船后，取得了海运提单。根据合同的约定，向北京幸运纤维板贸易有限公司的玲玲发出了货物已经装船的信函并附上海运提单的复印件，要求北京幸运纤维板贸易有限公司用电汇的方式支付此次合同的货款。

## 二、北京幸运纤维板贸易有限公司的信函

### （一）交单与付款（lucky-in 1）

From: Bill salesdepartment@pinetree.com.au
To: Lingling lingling@163.com
Date: 2019.08.05
Subject: shipment and payment
Attachment: Ocean Bill of Lading

Dear Lingling,

With reference to Contract No. SC-PINE2019010, we have just got the Ocean Bill of Lading and we are sending you the copy of Ocean Bill of Lading by fax and you can also find the copy of it in the attachment.

Meanwhile, please remit us the rest amount for the ordered goods, that is, USD18,701.50. The account is just the same as before.

Bank Name: HSBC Bank Australia, South Melbourne Branch
Address: Shop G16-G17, 265 Clarendon Street, South Melbourne, VIC 3205
Account Name: Pinetree Fibreboard Industries Co., Ltd.
Account No.: 172314-258

Please advise[1] us by e-mail after remittance.

The documents required will be sent to your address right away after we receive your remittance. We will inform[2] you of the tracking No. when the documents are delivered[3].

Best regards
Bill
Sales Department
Pinetree Fibreboard Industries Co., Ltd.

## Notes

1. advise *v.* 通知
   e.g. Please advise the date of shipment as soon as possible.
   请尽快通知装船日期。
2. inform *v.* 通知
   e.g. Can you inform me when to begin our final examination?
   你能通知我期终考试开始的时间吗？
3. deliver *v.* 发送
   e.g. The pizza will be delivered within 20 minutes.
   披萨将在 20 分钟内送达。

（二）交单与付款（lucky-out 1）

From: Lingling lingling@163.com
To: Bill salesdepartment@pinetree.com.au
Date: 2019.08.08
Subject: RE: shipment and payment

Dear Bill,

In reply to your letter on August 5 about the payment against Contract No. SC-PINE2019010, we have already remitted USD18,701.50 to your account in HSBC Bank Australia, South Melbourne Branch.

Please check your account in the next few days and send us e-mail to confirm[1] it.

As to the documents required, please send them to us right away.

The list of the documents required is as follows.

(1) Signed Commercial Invoice in 3 copies
(2) Signed Packing List in 3 copies
(3) Full set of clean on board Ocean Bills of Lading
(4) Certificate of Australian Origin issued by authorized institute of Australia
(5) Phytosanitary Certificate issued by Australian authorized institute
(6) Insurance Policy in duplicate

Have a nice day!

Sincerely
Lingling
Purchasing Manager
Beijing Lucky Fibreboard Trading Co., Ltd.

## Note

1. confirm　*v.* 确认
   e.g. I call you to confirm your reservation in our hotel.
   给您打电话是要确认您在我们酒店的预订。

（三）交单与付款（lucky-in 2）

From: Bill salesdepartment@pinetree.com.au
To: Lingling lingling@163.com
Date: 2019.08.10
Subject: RE: RE: shipment and payment

Dear Lingling,

We have received the amount USD18,701.50 remitted by your bank.

The documents against Contract No. SC-PINE2019010 have been sent to your address through DHL, and the tracking No. is AU20453689.

The list of the documents is as follows.

(1) Signed Commercial Invoice in 3 copies

(2) Signed Packing List in 3 copies

(3) Full set of clean on board Ocean Bills of Lading

(4) Certificate of Australian Origin issued by Australian Chamber of Commerce and Industry

(5) Phytosanitary Certificate issued by Department of Agriculture, Fisheries and Forestry

(6) Insurance Policy in duplicate issued by Allianz Australia Insurance Limited

Any complaints[1] about the goods should be informed to us within two weeks upon their arrival.

Best regards
Bill
Sales Department
Pinetree Fibreboard Industries Co., Ltd.

## 附 9.3a Hamburg Sud 船公司出具的海运提单

Shipper

Pinetree Fibreboard Industries Co., Ltd.
Address: No. 8 Pinetree Road, Melbourne, Australia
Tel: 61-3-85715322; Fax: 61-3-85715331

Consignee

Beijing Lucky Fibreboard Trading Co., Ltd.
Tel: 86-010-65771234; Fax: 86-010-65771233
Address: Room 801, International Trade Center, Chaoyang, Beijing, China

Notify Party

SAME AS CONSIGNEE

B/L NO. SUDU393501955096

HAMBURG SÜD GROUP

**www.hamburgsud.com**

**MULTIMODAL TRANSPORT BILL OF LADING**

Received in apparent good order and condition except as otherwise noted the total number of containers or other packages or units enumerated below for transportation from the place of receipt to the place of delivery subject to the terms hereof. One of the signed Bills of Lading must be surrendered duly endorsed in exchange for the Goods or Delivery order. On presentation of this document (duly) endorsed to the Carrier by or on behalf of the Holder, the rights and liabilities arising in accordance with the terms hereof shall (without prejudice to any rule of common law or statute rendering them binding on the Merchant) become binding in all respects between the Carrier and the Holder as though the contract evidenced hereby had been made between them.

| | | |
|---|---|---|
| Place of Receipt | Pre-carriage by | Originals to Be Released at<br>MELBOURNE, AUSTRALIA |
| Port of Loading<br>Melbourne, Australia | Vessel and Voyage Number<br>Maersk Virginia/530E | Freight Payable at<br>Melbourne, Australia |
| Port of Discharge<br>Pusan, Korea | Place of Delivery<br>Xingang, China | Number of Original Bs/L<br>THREE (3) |

**PARTICULARS AS DECLARED BY SHIPPER – CARRIER NOT RESPONSIBLE**

| Container Nos./Seal Nos. Marks and Numbers | No. of Containers/ Packages | Description of Goods | Gross Weight (MT) | Measurement ($M^3$) |
|---|---|---|---|---|
| SUDU5981109/0134842<br>NM | 1 CONTAINER<br>14 PACKAGES | FIBREBOARD | 24.75 MT | 32.66 $M^3$ |
| SUDU5978109/0134803<br>NM | 1 CONTAINER<br>11 PACKAGES | FIBREBOARD | 24.75 MT | 25.40 $M^3$ |

| | |
|---|---|
| FREIGHT & CHARGES | Number of Containers/Packages (in words) |
| FREIGHT PREPAID | TWO CONTAINERS/TWENTY-FIVE PACKAGES |
| | Shipped on Board Date: |
| | AUG 1, 2019 |
| | Place and Date of Issue: |
| | MELBOURNE, AUSTRALIA<br>AUG 1, 2019 |
| | AS AGENT FOR HAMBURG SUD |
| | ***Douglas*** |
| | **HAMBURG SUD AUSTRALIA PTY LTD** as Carrier |

### 附 9.3b 澳大利亚松树纤维板工业有限公司出具的商业发票（合同号：SC-PINE2019010）

**PINETREE**

**COMMERCIAL INVOICE**

BUYER: Beijing Lucky Fibreboard Trading Co., Ltd.
Room 801, International Trade Center,
Chaoyang, Beijing, China

DATE: July 28, 2019
CONTRACT NO.: SC-PINE2019010
L/C NO.: N/A
INVOICE NO.: PINE20190610

| **Commodity** | **Specification** | | | | **Price ($USD/M^3$)** | **Quantity** | | **Amount (USD)** |
|---|---|---|---|---|---|---|---|---|
| | *Grade* | *Length* | *Width* | *Thickness (MM)* | *CIF Xingang China* | *No. of Sheet* | *$M^3$* | |
| fibreboard | premium | 2,400 MM | 1,200 MM | 9 MM | 430 | 1,260 | 32.66 | 14,043.80 |
| fibreboard | premium | 2,400 MM | 1,400 MM | 6 MM | 490 | 1,260 | 25.40 | 12,446.00 |
| TOTAL | | | | | | 2,520 | 58.06 | 26,489.80 |

TOTAL AMOUNT: USD TWENTY-SIX THOUSAND FOUR HUNDRED EIGHTY-NINE AND CENTS EIGHTY ONLY.

ON BEHALF OF
PINETREE FIBREBOARD INDUSTRIES CO., LTD.

SIGNATURE: ***Bill***
DATE: July 28, 2019

PINETREE FIBREBOARD INDUSTRIES CO., LTD.
Address: No. 8 Pinetree Road, Melbourne, Australia
Tel: 61-3-85715322；Fax: 61-3-85715331

## 附 9.3c 澳大利亚松树纤维板工业有限公司出具的包装单（合同号：SC-PINE2019010）

**PINETREE**

**PACKING LIST**

BUYER: Beijing Lucky Fibreboard Trading Co., Ltd.
Room 801, International Trade Center, No. 92 Jianguo Road,
Chaoyang, Beijing, China

DATE: July 28, 2019
CONTRACT NO.: SC-PINE2019010
L/C NO.: N/A
INVOICE NO.: PINE20190610

| SHEET DIMENSIONS | SHEETS PER PACK | NO. OF PACKS | SHIPMENT QNANTITY (SHEETS) | NET WEIGHT (MT) | GROSS WEIGHT (MT) | VOLUME ($M^3$) | CONTAINER NO./ SEAL NO. |
|---|---|---|---|---|---|---|---|
| 2,400 MM × 1,200 MM × 9 MM | 90 | 14 | 1,260 | 23.65 | 24.75 | 32.66 | SUDU5981109/ 0134842 |
| 2,400 MM × 1,400 MM × 6 MM | 120 | 11 | 1,260 | 24.63 | 24.75 | 25.40 | SUDU5978109/ 0134803 |
| TOTAL | | 25 | 2,520 | 48.28 | 49.50 | 58.06 | |

TOTAL PACKS: TWENTY-FIVE (25) PACKS ONLY
TOTAL CONTAINERS: TWO (2) ONLY

ON BEHALF OF
PINETREE FIBREBOARD INDUSTRIES CO., LTD.

SIGNATURE: ***Bill***
DATE: July 28, 2019

PINETREE FIBREBOARD INDUSTRIES CO., LTD.
Address: No. 8 Pinetree Road, Melbourne, Australia
Tel: 61-3-85715322；Fax: 61-3-85715331

## 附 9.3d 澳大利亚商业与工业商会签发的原产地证书

**ORIGINAL**

| | |
|---|---|
| 1. Exporter | Certificate No.<br>387249258 |
| Pinetree Fibreboard Industries Co., Ltd.<br>Address: No. 8 Pinetree Road, Melbourne, Australia | Exporter's Reference<br>SC-PINE2019010 |
| 2. Consignee<br>Beijing Lucky Fibreboard Trading Co., Ltd.<br>Room 801, International Trade Center,<br>Chaoyang, Beijing, China | **BUYER (IF NOT CONSIGNEE)** |

| | | |
|---|---|---|
| 3. PORT OF LOADING | | **CERTIFICATE OF AUSTRALIAN ORIGIN**<br>AUSTRALIAN CHAMBER OF COMMERCE AND INDUSTRY<br>**ACCI**<br>LEVEL 3<br>COMMERCE HOUSE<br>24 BRISBANE AVENUE<br>BARTON ACT 2600<br>AUSTRALIA<br>TELEPHONE:<br>INTERNATIONAL: 61 2 6273 2311<br>LOCAL: 02 6273 2311<br>AUTHORISED TO ISSUE CERTIFICATES OF ORIGIN BY THE GOVERNMENT OF THE COMMONWEALTH OF AUSTRALIA. |
| Melbourne, Australia | | |
| 4. VESSEL/AIRCRAFT | 5. DATE OF DEPARTURE | |
| Maersk Virginia/530E | AUG 1, 2019 | |
| 6. SEA/AIRPORT OF DISCHARGE | 7. FINAL DESTINATION | |
| BUSAN, KOREA | XINGANG, CHINA | |

| 8. Marks and Numbers | 9. Number and Kind of Packages | 10. Description of Goods | 11. H.S. Code | 12. GROSS WEIGHT |
|---|---|---|---|---|
| NM | 25 PACKAGES × 40 CONTAINERS OF FIBREBOARD | | 44.11.14.25 | 49,500.0 KG |

*******************************************************************************

CONTAINER Nos.
SUDU5981109, SUDU5978109

| | |
|---|---|
| I, the undersigned, being duly authorized by the above exporter, and having made the necessary enquiries HEREBY CERTIFY THAT based on the rules of origin printed on the reverse hereof all the goods listed above originate in AUSTRALIA. I further declare that I will furnish to the Customs authorities of the importing country of their nominee, for inspection at any time such evidence as may be requested for the purpose of verifying this certificate.<br>The goods were produced/manufactured at<br>Melbourne<br>*******************************************************<br>SIGNATURE OF AUTHORISED OFFICER ***Bill*** | I, the undersigned, being duly authorized by the Australian Chamber of Commerce and Industry to sign documentary evidence of origin, hereby certify that on the basis of information supplied by the exporter and to the best of my knowledge and belief the country of origin of the above mentioned goods, based on the rules of origin claimed by the exporter, is AUSTRALIA.<br><br>SIGNATURE OF AUTHORISED OFFICER ***Michael*** |

## 附 9.3e　澳大利亚农业、渔业和林业部签发的植物检疫证书

**ORIGINAL**

Name and Address of Exporter(1)
Pinetree Fibreboard Industries Co., Ltd.
No. 8 Pinetree Road, Melbourne, Australia

No. 4X95610834

**Australian Government**

..................................

**Department of Agriculture, Fisheries and Forestry**

**PHYTOSANITARY CERTIFICATE**

Plant Protection Organisation of the Australian Government (5)

Declared Name and Address of Consignee/Notify Party: (2)
Beijing Lucky Fibreboard Trading Co., Ltd.
Room 801, International Trade Center,
Chaoyang, Beijing, China

| | |
|---|---|
| Place of Origin (7)<br>Melbourne | Code<br>3026 |
| Country of Final Destination (8)<br>CHINA | Code<br>CN |

To: the Plant Protection Organisation of (9)
CHINA

| | | |
|---|---|---|
| Declared Means of Conveyance (10)<br>Maersk Virginia/530E | Declared Point of Entry (11)<br>XINGANG | Import Permit Number (6)<br>NOT SUPPLIED |

| Distinguishing Marks and Container Numbers (12) | Number and Description of Packages (13) | Name of Produce/ Quantity Declared (14) | Botanical Name of Plants (15) | Commodity Code (16) |
|---|---|---|---|---|
| SUDU5981109, SUDU5978109 | 25 PACKAGES | FIBREBOARD | | 44.11.14.25 |

| | Number of Packages (total) (17) | Mass (total) (18) |
|---|---|---|
| | **25** | **49,500.0 KGS** |

This is to certify that the plants, plant products or other regulated articles described herein have been inspected and/or tested according to appropriate procedures and are considered to be free from the quarantine pests specified by the importing contracting party and to conform with the current phytosanitary requirements of the importing contracting party, including those for regulated non-quarantine pests. (19)

**DISINFESTATION AND/OR DISINFECTION TREATMENT (20)**

| Date (21) | Treatment (22) | Chemical (active ingredient) | Concentration (24) |
|---|---|---|---|
| *********************** | ***************** | ********************** | ****************************** |

| Duration and Temperature (25) | Additional Information (26) |
|---|---|
| ************************ | ******************************************************************************** |

Additional Declaration (27)
**NO ADDITIONAL DECLARATION**

| | | |
|---|---|---|
| Place of Issue (32)<br>**TULLAMARINE** | | Code<br>**3043** |
| Name of Inspector (28)<br>**KELLY ARNETT** | Inspection Date (29)<br>**25/07/2019** | Code<br>**3012** |
| Name of Authorised Officer (30)<br>**NICOLE TANNER** | Signature of Authorised Officer an Officer of the Dept (34)<br>*Tanner* | |

## 附 9.3f 安联（澳大利亚）保险公司出具的货物运输保险单

| | |
|---|---|
| Allianz | **Allianz Australia Insurance Limited**<br>Head Office: Sydney |

**CARGO TRANSPORTATION INSURANCE POLICY**

| | | | |
|---|---|---|---|
| INVOICE NO. | PINE20190610 | POLICY NO. | 3221335478965423 |
| CONTRACT NO. | SC-PINE2019010 | | |
| L/C NO. | N/A | | |
| INSURED: | Pinetree Fibreboard Industries Co., Ltd.<br>No. 8 Pinetree Road, Melbourne, Australia | | |

THIS POLICY OF INSURANCE WITNESSES THAT Allianz Australia Insurance Limited (HEREINAFTER CALLED "THE COMPANY") AT THE REQUEST OF THE INSURED AND IN CONSIDERATION OF THE AGREED PREMIUM PAID TO THE COMPANY BY THE INSURED, UNDERTAKES TO INSURE THE UNDERMENTIONED GOODS IN TRANSPORTATION SUBJECT TO THE CONDITIONS OF THIS POLICY AS PER THE CLAUSES PRINTED OVERLEAF AND OTHER SPECIAL CLAUSES ATTACHED HEREON.

| MARKS & NOS | QUANTITY | DESCRIPTION OF GOODS | AMOUNT INSURED |
|---|---|---|---|
| NM | 58.06 CBM | FIBREBOARD | USD29,138.78 |

| | |
|---|---|
| TOTAL AMOUNT INSURED: | USD TWENTY-NINE THOUSAND ONE HUNDRED AND THIRTY-EIGHT AND CENTS SEVENTY-EIGHT ONLY. |

| | | | | | |
|---|---|---|---|---|---|
| PERMIUM: | AS ARRANGED | DATE OF COMMENCEMENT: | AUG 1, 2019 | PER CONVEYANCE: | Maersk Virginia/530E |

| | | | | | |
|---|---|---|---|---|---|
| FROM: | Melbourne, Australia | VIA | Pusan, Korea | TO | Melbourne, Australia |

CONDITIONS:

Covering All Risks as per ICC "A" (1/1/2009).

IN THE EVENT OF LOSS OR DAMAGE WHICH MAY RESULT IN A CLAIM UNDER THIS POLICY, IMMEDIATE NOTICE MUST BE GIVEN TO THE

| | | |
|---|---|---|
| COMPANY'S AGENT AS MENTIONED HEREUNDER. CLAIMS, IF ANY, ONE OF THE ORIGINAL POLICIES WHICH HAVE BEEN ISSUED IN | 2 | ORIGINAL(S) |

TOGETHER WITH THE RELEVANT DOCUMENTS SHALL BE SURRENDERED TO THE COMPANY. IF ONE OF THE ORIGINAL POLICIES HAS BEEN

| | |
|---|---|
| ACCOMPLISHED. THE OTHERS TO BE VOID. | |
| Survey By:<br><br>Allianz China General Insurance Company Ltd.<br>ADDR: 10 Unit, 34 Building, International Finance Tower, 5 Pearl River West Road, Guangzhou<br>TEL: 86 20 8396 6788<br>FAX: 86 20 3891 1890 | **Allianz Australia Insurance Limited** |
| CLAIM PAYABLE AT XINGANG, CHINA IN USD | |
| ISSUING DATE JULY 28, 2019 | Authorized Signature *Allen Smith* |

## Note

1. complaint *n.* & *v.* 投诉

e.g. I have no complaints during my stay in the hotel.

我在本酒店的住宿期间没有投诉。

## 练习

### 一、将下列句子译成中文。

（一）信用证支付方式下的交单付款练习

1. Yesterday we submitted all the required documents to the negotiating bank, several discrepancies were found in the presented documents.
2. Under the field "FREIGHT AND CHARGES" it reads "FREIGHT TO COLLECT" and it should be "FREIGHT PREPAID".
3. The DATE OF SHIPMENT on B/L is later than the LATEST DATE OF SHIPMENT (field 44c) on L/C.
4. The port of loading is not in compliance with the L/C.
5. The name of the exporter in the invoice and the beneficiary in the L/C is not the same.
6. The description of goods in the invoice does not comply with the L/C.
7. We have approached the issuing bank and the bank agrees to accept the discrepancies.
8. You still have to pay USD100 to the issuing bank for the discrepancy fee.

（二）电汇支付方式下的交单付款练习

1. Please find the copy of the B/L in the attachment.
2. Please remit us the amount USD15,360 to our account in Bank of China, Qingdao Branch.
3. We have sent the documents required to your address through EMS and tracking No. is NG304893689.
4. The list of the documents sent by forwarder is as follows.
5. The documents required are sent to your address right away after we receive your remittance.
6. Please check your account in the next few days and send us e-mail to confirm it.

（三）托收支付方式下的交单付款练习

1. We have chosen Bank of China as the remitting bank.
2. The documents required have been sent to the collecting bank by forwarder through Bank of China.

## 二、将下列句子译成英文。

（一）信用证支付方式下的交单付款练习

1. 在向议付行提交的单据中，发现了几处不符点。
2. 在提单的运费与费用栏目里，填写的是“运费预付”，但应该填写“运费到付”。
3. 提单里目的港的名称与信用证的要求不相符。提单上填写的目的港是“中国青岛”，而信用证里的目的港是“中国广州”。
4. 发票中的货物描述与信用证里的货物描述不相符。
5. 我公司交单时已经迟于信用证规定的交单期。请与开证行沟通，使开证行同意付款。
6. 我公司同意接受你公司提出的单据不符点，并将与开证行沟通，使开证行接受单据的不符点。
7. 我公司不同意接受你公司提出的单据不符点，即提单中的箱数与装箱单中的箱数不相符。
8. 银行同意接受你方提出的单据不符点，但要求扣除 100 美元的不符点费用。

（二）电汇支付方式下的交单付款练习

1. 提单的复印件已经通过传真于 6 月 24 日发给你方了。
2. 请把其余货款 36 250 美元汇入我公司在交通银行青岛分行的账户。
3. 请向我公司在中国银行天津分行的账户汇款 13 200 美元。
4. 我公司已经向你公司在中国银行青岛分行的账户汇款 325 000 美元。
5. 请告知我方你公司的银行名称和账户，以便我方向你公司汇款。
6. 货物的单据已经通过联邦快递发出，运单号为 HD45682123。

（三）托收支付方式下的交单付款练习

1. 我方已经选择了交通银行作为托收行。
2. 要求的单据已经通过交通银行以快递的方式发给了代收行。

## 技能训练

### 根据业务情境和信息写信。

（一）业务情境

1. 江苏通达轮胎有限公司将合同 LLLT20190608 项下大力神轮胎贸易公司订购的货物装运完毕后，李辉制作并取得了包括海运提单在内的信用证要求的所有单据，在信用证有效期内向议付行——中国银行无锡分行交单议付。

但交单后，中国银行无锡分行告知李辉所提交的单据有不符点。要求江苏通达轮胎有限公司在交单期内提交符合要求的单据。

但由于交单期临近，如果修改单据再提交给议付行可能造成逾期交单。于是，李辉向大卫·桑德伯格写信请求对方联系开证行，使开证行接受单据的不符点。

2. 大卫·桑德伯格收到李辉请求与开证行联系的信函后，及时与开证行联系。开证行同意接受单据的不符点，但需要扣除 120 美元的费用。

大卫·桑德伯格写信向李辉说明了这些情况。

（二）信息

1. 议付行提出的单据不符点：

（1）单据的货物描述与信用证不相符；

（2）提单的装运期迟于最迟装运期。

2. 不符点费用：USD120.00。

（三）任务

根据以上的业务情境和信息写信。

1. 李辉写信告知大卫·桑德伯格提交的单据存在不符点，请求对方与开证行联系接受不符点交单。

信函应包括以下要点：

（1）提及合同号 LLLT20190608 项下单据；

（2）说明单据存在不符点；

（3）具体说明单据存在的不符点及原因；

（4）说明由于交单期临近，修改单据可能造成逾期交单；

（5）请求大卫·桑德伯格与开证行联系，使开证行接受不符点付款；

（6）表示感谢。

2. 大卫·桑德伯格回复李辉：单据的不符点的处理结果。

信函应包括以下要点：

（1）提到李辉关于单据不符点的来信；

（2）同意李辉提出的要求；

（3）告知李辉已经与开证行联系，开证行同意接受单据的不符点并付款，但需要扣除不符点费用；

（4）请李辉交单后告知运单号；

（5）表示感谢。

## 补充阅读

信函 1：卖方交单

业务背景：青岛兴旺手工艺品有限公司的销售经理李华在将货运单据提交银行后，及时通知法国优雅贸易有限公司总经理海伦。

From: lihua@handicraftschina.com

To: helen1219@hotmail.com

Date: 2019.06.12
Subject: shipping documents

Dear Helen,

I have just presented the documents required to the negotiation bank (Bank of China, Qingdao China).

The documents presented are as follows:

(1) Full set of clean on board Bill of Lading in three originals

(2) Signed Commercial Invoice in triplicate

(3) Signed Packing List in triplicate

(4) Certificate of Origin by CCPIT in duplicate

(5) Insurance Policy in duplicate

The documents will reach the issuing bank in due course.

If you have any problem with the documents upon receipt of them, please inform us as soon as possible.

Yours sincerely
Li Hua
Sales Manager
Qingdao Xingwang Handicrafts Co., Ltd.
Address: No. 1251 Xingwang Road Qingdao, Shandong, China
Tel: 86-0532-8745618; Fax: 86-0532-8745617

信函 2：卖方要求买方付款后发货

业务背景：淄博海来特锥形钢管有限公司在将印度 API 钢管有限公司的订单生产完毕后，公司的销售经理大卫向印度 API 钢管有限公司总经理曼珠先生发出信函，要求付清其余货款后发货。

From: davidli@steelpipechina.com
To: mundra@indiapipe.com
Date: 2019.05.30
Subject: payment for Order No. AT2019002

Dear Mr. Mundra,

Regarding your Order No. AT2019002 for 5,000 pieces of tapered steel pipe, the goods have been finished now.

Please remit the remaining amount of the payment to our following account just as before.

Bank Name: Industrial and Commercial Bank of China Beijing Municipal Branch,

Beijing, PRC

Address: No. 55 Fuxingmen Street Xicheng District, Beijing, China

Account Name: Zibo Highlight Tapered Steel Pipe Co., Ltd.

Account No.: 6571424016

SWIFT CODE: ICBKCNBJBJM

We will deliver the goods to you upon receipt of your remittance.

If you have any question about the ordered goods, don't hesitate to let us know.

Regards

David Li

Sales Manager

Zibo Highlight Tapered Steel Pipe Co., Ltd.

Address: No. 1251 Nanshan Road, Zibo, Shandong, China

Tel: 86-0533-8265184; Fax: 86-0533-8265173

# 任务十

# 投诉与索赔

# Complaint and Claim

## 学习目标

1. 了解投诉与索赔的相关知识；
2. 掌握投诉与索赔信函的写作要点；
3. 熟悉投诉与索赔信函的常用词语和句子；
4. 能够阅读和撰写有关投诉与索赔的信函。

## 背景知识

投诉与索赔不是国际贸易业务中必然会发生的事件。如果交易双方都能严格按合同规定履行各自的义务，那么投诉与索赔是可以避免的。但是，在实际业务中，由于种种原因，当事人不按规定履行合同的义务或由于失误或疏忽没有能够履行合同的义务也是常常发生的。在这样的情况下，买方或卖方会向对方或其他当事人提出投诉或索赔。

### 一、常见的索赔情形

（一）买方向卖方索赔

（1）卖方不交货；

（2）延迟交货；

（3）所交货物与合同规定不相符。

（二）卖方向买方索赔

（1）买方无理拒收货物；

（2）不按合同规定派船接货；

（3）拒绝支付货款。

（三）买方或卖方向承运方提出索赔

（1）由于装卸发生的货物损失；

（2）运输途中由于照料不当造成的货物损失。

（四）买方或卖方向保险公司提出索赔

货物在运输过程中发生的承保险别以内的风险造成的损失。

对于买卖双方之间的索赔，双方首先应该友好协商进行处理。如果协商不成，可以提交仲裁或法院进行处理。对属于承运方的责任，或者属于保险公司赔偿范围的索赔，买方或卖方应该分清责任归属，及时向有关责任方进行索赔。

## 二、索赔证据

索赔时，索赔方应准备好索赔的证据，否则，可能遭到对方的拒赔。

常用的索赔证据包括合同、买卖双方的往来函电、权威或约定的商检机构出具的商检证明等。

## 三、索赔期限

在合同中，要明确规定索赔的期限，比如，收到货物后的30天内提出索赔。超出索赔期限，对方可以拒绝索赔要求。

# 写作提示

投诉或索赔信函的业务情境繁多，但信函的写作内容包括的要点通常如下。

## 一、投诉或索赔信函

（1）提及所投诉或索赔的对象，给出合同号或订单号；

（2）说明投诉或索赔的原因；

（3）说明投诉或索赔的证据，并附上；

（4）提出自己的处理方案或赔偿要求；

（5）希望对方尽快答复。

## 二、回复投诉或索赔信函

（1）提及对方的投诉或索赔信函；

（2）表示道歉或遗憾；

（3）解释问题出现的原因；

（4）同意或拒绝对方的投诉或索赔；

（5）提出自己的处理意见；

（6）等待对方回复。

## 示范信函

# CASE 1 Weifang Baoda Textiles Co., Ltd.

## 一、信函的业务背景

孟加拉国缝得好服装有限公司收到了潍坊宝达纺织品有限公司的发货，但发现其中有两包货物不是所订购的货物。于是，丽莎写信要求对方换货。

## 二、潍坊宝达纺织品有限公司的业务信函

（一）投诉与索赔（baoda-in 1）

From: Lisa lisa@stitchwell.com
To: Albert albert@163.com
Date: 2019.07.08
Subject: wrong delivery[1] under Contract No. XS-2019001
Attachment: photos of the wrong delivered goods

Dear Albert,

We have just received the goods under Contract No. XS-2019001. But unfortunately[2] we found that two bags of the goods delivered are not the goods we ordered, while the item for which the style No. is XS-FLANNEL-03 is short of[3] two bags.

Please send two bags (200 yards) of the goods for which the style No. is XS-FLANNEL-03 to us immediately to replace[4] the wrong goods. We are in urgent[5] need of the fabrics to work on[6] the order for our customer.

Your early reply will be greatly appreciated[7].

Regards
Lisa
Purchasing Manager
Stitchwell Garments Co., Ltd.

### Notes

1. wrong delivery 错发货
2. unfortunately *adv.* 不幸地
3. short of 短少

e.g. I am getting short of money because of out of job.

我现在因为没有工作缺钱了。

4. replace *v.* 代替

e.g. Nowadays e-mails have replaced letters for daily communication.

当今的日常交流中，电子邮件已经代替了书信。

5. urgent *adj.* 紧急的

e.g. The issue is urgent according to the officials at the Department of Commerce.

根据商务部官员的说法，问题十分紧急。

6. work on sth. 为……工作

e.g. I worked all night on that article.

我整夜为写那篇文章工作。

7. be appreciated 感谢的，感激的

e.g. I am appreciated for your great help.

我非常感激你的帮助。

（二）投诉与索赔（baoda-out 1）

From: Albert albert@163.com

To: Lisa lisa@stitchwell.com

Date: 2019.07.10

Subject: RE: wrong delivery under Contract No. XS-2019001

Dear Lisa,

In reply to your letter on July 8 about the wrong goods delivery, we are very sorry about the inconvenience[1] caused by wrong delivery.

After careful investigation, we found that the incident was caused by the following fault by one of our staff. The staff member responsible for packing put the goods under another order into the goods you ordered by mistake[2].

We will ship the correct goods, that is, 200 yards fabrics for which the style No. is XS-FLANNEL-03 to you by airfreight[3] right away.

As to the wrong delivered goods, we propose two alternative[4] solutions[5]. One is that we sell the goods to you at low price, that is, USD1 per yard; the other is that you return the goods to us and the freight is for our account[6].

Please advise us when you receive the goods delivered by air.

We apologize[7] again for the inconvenience caused by the wrong delivery.

Yours sincerely

Albert

Sales Manager
Weifang Baoda Textiles Co., Ltd.

## Notes

1. inconvenience　*n.* 不方便
   e.g. I am sorry for the inconvenience caused by water cut.
   对于停水造成的不便，我非常抱歉。
2. by mistake　错误地
   e.g. He has been arrested by police by mistake.
   他已经被警察误抓。
3. by airfreight　通过空运
   e.g. This post requires 2 years working experience in airfreight or ocean forwarding industry.
   该岗位要求具有两年空运或海运行业的工作经验。
4. alternative　*n. & adj.* 可选择（的）
   e.g. Humans are looking for alternative sources of energy.
   人类正在寻找可替代的能源。
5. solution　*n.* 解决方案
   e.g. The two countries are seeking for a peaceful solution to the frontier issue.
   这两个国家正在寻找边境问题的和平解决方案。
6. for our account　由我方承担费用
   e.g. The charges of the samples are for our account.
   样品费用由我们承担。
7. apologize　*v.* 道歉

（三）投诉与索赔（baoda-in 2）

From: Lisa lisa@stitchwell.com
To: Albert albert@163.com
Date: 2019.07.12
Subject: RE: RE: wrong delivery under Contract No. XS-2019001

Dear Albert,

Thank you for your quick response.

We agree on your proposal[1] that the wrong delivered goods will be sold at USD1 per yard to us, and we will remit the amount USD200.00 to your account by T/T.

We will advise you when receiving the goods delivered by air.

Thank you for your cooperation.

Regards
Lisa
Purchasing Manager
Stitchwell Garments Co., Ltd.

**Note**

1. proposal *n.* 提议

e.g. Please give your proposal on present educational reform issues.

请给出关于当前教育改革问题的提议。

# CASE 2 Beijing Lucky Fibreboard Trading Co., Ltd.

## 一、信函的业务背景

北京幸运纤维板贸易有限公司在收到货物后，发现靠近托盘底部的纤维板发霉。为此，写信给澳大利亚松树纤维板工业有限公司，要求对方查明事件的原因。

## 二、北京幸运纤维板贸易有限公司的信函

（一）投诉与索赔（lucky-out 1）

From: Lingling lingling@163.com
To: Bill salesdepartment@pinetree.com.au
Date: 2019.08.25
Subject: claim[1] for the goods under Contract No. SC-PINE2019010
Attachment: Survey Report[2]

Dear Bill,

With reference to the goods under Contract No. SC-PINE2019010, we've just received the goods. However, we regretfully find that some of the fibreboard near the bottom of the pallet[3] are soaking[4] and mouldy[5].

We've asked Beijing Customs District P.R. China[6] to survey this incident and the surveyor's[7] opinion is that it is caused by water permeation[8].

Please investigate[9] the incident and provide us with your explanation as soon as possible.

If it falls within your responsibility[10] we will have to lodge a claim against you[11] for the damage of the goods.

As to the amount, we would claim for USD500.00 on the goods after evaluating[12] the loss[13].

We are enclosing the Survey Report issued by Beijing Customs District P.R. China.

Await your quick response.

Yours sincerely
Lingling
Purchasing Manager
Beijing Lucky Fibreboard Trading Co., Ltd.

## Notes

1. claim *n.* & *v.* 索赔
   表示索赔的说法有：claim，raise a claim，lodge a claim，make a claim。
   e.g. (1) We would claim for USD5,000 against you on the goods ordered.
   我方就订购的货物向你方提出 5 000 美元的索赔。
   (2) We have to lodge a claim against you for the low quality of the 100 MT rice.
   由于 100 吨大米的质量低劣，我方不得不向你方提出索赔。
   (3) We shall make a claim against you for the shortage of the goods.
   由于短重，我方将向你方提出索赔。
2. survey report 调查报告
   索赔时，需要由调查人出具调查报告作为索赔的依据。
3. pallet *n.* 托盘
4. soaking *adj.* 湿透的
   e.g. I am soaking in the heavy rain.
   在大雨里，我湿透了。
5. mouldy *adj.* 发霉的
   e.g. The cheese is mouldy, so throw it away!
   奶酪发霉了，扔掉！
6. Beijing Customs District P. R. China 中华人民共和国北京海关
   2018 年 4 月出入境检验检疫管理职责和队伍划入海关总署。
7. surveyor *n.* 调查人
8. water permeation 渗水
9. investigate *v.* 调查
   e.g. The police are investigating the incident.
   警方正在调查此事件。
10. responsibility *n.* 责任
11. lodge a claim against you 向你方提出索赔
    e.g. We refrain from lodging a claim against you considering our friendship.
    考虑到我们之间的友谊，我方不向你方提出索赔。

12. evaluate *v.* 估价

e.g. It is hard to evaluate the loss caused by the fire.

火灾引起的损失难以估计。

13. loss *n.* 损失

e.g. The death of her husband is a great loss to the whole family.

她丈夫的去世对于整个家庭是巨大的损失。

（二）投诉与索赔（lucky-in 1）

From: Bill salesdepartment@pinetree.com.au

To: Lingling lingling@163.com

Date: 2019.08.26

Subject: RE: claim for the goods under Contract No. SC-PINE2019010

Dear Lingling,

In reply to your letter on August 25 about claim on the goods under Contract No. SC-PINE2019010, we've checked the detailed records of production and the conditions of your ordered goods before shipment and find nothing was wrong with[1] it.

Then, we contacted the shipping company and learnt that the ship encountered[2] rainstorm during the voyage which resulted in[3] water permeation of some of the containers in the ship.

So we are not responsible for[4] the damage of the goods, but you can contact the agency[5] of the Insurer[6](ALLIANZ CHINA GENERAL INSURANCE COMPANY LTD.[7]) to make a claim.

Please contact the Surveyor[8] of the agency of the Insurer in China as soon as possible.

Information of the Surveyor of the Insurer in China

Contact person: Li Qiang

Agency of the Insurer: Allianz China General Insurance Company Ltd.

Tel: 86-20-83966788

Fax: 86-20-38911890

E-mail: liqiang@sina.com.cn

If you have any other problems about the delivered goods, please let us know.

Best regards

Bill

Sales Department

Pinetree Fibreboard Industries Co., Ltd.

## Notes

1. be wrong with sth. 某事物存在问题
   e.g. Something is wrong with my computer.
   我的电脑有些问题。
2. encounter *v.* 遭遇
   e.g. Whatever profession you take, you are bound to encounter difficulties.
   不管你从事什么职业，你注定会遇到困难。
3. result in 导致
   e.g. My carelessness resulted in my failure in the exam.
   我的粗心导致了考试的失败。
4. be responsible for sth. 对某事负责
   e.g. I am responsible for this accident.
   我对这个事故负责。
5. agency *n.* 代理
   e.g. The company intends to hire a sales manager through an employment agency.
   公司打算通过职业中介机构聘用一名销售经理。
6. insurer *n.* 保险人
   保险人指接受投保人的申请，与投保人订立保险合同，并承担赔偿责任的保险公司。
7. Allianz China General Insurance Company Ltd. 安联财产保险（中国）有限公司
   安联财产保险（中国）有限公司由德国安联保险公司单独出资，总部设于广州的外商独资保险公司。
8. surveyor *n.* 勘察员
   勘察员此处指保险勘察员。主要工作是被保险财物出险后，负责进行现场勘察。

## 练习

**一、将下列句子译成中文。**

1. We find that 3 cartons of the delivered goods are not the goods we ordered.
2. The item XD-2041 is in short of 5 cases.
3. We found that the packages of 9 bales had been broken.
4. We request you to replace the wrong delivered goods as soon as possible.
5. We will lodge a claim against you for the ordered goods for USD520.00.
6. We claim USD800.00 against you for the loss caused by short weight.
7. We will appreciate it if you could look into the matter and let us know your disposal as soon as possible.
8. We are sorry for the inconvenience caused by wrong delivery.
9. We regret what happened to your ordered goods.

10. We assure you that care will be taken in your future orders.
11. Your claim and the surveyor's report are now having our careful consideration and we apologize for this incident.
12. We regret to say that we are not responsible for the damage of the goods.

**二、将下列句子译成英文。**

1. 我方发现收到的货物中有两箱不是我方订购的货物。
2. 我方发现货物的质量低于样品的质量。
3. 我方发现收到的货物缺少两箱。
4. 因为错发货，我方要求你方尽快换货。
5. 因为货物的质量问题，我方向你方提出索赔 2 000 美元。
6. 因为短重我方要向你方提出索赔，金额为 300 美元。
7. 我们已经对你方提出的包装问题进行了仔细的检查。
8. 我方对由于货物的质量问题引起的不便表示歉意。
9. 很遗憾，我方不对货物的损失负责，你方可以向保险公司提出索赔。
10. 我们抱歉地说不能接受你方关于短量的索赔。
11. 船公司应该对货物在运输中的损坏负责。
12. 我方将向你方账户汇入 2 000 美元作为赔偿。

## 技能训练

### 根据业务情境和信息写信

（一）业务情境

1. 大力神轮胎贸易公司在收到了合同 LLLT20190608 项下的货物后，发现有两条轮胎的规格与合同不相符。于是，大卫•桑德伯格发出信函告知江苏通达轮胎有限公司并要求尽快换货。

2. 江苏通达轮胎有限公司的李辉在收到大卫•桑德伯格要求换货的信函后，回信表示道歉，并告知将立即通过空运的方式将正确规格的轮胎发运，同时，请大卫•桑德伯格将规格不符的两条轮胎退回，运费由江苏通达轮胎有限公司支付。

（二）信息

1. 两条规格与合同不符的轮胎的规格：245/50R18，正确的规格：10.00R20；
2. 错发货原因：装货人员的工作失误。

（三）任务

根据以上的业务情境和信息写信。

1. 大卫•桑德伯格写信告知收到的货物中有两条轮胎的规格与合同不相符，要求换货。

信函应包括以下要点：

（1）提及合同号 LLLT20190608 项下的商品；

（2）告知到货后发现有两条轮胎的规格与合同不符；

（3）附上规格与合同不符的两条轮胎的照片；

（4）要求李辉换货；

（5）希望李辉尽快处理此事。

2. 李辉回复大卫·桑德伯格要求换货的信函。

（1）提及大卫·桑德伯格要求换货的信函；

（2）表示道歉；

（3）解释发错货的原因：装货人员的工作失误；

（4）同意大卫·桑德伯格的换货要求，通过空运的方式将正确规格的两条轮胎发运；

（5）请大卫·桑德伯格将两条规格不符的轮胎退回，运费由江苏通达轮胎有限公司支付；

（6）再次表示道歉。

## 补充阅读

信函 1：迟交货引起的投诉

业务背景：中国的一家贸易公司（青岛鱼山贸易有限公司）与日本的一家智能玩具生产企业（三友智能玩具公司）签订了订货合同。交货期已过，但三友智能玩具公司仍然没有发货。

From: alice0512@yushantrading.com
To: tunkis@smarttoy.com
Date: 2019.12.17
Subject: late delivery of Purchase Order No. 19031

Dear Mr. Tunkis,

I would like to remind you that we have not received any information about the goods of Purchase Order No. 19031.

The latest date of shipment for the goods mentioned above is by the end of November according to the Purchase Order. You promised to deliver the goods before December 15 in your last email.

As you know, the smart toys are seasonal goods and our customers are in urgent need of the goods for the selling season. If the goods can not be put on the market on time, it will be tough to sell them out in spite of good design and quality.

If the goods ordered can not reach us by December 20, we will have to lodge a claim against you.

Please tell us your solution as soon as possible.

Yours sincerely
Alice Chen
General Manager
Qingdao Yushan Trading Co., Ltd.
Address: No. 6381 Yushan Road, Qingdao, Shandong, China
Tel: 86-0532-8185678; Fax: 86-0532-8185677

信函 2：卖方对迟交货投诉的回复

业务背景：日本的三友智能玩具公司的销售经理呐呐在收到青岛鱼山贸易有限公司的总经理爱丽斯关于迟交货的信函后，回信说明迟交货的原因。

From: tunkis@smarttoy.com
To: alice0512@yushantrading.com
Date: 2019.12.18
Subject: RE: late delivery of Purchase Order No. 19031

Dear Alice,

With reference to your letter on December 17, we are very sorry for the inconvenience caused by late delivery.

As you know, this is a very busy season for us and it is also a busy season for shipment.

Now we are fully engaged in a lot of orders and we have done our utmost to work for your order and will finish the packing of the ordered goods on December 19.

We have to deliver the goods by air and have already booked space on December 20. We will inform you as soon as the goods are shipped.

We are sorry again for the late delivery and willing to provide you 10 pieces of the smart toys ordered as compensation.

Sincerely
Okada Nana
Sales Manager
Sanyu Smart Toy Corporation
Address: 1-33-2-204，Minamitokiwadai, Itabashi-ku, Tokyo 174-0072 Japan
Tel: 81-3-53447866; Fax: 81-3-53447869

信函 3：由于包装破损引起的索赔

业务背景：中国的一家草编工艺品生产企业（青岛兴旺手工艺品有限公司）与法国的一家手工艺品贸易公司（优雅贸易有限公司）签订了草编工艺品的购销合同。优雅贸易有限公司在收到货后，发现有部分货物损坏。于是，优雅贸易有限公司的总经理海伦写信给青岛兴旺手工艺品有限公司的销售经理李华说明货物损坏的情况。

From: helen1219@hotmail.com
To: lihua@handicraftschina.com
Date: 2019.07.02
Subject: damage of the goods under Sales Contract No. 2019-025

Dear Lihua,

Regarding the goods under Sales Contract No. hc2019008, we have just received the 8,000 pieces of straw knitting handicrafts which are shipped by HANJIN BUDDHA 0009W. We regretfully found that the paper boxes of 20 pieces of the goods are broken and the goods inside are damaged.

We have to claim USD84.00 against you for the damaged goods, or we will return the goods to you and ask for replacement.

Please let us know your decision on this matter as soon as possible.

Yours sincerely
Helen Keller
General Manager
Elegance Trading Limited, France
Address: No. 1203 Garden Road, Paris, France
Tel: 33-1-8185678; Fax: 33-1-8185677

信函 4：卖方回复包装破损引起的索赔

业务背景：青岛兴旺手工艺品有限公司的销售经理李华在收到了法国优雅贸易有限公司的总经理海伦关于货物损坏并要求索赔的信函后，进行了回复。

From: lihua@handicraftschina.com
To: helen1219@hotmail.com
Date: 2019.07.03
Subject: RE: damage of the goods under Sales Contract No. 2019-025

Dear Helen,

Regarding your letter yesterday about the damage of 20 pieces of straw knitting handicrafts, I am sorry for what happened to the goods shipped.

We have looked into this matter and found that the goods were carefully packed by our staff and were in good condition before shipment. So we are sure that the damage happened during the ocean transit.

In this case, there is no ground for us to be responsible for the damaged goods. Please approach the Shipping Company and find the cause of the incident.

If you have any doubt on our explanation, please let me know.

Regards

Li Hua

Sales Manager

Qingdao Xingwang Handicrafts Co., Ltd.

Address: No. 1251 Xingwang Road, Qingdao, Shandong, China

Tel: 86-0532-8745618; Fax: 86-0532-8745617

# 情境三　商务关系的维护
# Maintenance of Business Relations

# 任务十一

# 商务拜访

# Business Visit

## 学习目标

1. 了解商务拜访的相关知识；
2. 掌握商务拜访信函的写作要点；
3. 熟悉商务拜访信函中常用的词语和句子；
4. 能够阅读与撰写商务拜访的信函；

## 背景知识

在商务活动中，商务拜访是重要和常见的。市场调查、新品推广和客户关系维护都需要拜访客户。

商务拜访的方式多数以面对面的方式进行，但是在拜访前，往往先要进行口头沟通或书面沟通。

商务拜访可以由买方提出，也可以由卖方提出。双方会面的场所包括展览会、卖方的工厂或买方的办公场所等。

拜访前要做好充分的准备，以保证商务拜访的效果，另外，在拜访过程中，要注意着装、礼仪，给对方留下好的印象。

### 一、拜访前的准备

（1）明确拜访目的；
（2）安排参加拜访的人员；
（3）准备拜访资料，卖方准备好产品样品；
（4）双方进行沟通，安排拜访日程；
（5）准备好必要的礼品。

## 二、拜访过程

（1）注意着装和礼仪；
（2）控制好拜访的时间；
（3）交谈内容应与拜访目的一致。

## 写作提示

商务拜访的信函通常包括如下情境和要点：

### 一、卖方邀请买方参加展览会

（1）问候；
（2）邀请对方参加展览会；
（3）告知展览会的时间、地点和公司展位等信息；
（4）询问对方是否能接受邀请；
（5）期待回信。

### 二、买方对卖方邀请参加展览会的回复

（1）感谢对方的邀请；
（2）说明参加或不能参加展览会；
（3）如果参加，告知对方自己的行程安排；
（4）如果不能参加，告知对方原因。

### 三、买方要求参观卖方的工厂

（1）问候；
（2）告知自己参观工厂的打算；
（3）询问对方是否方便接待；
（4）期待回信。

### 四、卖方对买方要求参观工厂的回复

（1）问候；
（2）如果方便接待，告知对方公司接待的行程安排；
（3）如果不方便接待，说明原因；
（4）期待与对方的会面。

示范信函

# CASE 1　Weifang Baoda Textiles Co., Ltd.

## 一、信函的业务背景

潍坊宝达纺织品有限公司将要参加第 126 届中国进出口商品交易会（见图 11.1）。有一些新的产品想要介绍给客户——孟加拉国缝得好服装有限公司。因此，阿尔伯特想邀请缝得好服装有限公司的丽莎在交易会上见面。

图 11.1　中国进出口商品交易会

## 二、潍坊宝达纺织品有限公司的业务信函

（一）邀请买方参加展览会（baoda-out 1）

From: Albert albert@163.com

To: Lisa lisa@stitchwell.com

Date: 2019.10.14

Subject: invitation to China Import & Export Trade Fair

Dear Lisa,

We are going to attend[1] the 126th China Import & Export Fair[2] from October 31 to November 4, 2019.

Because we have developed some new products such as ironing-free[3] fabrics, elastic fabrics, we would like to invite you to come to Guangzhou to visit our booth in the Fair. The information of the Fair and our booth No. are as follows.

**The 126th China Import & Export Fair**

**Venue: No. 382 Yuejiang Zhong Road, Haizhu District, Guangzhou City, Guangdong Province, China**

**Booth No.: 14.4124**

Please tell us whether you will come and the schedule of your trip if you do, we will pick you up at the airport and arrange the accommodations[4] for you.

I expect your reply and hope to see you in the Fair.

Best regards
Albert
Sales Manager
Weifang Baoda Textiles Co., Ltd.

## Notes

1. attend *v.* 参加
   e.g. Bob won't be able to attend your class this afternoon.
   鲍勃今天下午不能上您的课了。
2. China Import & Export Fair 中国进出口商品展览会
3. ironing-free 免烫
4. accommodation *n.* 住宿
   e.g. They provided comfortable accommodations for visitors.
   他们为来访者提供了舒适的住宿。

（二）邀请买方参加展览会（baoda-in 1）

From: Lisa lisa@stitchwell.com
To: Albert albert@163.com
Date: 2019.10.15
Subject: RE: invitation to China Import & Export Trade Fair

Dear Albert,

Thank you for your invitation letter on October 14, 2019.

I appreciate your kind invitation to the 126th China Import & Export Fair and I am eager to see you and your newly developed fabrics.

As I am busily engaged in business affairs, I will not be free by the end of this month. Hence, it is quite possible for me to visit the Fair in the first few days of November.

I will confirm the schedule of my trip to China in the next few days.

Thank you a lot.

Best regards
Lisa
Purchase Manager
Stitchwell Garments Co., Ltd.

# CASE 2　Beijing Lucky Fibreboard Trading Co., Ltd.

## 一、信函的业务背景

北京幸运纤维板贸易有限公司的采购部经理玲玲打算参观澳大利亚松树纤维板工业有限公司的生产工厂（见图 11.2）。

**图 11.2　澳大利亚 MDF 工厂**

## 二、北京幸运纤维板贸易公司的信函

（一）商务拜访（lucky-out1）

From: Lingling lingling@163.com
To: Bill salesdepartment@pinetree.com.au
Date: 2019.11.04
Subject: request for visiting the factory

Dear Bill,

We would like to visit your factory sometime this year so as to know more about the products and have business negotiation about future orders.

Please tell me the time which is convenient for you in order for us to arrange the upcoming business trip.

Meanwhile, please send us the invitation letter which is a necessary document for us to get the visa[1].

Best regards
Lingling
Purchase Manager
Beijing Lucky Fibreboard Trading Co., Ltd.

## Note

1. Visa *n.* 签证

e.g. Getting a visa isn't as simple as you might suppose.
获得签证并不像你想的那样简单。

（二）商务拜访（lucky-in 1）

From: Bill salesdepartment@pinetree.com.au
To: Lingling lingling@163.com
Date: 2019.11.06
Subject: Re: request for visiting the factory
Attachment: Invitation Letter[1]

Dear Lingling,

We are pleased to invite you to visit our factory for business negotiation[2] and we sincerely hope that the upcoming visit will make a deep impression on you about our factory.

It is convenient for us to accommodate[3] you in December or in January, 2020, so please arrange your trip accordingly.

We shall make all necessary arrangement for your visit and all of the expenses during your visit, including accommodations will be on our account.

Meanwhile, we are attaching the Invitation Letter for your confirmation.

We are looking forward to meeting you in the near future.

Best regards,
Bill
Sales Department
Pinetree Fibreboard Industries Co., Ltd.

## 附 11.1　Invitation Letter

To: The Australian Embassy in China

Dear Sir or Madam:

We are very pleased to invite Miss Wang Lingling come to our factory for visiting and business negotiation. The business trip will start from ***to ***. And because the long business co-operation in future between Beijing Lucky Fibreboard Trading Co., Ltd. and us, they will come to Australia for many times.

Please note, however, that we don't assume any legal or financial responsibility regarding the presence of Wang Lingling in Australia. All expenses of her journey to/from Australia will be borne by us.

Her personal details are as below:
Name: Wang Lingling
Date of birth: May 5th, 1980
Citizenship: China
Passport: E05048296

Yours sincerely
David Morgan
General Manager
Pinetree Fibreboard Industries Co., Ltd.

## Notes

1. invitation letter　邀请函
2. business negotiation　商务谈判
3. accommodate　*v.* 向某人提供住宿，接待
   e.g. There is usually room to accommodate up to 80 visitors.
   通常有可接待多达 80 位来访者的房间。

## 练习

**一、将下列句子译成中文。**

1. We are going to attend the 9th Guangzhou International Wire and Cable Fair from November 6 to November 9.
2. We would like to invite you to come to Guangzhou to visit our booth in the Fair.
3. Our booth No. is B-016, which is on the second floor of the building.
4. The fair will be held at Hong Kong Convention and Exhibition Center, which is opposite

the Victoria Harbor.
5. Please tell us your schedule, we will pick you up at the airport and arrange the accommodations for you.
6. As I am busily engaged in business affairs, I am afraid that I can not go to the fair.
7. Thank you for the kind invitation and I look forward to seeing you be in the fair.
8. We would like to visit your factory in October to know more about the products.
9. Please send us the invitation letter which is a necessary document for us to get the visa.
10. It is convenient for us to accommodate you in December, so please arrange your trip accordingly.

**二、将下列句子译成英文。**

1. 我们将参加今年 4 月在德国法兰克福举行的第 1 届国际包装材料展览会。
2. 我们高兴地邀请你公司到北京参加本次旅游用品展览会。
3. 届时，我将告知你方在展览会的展位号。
4. 展览会的举办地点在美国纽约国际会议展览中心。
5. 我们会告知你方日程安排，请合理安排行程。
6. 由于我公司将参加在香港举行的国际服装展，恐怕不能参加贵方邀请的展会。
7. 感谢你方的邀请，期待与您见面并看到贵公司新开发的产品。
8. 我们想邀请你参观工厂，请告知方便的时间以便我们安排活动日程。
9. 我公司将向你方发出邀请函，请注意查收并准备签证材料。
10. 我公司拟定的日程安排请见附件，请反馈意见。

## 技能训练

### 根据业务情境和信息写信

（一）业务情境

江苏通达轮胎有限公司是一家生产汽车轮胎的企业，近来，公司研发了新产品并将参加在香港会议展览中心（见图 11.3）举行的汽车配件展览会。李辉打算邀请大卫去展览会，了解公司的新产品。

（二）信息

1. 展会名称：第 22 届国际汽车配件展览会
2. 香港会议展览中心：香港湾仔区博览道 1 号
3. 展会时间：2019.10.01-2019.10.04
4. 公司的展位号：B-019

图 11.3　香港会议展览中心

（三）任务

1. 李辉想邀请大力神轮胎贸易公司的总经理大卫参加即将在香港举行的展览会。

信函包括如下要点：

（1）打算参加在香港会议展览中心举行的汽车配件展览会；

（2）邀请大卫参加展览会；

（3）告知大卫展览会的时间、地点及展位等信息；

（4）期待大卫 • 桑德伯格回信。

2. 大卫回复李辉的邀请

信函包括如下要点：

（1）感谢对方的邀请；

（2）自己将参加展览会；

（3）告知李辉赴展会的日程安排；

（4）期待与对方的见面。

## 补充阅读

信函：商务拜访

业务背景：中国一家钢管生产企业（淄博海来特锥形钢管有限公司）销售经理大卫要去印度孟买参加孟买中国商品展览会（见图 11.4）。大卫向印度的客户孟卓写信邀请其参加该展览会。

From: Davidli@steelpipechina.com
To: Mundra@indiapipe.com
Date: 2019.03.12
Subject: invitation letter for attending the exhibition

Dear Mundre,

Our company will attend the 10th Asia Machinery Exhibition in Mumbai, India next month. As you are our old friends, I sincerely invite you to come to the Exhibition if it is convenient for you.

I am sure that it will bring you a big surprise because we have some new development in our products.

Hope to see you soon in India.

Regards  
David Li  
Sales Manager  
Zibo Highlight Tapered Steel Pipe Co., Ltd.  
Address: No. 1251 Nanshan Road Zibo, Shandong, China  
Tel: 86-0533-8265184; Fax: 86-0533-8265173

图 11.4　印度孟买中国商品展览会

# 任务十二

# 客户满意度调查

# Investigation of Customers' Satisfaction

## 学习目标

1. 了解客户满意度调查的相关知识；
2. 掌握客户满意度调查信函的写作要点；
3. 熟悉客户满意度调查信函中常用的词语和句子；
4. 能够阅读与撰写客户满意度调查的信函；

## 背景知识

在当今的市场经济中，竞争不仅仅是产品的质量和价格，企业提供的服务也是决定竞争地位的重要因素。为此，企业需要对客户进行满意度调查以取得关于自身产品、服务的数据，以改进产品的质量、创新产品、提高管理效率和服务水平。

卖方可以通过信函或电话与买方进行沟通，了解产品在市场的销售情况以及买方对售后服务的满意程度，即客户回访。客户回访有电话回访、电子邮件回访及当面回访等不同形式。从实际的操作效果看，电话回访结合信函回访是最有效的方式。

客户满意度调查可以让客户填写问卷，或让客户直接通过邮件回复对公司产品与服务的评价与建议。

客户满意度调查的主要目的是通过了解产品在市场的销售情况及时对产品的优点和缺点进行掌握，为产品的改进提供必要的信息。另外，通过对买方对售后服务的满意程度的了解，可以及时对本公司在管理上存在的问题进行跟进，为改善公司的管理提供有用的信息。

客户满意度调查可以增进买卖双方的友谊，对于稳定和进一步发展双方的贸易关系十分重要。

## 写作提示

客户满意度调查的信函通常包括如下情境和要点：

### 一、卖方对买方的满意度调查

（1）提及已经销售的某种产品；
（2）询问买方对产品的使用情况和满意度；
（3）（可选择）附上产品满意度调查表并请买方填写；
（4）期待对方的回复。

### 二、买方的反馈

（1）感谢卖方的询问；
（2）回答对产品的满意度和市场销售情况；
（3）提出产品、服务方面的问题并提出改进意见；
（4）（可选择）附上反馈的产品满意度调查表。

## 示范信函

## CASE 1　Weifang Baoda Textiles Co., Ltd.

### 一、信函的业务背景

潍坊宝达纺织品有限公司与孟加拉国缝得好服装有限公司已经做成了几笔业务。阿尔伯特为了解客户对本公司产品和服务的满意度，写信给缝得好服装有限公司的丽莎向其进行客户满意度调查。

### 二、潍坊宝达纺织品有限公司的业务信函

（一）客户满意度调查（baoda-out 1）

From: Albert albert@163.com
To: Lisa lisa@stitchwell.com
Date: 2019.10.14
Subject: your feedback about our products
Attachment: Survey form[1] about customer's satisfaction

Dear Lisa,

Long time no see!

I would like to have your feedback about our fabrics.

Please tell us the selling situation of our products and the overall competitiveness[2] such as quality, price.

What's more, are you satisfied with our delivery, after-sale service[3]? If you are not satisfied, will you tell us what should be done to improve them?

Please fill the form in the attachment. Your feedback will be helpful for us to improve the products and service.

I hope to have your new orders in the near future.

Best regards
Albert
Sales Manager
Weifang Baoda Textiles Co., Ltd.

**附 12.1　客户满意度调查表**

| **survey about customer's satisfaction** | | | | | |
|---|---|---|---|---|---|
| **item** | | ***very satisfied*** | ***satisfied*** | ***OK*** | ***bad*** |
| | | | | | |
| **1** | **competitiveness** | | | | |
| **2** | **quality** | | | | |
| **3** | **packing** | | | | |
| **4** | **price** | | | | |
| **5** | **delivery** | | | | |
| **6** | **after-sales** | | | | |
| **please tick the box if you consider it deserves.** | | | | | |
| **Your Advice:** | | | | | |

## Notes

1. survey form 调查表
2. competitiveness *n.* 竞争力
   e.g. Scientific know-how, innovation and technical capability are critical to maintaining the nation's competitiveness and productivity.
   科学知识、创新和技术能力对保持一个国家的竞争力和生产率至关重要。
3. after-sale service 售后服务

（二）客户满意度调查（baoda-in 1）

From: Lisa lisa@stitchwell.com
To: Albert albert@163.com
Date: 2019.10.15
Subject: RE: your feedback about our products
Attachment: Survey form about customer's satisfaction

Dear Albert,

Thank you for your inquiry about the fabrics we ordered from you.

In general, our customers are quite satisfied with the quality of your fabrics.

However, I must tell you some problems raised by our customers.

Colour fastness for some dark fabrics does not comply with the standard, so please seek for solution to this problem.

Some of the fabrics we ordered have flaws[1], please improve the checking process to ensure the quality.

As to the price, you are losing the advantage due to the competition from Southeast Asian countries, such as Vietnam, Myanma and India. Therefore, you have to manage to reduce the cost to maintain competitiveness.

The after-sale service is quite satisfactory except for responding speed[2]. You have to quicken the responding speed when problem occurs.

Please see the attachment for detailed comment by us.

Best regards
Lisa
Purchase Manager
Stitchwell Garments Co., Ltd.

## Notes

1. flaw *n.* 瑕点，缺陷
2. responding speed 响应速度

# CASE 2 Beijing Lucky Fibreboard Trading Co., Ltd.

## 一、信函的业务背景

北京幸运纤维板贸易有限公司采购部经理玲玲写信告诉比尔产品在中国市场的销售情况。

## 二、北京幸运纤维板贸易公司的信函

客户满意度调查 (lucky-out1)

From: Lingling lingling@163.com

To: Bill salesdepartment@pinetree.com.au

Date: 2019.11.04

Subject: market situation of MDF[1]

Dear Bill,

How are you recently?

Thanks to our mutual efforts we have established business relations with each other and I hope we can cooperate in the future.

Now I would like to respond the inquiry about your products by telling you the situation of your products in China market.

The customers are quite satisfied with the quality of MDF manufactured by your company.

Due to the development of housing market the demand for MDF is increasing fast. Although market competition is strong, your products have advantage in quality and environmental standard[2].

Although the prices of your products are higher than similar products, the consumers accept them due to their quality standard. They are sold well in China.

New demand for door components[3] are increasing, it opens new markets for your products. We hope that you will supply new products through innovation to keep the advantage.

Best regards

Lingling

Purchase Manager
Beijing Lucky Fibreboard Trading Co., Ltd.

## Notes

1. MDF 中密度板
   全称为 Medium Density Board
2. environmental standard 环保标准
3. door components 门的组件

## 练习

### 一、将下列句子译成中文。

1. I would like to have your feedback about our products.
2. Will you tell us the selling situation about our products?
3. We would like to have your feedback about our products and services.
4. Our customers are quite satisfied with the quality of your products.
5. As to the price, you are losing the advantage due to the competition from Southeast Asian countries.
6. You have to manage to reduce the cost to maintain competitiveness.
7. The responding speed has to be improved.
8. The delivery time is not satisfactory. You have to increase the production efficiency.
9. The environmental standard is of great concern to the customers.
10. The high end market is enlarging because of the increase of income level.

### 二、将下列句子译成英文。

1. 请填写附件里的客户满意度调查表，告诉我们对产品及服务是否满意。
2. 我们的产品在美国的销售情况如何？
3. 请提供你对我们产品及服务的反馈，包括商品符合度、店家服务态度、物流发货速度以及配送中服务。
4. 消费者对贵公司产品的包装不太满意，请对包装重新进行设计。
5. 请改进包装，以保证产品在长途运输中不会损坏。
6. 对于装饰材料，消费者对其环保标准越来越重视。
7. 你公司产品已经失去了价格上的优势。
8. 对于智能玩具，低端产品市场在萎缩，而中高端产品市场在扩大。
9. 希望贵公司加强在产品研发上的投入、不断开发新产品，这样才能保持竞争优势。
10. 希望贵公司能够改进物流，提高发货速度。

## 技能训练

### 根据业务情境和信息写信

（一）业务情境

江苏通达轮胎有限公司想了解美国客户大力神公司对本公司产品与服务的满意度，销售经理李辉向大力神公司的总经理大卫询问相关情况。

大卫回信告诉李辉客户对产品的反馈。

（二）信息

1. 家用汽车轮胎的价格优势正在丧失，面临其他国家轮胎生产企业的竞争；
2. 建议开发重型机械的轮胎产品，以争取市场优势。

（三）任务

1. 李辉向大卫询问对本公司产品与服务的满意度。

信函应该包括如下要点：

（1）问候；

（2）询问本公司产品在美国市场的销售情况及产品的优缺点；

（3）询问其他方面的情况：如售后服务、交货时间等；

（4）表示感谢。

2. 大卫回复关于客户满意度调查的信函。

信函应该包括如下要点：

（1）告知李辉公司的轮胎在美国市场的销售情况及产品的优缺点；

（2）表明对售后服务、交货时间等方面的满意程度；

（3）建议：开发重型机械的轮胎产品。

## 补充阅读

信函：客户回访

业务背景：日本的三友智能玩具公司总经理呐呐向青岛鱼山贸易有限公司的总经理发出回访信函，想了解本公司产品的使用情况。爱丽斯回信告知其公司产品在中国的销售情况及需要改进的问题。

From: Alice0512@yushantrading.com
To: Tunkis@smarttoy.com
Date: 2019.10.12
Subject: RE: Feedback about our smart toys

Dear Nana,

Now I would tell you the selling situation of your smart toys in China.

As you know, the competition in smart toy market is becoming stronger and stronger because lots of manufactures have entered this market. Similar products are everywhere. The solution to this matter is to keep your comparative advantage through innovation, that is , to develop new products.

There is another problem I want to mention. Some toys were damaged in the recent order due to the poor packing. So I suggest that the outer packing should be changed to 3-layer corrugated carton. The 2-layer corrugated carton packing is not suitable for long distance shipping.

Yours sincerely

Alice Chen
General Manager
Qingdao Yushan Trading Co., Ltd.
Address: No. 6381 Yushan Road Qingdao, Shandong, China
Tel: 86-0532-8185678; Fax: 86-0532-8185677

# 任务十三

# 新产品介绍与促销

# Introduction and Promotion of New Products

## 学习目标

1. 了解新产品介绍与促销的相关知识；
2. 掌握新产品介绍与促销信函的写作要点；
3. 熟悉新产品介绍与促销信函中常用的词语和句子；
4. 能够阅读与撰写新产品介绍与促销的信函。

## 背景知识

无论处于何种行业的企业，要想在激烈的市场竞争中生存和发展，它就必须创新自己的产品。面对激烈的市场竞争，新产品的开发和推广对于企业的生存和发展尤其重要。

对于老客户，要适时地推介新产品，扩大新产品的销路，增强企业的市场竞争力。当公司推出新产品时，对外贸业务员来说是一次不错的营销机会。

首先，你可就新产品跟客户拉近关系，维护好与客户的关系；其次，新产品比较容易吸引客户眼球，引起下单的兴趣，尤其是针对那些尚未下单的客户，新产品出来后是推动其下单的良好契机；最后，新产品推出后，公司一般会有一些新的推广措施，如此也会增加外贸业务员的销售机会。

有新产品就可以向客户推荐，先询问客户老产品用得怎么样，然后再引出新产品的话题。首先，介绍新产品的性能以及优势；其次，说明新产品的优势是否能给客户带来更大的利益；最后，介绍价格，新产品的价位会高一些，可以向客户表明折扣等促销手段。

另外，网站是进行产品宣传的重要媒介，做精美的网页，给客户提供链接，将图片、视频和文字有机地结合在一起，想办法体现产品的特色，效果才能达到最佳。

## 写作提示

新产品介绍与促销的信函通常包括如下要点：

### 一、出口商发出的介绍和促销新产品的信函

（1）介绍新产品，尤其是新产品的特点和市场前景；
（2）附上新产品的图片、说明或告知新产品的网址；
（3）报新产品的价格，并说明有无促销手段；
（4）如果客户感兴趣，请进一步咨询或提供样品。

### 二、进口商回复介绍和促销新产品的信函

（1）感谢对方的来信；
（2）说明对新产品是否感兴趣；
（3）如果对新产品感兴趣，对新产品进一步咨询或索要样品。

## 示范信函

# CASE 1　Weifang Baoda Textiles Co., Ltd.

### 一、信函的业务背景

潍坊宝达纺织品有限公司开发了一种高支高密的色织面料。阿尔伯特写信给缝得好服装公司的丽莎，向她推荐该种新产品。

### 二、潍坊宝达纺织品有限公司的业务信函

（一）新产品介绍与促销（baoda-out 1）

From: Albert albert@163.com
To: Lisa lisa@stitchwell.com
Date: 2019.12.12
Subject: our new products
Attachment: the photo of our new product

Dear Lisa,

How are you?

Now we have developed some new products and I would introduce the new features[1] of them.

The fabrics are woven by super thin yarn count[2], which is 130s. It is as thin as thread made by spiders. The fabrics woven by this kind of yarn is as thin as the wings of cicadas. The quality standard complies with international standard. They are used for shirts of high end market[3].

With the economic development, the incomes of many people are increasing and consumption is upgrading[4]. It means more people will buy clothes which are of good quality. So this is a good opportunity for our new products.

As to the price, the new products will be higher than ordinary fabrics. But we have promotion[5] in order to open new market.

Please see the detailed specifications and pictures in the attachment, you can also visit our website (www.baodatextile.com) to know more about our new products.

If you are interested in them, don't hesitate to have further inquiry.

Best regards
Albert
Sales Manager
Weifang Baoda Textiles Co., Ltd.

**附 13.1　新产品（高支高密衬衫）图示**
**new product**

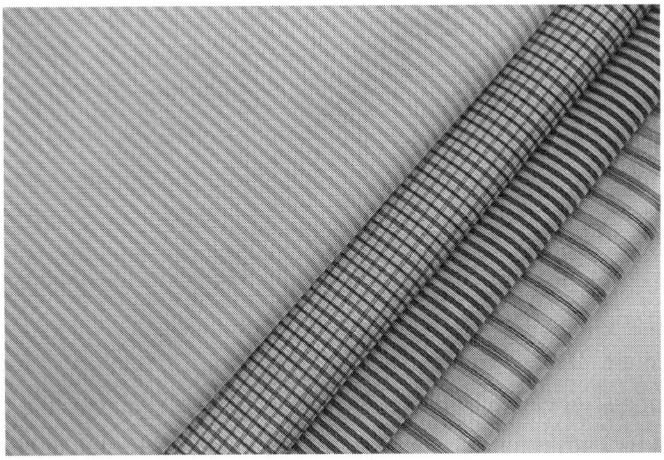

## Notes

1. feature　*n.* 特征
   e.g. The spacious gardens are a special feature of this property.
   宽敞的花园是这处房产的一个特征。
2. yarn count　棉纱支数

3. high end market 高端市场
4. upgrade *v.* 升级
   e.g. Medical facilities are being reorganized and upgraded.
   医疗设施正在被重组和升级。
5. promotion *n.* 促销
   e.g. In cosmetic industry, enterprises spend a lot of money on advertising and promotion.
   在化妆品行业，企业在广告和促销方面花费大量金钱。

# CASE 2 Beijing Lucky Fibreboard Trading Co., Ltd.

## 一、信函的业务背景

澳大利亚松树纤维板工业有限公司开发出一种用于室内门的系列新产品。为此，比尔写信将该系列产品介绍给玲玲。

## 二、北京幸运纤维板贸易公司的信函

（一）新产品介绍与促销（lucky-in 1）

From: Bill salesdepartment@pinetree.com.au
To: Lingling lingling@163.com
Date: 2019.11.06
Subject: our new door components series
Attachment: the photo of door components series

Dear Lingling,

How are you recently?

How about our products selling in China market?

Recently, we developed some new products which are used for doors and I am pleased to introduce them for you.

Pinetree Medium Density Fibreboard (MDF) Door Components[1] are produced from specifically formulated grades of MDF to provide the best solutions for their applications. These can be used for both commercial and residential purposes to suit all modern door types.

Our new products are divided into two series. One is door skins series and the other is door cores series.

Due to the new feature of our door cores series, here I would especially like to introduce them to you.

The Pinetree MDF door cores are used where a lower finished door weight is critical. It is 20% lighter in weight than regular MDF but maintains the excellent strength quality, surface smoothness, stability and provides a uniform substrate for overlaying[2].

Please see the photo of the new products in the attachment. If you have any interest in them I will send samples to you.

Best regards,
Bill
Sales Department
Pinetree Fibreboard Industries Co., Ltd.

**附 13.2　door cores series**

## Notes

1. door components 门的组件
2. overlay *n.* & *v.* 覆盖
   e.g. An overlay of wood covers the brick wall.
   一层木板覆盖着砖墙。

## 练习

**一、将下列句子译成中文。**

1. We have developed some new products which I am sure that they will interest you.
2. We developed some new fabrics which are for young people in the US market.
3. These newly developed smart toys have some new features which are designed for 4 to 6 years old children.
4. Our new tire has better performance in abrasion resistance.
5. The new Medium Density Fibreboard for Door can be used for both commercial and residential purposes to suit all modern door types.

6. Although some new features are added to the new products, the prices are not much higher than the traditional ones.
7. We have promotion for the new products in order to open European market.
8. We can give you 3% discount for the new model.
9. We can offer you 5% commission for the promotion of our new products.
10. If you have any interest in the new model I will send samples to you.

**二、将下列句子译成英文。**

1. 我们新研发了一种免烫面料，面向中高端商务人群。
2. 我们的新产品是针对非洲市场而开发的。
3. 新产品在环保标准方面达到了 E0 级。
4. 新品手机的 CPU 性能比原产品提升了 75%，内存达到 128GB。
5. 比起以前的智能玩具产品，新产品在人机互动方面更加智能。
6. 这种用于工程机械的轮胎，具有更强的耐磨性能。
7. 新开发的智能玩具的价格比以前的产品大约高 10%。
8. 为了打开新市场，我们进行促销，新品的价格不高于原产品的价格。
9. 如果我们为你的新产品做推广，可以给我们百分之几的佣金？
10. 我们对你公司新开发的型号 D-159 的智能手机感兴趣，请寄样品。

## 技能训练

### 根据业务情境和信息写信

（一）业务情境

江苏通达轮胎有限公司新开发了一种轮胎（见图 13.1），李辉向大卫推荐该产品。

**图 13.1　江苏通达轮胎有限公司新产品**

（二）信息

新产品的特点：

1. 具有胎面耐磨性能好，卓越的横向牵引性能等优点。
2. 适用于高速公路、国道、省道等综合路况的驱动轮使用。

（三）任务

根据给定的业务情境和信息，撰写信函介绍公司的新产品。

信函应该包括如下要点：

1. 问候；
2. 告知公司推出了新产品；
3. 详细介绍新产品的特点和市场前景；
4. 告知新产品的价格和促销手段；
5. 如果对新产品感兴趣，可以寄样品（或到展览会）。

## 补充阅读

信函：新产品介绍与促销

业务背景：三友智能玩具公司销售经理呐呐先生向青岛鱼山贸易有限公司的总经理爱丽斯介绍公司新研发的智能玩具（见图 13.2）。

**图 13.2　智能玩具新品**

From: Tunkis@smarttoy.com
To: Alice0512@yushantrading.com
Date: 2019.10.12
Subject: new arrival of smart toy

Dear Alice,

Hope everything is good for you.

I would introduce our newly developed product to you.

It is a smart dog! Some features have been added to our new product. It can dance and utter interesting voice. The more amazing feature is that it can answer questions!

It is an amazing smart toy which can be an intimate companion of children.

I will send you the sample of the new smart dog to let you have better understanding about it.

As to the price, it is not higher than the one you ordered last time.

Look forward to hearing from you soon.

Yours sincerely
Okada Nana
Sales Manager
Sanyou Smart Toy Co., Ltd.

# 参考文献
# Reference


[1] 程同春. 新编国际商务英语函电. 3 版. 南京：东南大学出版社，2016.
[2] 傅龙海. 外贸英语函电实务精讲. 北京：中国海关出版社，2013.
[3] 葛萍. 外贸英语函电. 4 版. 上海：复旦大学出版社，2017.
[4] 王维平. 商务英语函电. 2 版. 北京：机械工业出版社，2013.
[5] 易露霞. 外贸英语函电. 3 版. 北京：清华大学出版社，2016.
[6] 于晓云. 外贸函电. 北京：首都经济贸易大学出版社，2015.
[7] 赵银德. 外贸函电. 3 版. 北京：机械工业出版社，2016.